Tobacco Goes to College

Tobacco Goes to College

Cigarette Advertising in Student Media, 1920–1980

Elizabeth Crisp Crawford

McFarland & Company, Inc., Publishers

Jefferson, North Carolina

LIBRARY OF CONGRESS CATALOGUING-IN-PUBLICATION DATA

Crawford, Elizabeth Crisp, 1977–
Tobacco goes to college : cigarette advertising in student media,
1920–1980 / Elizabeth Crisp Crawford.
p.   cm.
Includes bibliographical references and index.

ISBN 978-0-7864-6819-5 (softcover : acid free paper) ∞
ISBN 978-1-4766-0365-0 (ebook)

1. Advertising—Cigarettes—United States—History—20th century.
2. College students—Tobacco use—United States—History—20th century.
3. College publications—United States—History—20th century.
4. Tobacco industry—United States—History—20th century.   I. Title.

HF6161.T6C73 2014   659.19'6797309730904—dc23   2014004621

BRITISH LIBRARY CATALOGUING DATA ARE AVAILABLE

On the cover: Chesterfield advertisement with Jo Stafford and Perry Como
in the University of Tennessee 1947 season football programs
(by permission of University of Tennessee Special Collections)

Manufactured in the United States of America

*McFarland & Company, Inc., Publishers
Box 611, Jefferson, North Carolina 28640
www.mcfarlandpub.com*

For Dorothy H. Crisp, who lived the history that I tell.

Table of Contents

PART III
CONCLUSION

Acknowledgments

I would like to express my sincere gratitude to all of the faculty and colleagues who helped me with this research. Specifically, I would like to thank Dr. Ron Taylor and the rest of my dissertation committee members at the University of Tennessee for advising me while I performed the initial research for this project. In addition, I would like to thank Dr. James W. Neuliep at St. Norbert College for suggesting that I pursue graduate studies and Dr. Joyce Wolburg at Marquette University for sparking my interest in advertising. I would also like to thank Dr. Ross Collins at North Dakota State University for encouraging me to write this book. Lastly, I would like to thank my family, especially my parents and my husband, Jeremy Jackson, whose encouragement made this work possible.

Preface and Introduction

Advertising is as essential to media as editorial content. The media need both to survive. However, a conflict of interest can arise when an advertiser becomes so powerful that it can shape media content and control editorial policy. From the 1920s to the 1960s, cigarette advertisers had a strong financial grip on student media. And, through its support of the campus paper and other campus media, the industry had power over colleges and universities across the nation. In fact, the tobacco industry's strength was so great many doubted whether student newspapers and other campus media could survive without tobacco money. When the Tobacco Institute, the organization that governed the tobacco industry, decided to pull the advertising in June 1963, nearly 2,000 student publications needed to recover up to 50 percent of their revenue because of the loss of the cigarette accounts.[1]

Although student newspapers are the main focus of this book, tobacco's presence on campus permeated more than just the student paper. Cigarette brands were promoted at football games, on campus radio and through campus representatives, and promotional items were placed on campus in locations such as university stores and student unions. For many years the tobacco industry employed students and professors to research tobacco marketing and tobacco as an agricultural product. It is important to understand the enormous scope of the tobacco industry's power to understand how it could execute its extensive marketing plan on college campuses. Tobacco had an especially close relationship with colleges and universities in the Southeast.

At about the same time as the Tobacco Institute pulled the cigarette ads, it also started to reduce its funding of university research. The reasons for this are twofold. First, filtered cigarettes did not require high-quality tobacco. Therefore, agricultural research was less important. Second, marketing research was required for tobacco advertising campaigns. Without the campaigns, there was no need to fund tobacco-related marketing research on campus.

This book is divided into three parts. The first part explores cigarette advertising in the student press in its historical and legal context. It provides the reader with the proper context for understanding the advertisements. It also summarizes the extensive industry and legal documents that relate to cigarette marketing on campus. The second part examines the advertisements themselves. The advertisements are examined to establish the frequency and extent of their placement and the creative strategies that were used. The third part analyzes the advertising strategies that were used in the campus media and the marketing strategies that were used to reach young smokers after cigarette advertising was banned from campus, and includes a conclusion for the book.

1

NEWSPAPERS, DOCUMENTS AND HISTORICAL RECORDS

This book uses a variety of documents that are available from university libraries and Internet archives that house electronic versions of the Tobacco Institute's archives. University archives house a variety of important documents related to the tobacco industry's marketing and advertising efforts on campus. Archive holdings include copies of the advertisements that were published in student papers as well as other documents related to media sales. Some university archives, especially land grant institutions in the southeast, also contain documents related to tobacco experiment stations on university campuses.

To conduct the research for this book, information was compiled from the physical and electronic archives at universities across the nation. The universities include Bard College, Brown University, Fordham University, Indiana University, Ithaca College, Loyola University Chicago, Miami University, MIT, North Dakota State University, Princeton University, San Diego State University, Southern Methodist University, Penn State University, the State University of New York at Buffalo, the University of Iowa, the University of Minnesota, the University of Tennessee, William & Mary, Vassar College, and Xavier University. Although university archives were essential to this book, the most important cache of internal industry documents was made available through the 1998 Master Settlement Agreement.

MASTER SETTLEMENT AGREEMENT AND TOBACCO ARCHIVES

The Master Settlement Agreement (MSA) was signed in November 1998 by the tobacco industry and the attorneys general in 46 states and five U.S. territories. The agreement resolved lawsuits filed by the attorneys general against the tobacco industry and provided funds to the states to compensate them for taxpayer money that was spent on patients and family members with tobacco-related diseases. Among the many other provisions limiting cigarette advertising and promotion, the tobacco companies also agreed to make many of their internal documents available to the public. The major vehicle that the tobacco companies use to make their documents available is the Internet. For instance, the MSA states:

> The Original Participating Manufacturers will maintain at their expense their Internet document websites accessible through "TobaccoResolution.com" or a similar website until June 30, 2010. The Original Participating Manufacturers will maintain the documents that currently appear on their respective websites and will add additional documents to their websites.[2]

The individual tobacco companies were required to continue to update the documents until 2010. The MSA continues by stating:

> Unless copies of such documents are already on its website, each Original Participating Manufacturer and Tobacco-Related Organization will place on its website copies of documents produced in any production of documents that takes place on or after the date 30 days before the MSA Execution Date in any federal or state court civil action concerning smoking and health. Copies of any documents required to be placed on a website pursuant to this subsection will be placed on such website within the later of 45 days after the MSA Execution Date or within 45 days after the production of such documents in any federal or state court action concerning smoking and health. This obligation will continue until June 30, 2010.[3]

However, there are certain documents that the MSA does not require the tobacco industry to post. The MSA states:

(1) it continues to claim to be privileged, a trade secret, confidential or proprietary business information, or that contain other information not appropriate for public disclosure because of personal privacy interests or contractual rights of third parties; or

(2) continue to be subject to any protective order, sealing order or other order or ruling that prevents or limits a litigant from disclosing such documents.[4]

INTERNET-BASED TOBACCO DATABASES

As part of the Master Settlement Agreement between the states and the tobacco companies, the industry was required to make the documents used during the various tobacco trials available. Two major Internet archives were used for this book: Tobacco Documents Online and The Legacy Tobacco Documents Library.

Tobacco Documents Online (TDO) was created to provide standard document descriptions and uniform searching of the industry documents made public by the MSA. TDO provides powerful searching across all the companies and access to high-quality images, as well as the ability to collect and annotate documents. These tools were built for document researchers and are available to anyone with a web browser.[5] Each entry in this book that is based on an original industry document contains a footnote with the document website and a Bates number. Documents from the digital tobacco industry archives can be easily found by searching for this identification number in the search field of the website.

The Legacy Tobacco Documents Library (LTDL) at the University of California, San Francisco, contains millions of documents related to advertising, manufacturing, marketing, sales, and scientific research of tobacco products. The LTDL includes more than 13 million documents posted on tobacco industry websites in accordance with the Master Settlement Agreement.[6] Visitors can search, view, and download these documents from this website.[7] Like other electronic tobacco archives, documents from LTDL can be retrieved by searching for the documents' Bates numbers.

MARKETING RESEARCH

Before an advertising campaign is launched, advertisers do extensive research to develop advertising that will resonate with their target audience. Once an advertising campaign is launched, the research continues to ensure the effectiveness of the advertising and measure sales during the campaign. If sales do not increase during a campaign, an advertiser might reevaluate the message strategy and creative execution or the medium, such as a newspaper, that it is using to advertise.

In addition to advertising in student publications, the Tobacco Institute promoted smoking by employing marketing representatives to distribute free cigarettes on campus.[8] The cigarette brands usually selected fraternity or sorority members or other influential students to promote products, or they employed the campus public relations professionals to promote their brands. These campus representatives were often rewarded with cash or other premiums.[9]

However, what is less well known is that the Tobacco Institute employed students and faculty to help with its market research. For instance, American Tobacco Company created the Student Marketing Institute (SMI) to help create and evaluate marketing efforts on campus. Lucky Strike, Tareyton, and Pall Mall benefited from student research that was super-vised by a faculty advisor.[10]

Every year, the SMI supplied American Tobacco Company with results from a campus survey that gathered data about college freshmen. The survey distributed during welcome week inquired about the incoming freshman's smoking habits and brand preferences. The campus representatives and market researchers also coordinated sponsorships of special events on campus and merchandising at campus retailers.[11]

AGRICULTURAL RESEARCH

By the 1950s, the tobacco industry had collaborated with many universities in the South to learn how to improve tobacco cultivation. The primary experiment stations were located at universities in North Carolina, South Carolina, Tennessee, and Kentucky.[12] Because of the research funding, these universities tended to welcome tobacco advertising and marketing efforts more than the others. And, for the most part, they were in need of the funding. This was certainly the case at the University of Tennessee.

During the first decade of the Tobacco Experiment Station's existence at the University of Tennessee, its primary goals related to the establishment of the facility. Although experimental studies had been conducted during this period, no significant breakthroughs were reported. During the war years, the station lost much of its manpower. The work at the station came almost to a standstill and was in desperate need of direction.[13] However, the changes brought about by World War II that necessitated the production of more tobacco and the technology that would make this possible would set the stage for the station's work over the next twenty-five years. According to Charles Click, the work conducted at the station during these years was the most influential in the station's history. Advances in plant breeding and agronomics resulted in a number of major discoveries that were beneficial to the tobacco farmer.[14]

After the 1964 U.S. Surgeon General's Report, tobacco production in the United States changed drastically. The change from unfiltered cigarettes to the filtered low-tar version enabled cigarette manufacturers to use a lower quality tobacco in their product.[15] This trend also resulted in an increased use of foreign tobaccos imported from Africa, Asia and Latin America. Therefore, the tobacco station changed its focus from creating new varieties and better quality tobacco to cultivating more tobacco at a reduced cost.[16]

The contributions made by the University of Tennessee Tobacco Experiment Station and experiment stations at other universities in the Southeast to the American tobacco industry are immeasurable.[17] The role played by the Tennessee station in increasing American tobacco production helped to place tobacco near the top of the list of U.S. agricultural exports. The economic benefit derived from the increased production made tobacco one of the most essential U.S. agricultural exports in the Southeast. From the early advances made against black root rot disease to the high yield varieties that are popular today, the station's tobacco breeding program has had a large influence on the tobacco industry in the United States.[18]

Tobacco and cigarettes were a major part of college life from 1920s to the 1960s. Cigarette advertisements in the student newspapers are just one visible example of the symbiotic relationship that existed between cigarette manufacturers and colleges and universities across the United States. The university provided research and a target market to the advertisers.

The advertisers provided funding for research and student media, primarily the newspaper. Both parties benefitted from the arrangement and neither party seemed willing to question the system that existed.[19]

Therefore, when evaluating the advertisements in the campus newspaper, the reader is getting a glimpse of a real relationship between the university and an advertiser. From the 1920s to the 1960s, advertising was often created in a very hierarchical manner. The advertiser created a message to communicate specific product features to a market. However, industry documents show that the Tobacco Institute was innovative in its approach. The documents indicate that research conducted by college students themselves inspired many of the ideas for the advertising message designs.[20] This practice is evident in the advertisements that specifically mention the students who created jingles or other creative elements featured in the ads.

Conclusion

A variety of documents from numerous institutions were required to compile the information for this book. The breadth of research represents the wide scope of the issue. The tobacco industry had a prominent place on college and university campuses. The extensive relationship is documented by millions of pieces of evidence that relate to the many areas of the university that the tobacco industry infiltrated. Even though the scope of this research is limited to cigarette advertising in the student media, the bigger issues can be seen through this limited lens.

The national cigarette advertising campaigns that ran in student newspapers were coordinated by the best agency talent that Madison Avenue had to offer.[21] The cigarette brands' research and marketing techniques that made use of deep consumer insights were truly ahead of their time. Even though it is easy to be critical of tobacco and their marketing practices, the advertisements that were placed in the student media are an essential piece of advertising history. The pioneering methods that the industry used to develop the ads made some of these campaigns the best of their time. The history of cigarette advertisements in the student media deserves our attention because of the advertisers' ability to control the media they supported, our criticism because of the dangerous product they advocated, and our admiration for their quality and innovation.

PART I

CIGARETTES AND THE CAMPUS PRESS: HISTORY AND REGULATION

1

The History of the Cigarette
The Birth of the Industry and Its Opposition

When Thorwald Dockstader—sophomore, epicure, and sportsman—first took up smoking, he did not simply choose the first brand of cigarettes that came to hand. He did what any sophomore, epicure, and sportsman would do: He sampled many brands until he found the very best—a mild, rich, flavorful smoke—an endless source of comfort and satisfaction—a smoke that never palled, never failed to please—a smoke that age could not wither nor custom stale—a filter cigarette with an unfiltered taste—Marlboro of course!
—Text from a Marlboro Advertisement, *The Orange and White,* 1963.

Professors smoking pipes, an English student at a typewriter smoking a cigarette, a young co-ed asking her new beau for a light... In years past, smoking was ingrained in the collegiate experience. Due to a long tradition of being associated with intellectualism, cigarette smoking and higher education seemed to be a natural fit. However, the link between cigarettes and college life was no accident. Cigarette manufacturers carefully managed the association over a span of five decades. The tobacco industry promoted smoking through extensive cigarette marketing on campus. And, advertising in student newspapers served as a primary promotional venue.

College and university student newspapers were the perfect advertising venue for cigarette brands. To survive, student newspapers and other student media needed to keep costs down. Colleges and universities were often unable to offer the student press the funding that it needed. Therefore, the student media was forced to generate revenue through other means. However, obtaining the needed funding could be challenging. For instance, newspaper readers are less likely to pay the same price for student journalism as for mainstream newspapers. And small circulation numbers make it harder to get high prices for advertising.

Although the student press faced many challenges, its strategic advantage has always been a young audience. Brand preferences are formed when people are young. Younger readers are more open to trying new things, are more image conscious, and tend to follow new trends. And, above all, they are impressionable.[1]

Financially strapped and desperate for advertising revenue, student newspapers were eager to accept advertising dollars from the tobacco industry. The campus newspapers' national sales representatives sold large amounts of advertising space in student publications across the nation to cigarette companies eager to attract new college-aged smokers. Both the national advertising representatives and the tobacco industry made handsome profits from the arrangement while the struggling student papers barely earned enough revenue to print the extra pages that the tobacco industry required for their large advertisements.[2]

From 1920 to 1963, student newspapers provided tobacco marketers with the ideal target audience for their finely crafted messages about tobacco. Tobacco advertising campaigns filled student newspapers with stories about Hollywood actors and actresses and their favorite brands, college contests sponsored by cigarette brands, comic strips and advertorials featuring popular cigarettes, and testimonials about the benefits of smoking. Numerous students responded to the messages. Cigarette smoking steadily increased in acceptance and popularity on campus.

Because of the health risks associated with smoking, academic researchers and government agencies have monitored cigarette advertising, particularly advertising that targets a young audience. Before government entities such as the Federal Trade Commission, Food and Drug Administration, and the U.S. Surgeon General began to take a more aggressive stance against cigarette advertising, the tobacco industry was able to market its product as it pleased, without warnings or restraints.

The topic of cigarette advertising has been a popular subject of research in many fields of study, including mass communication, business, political science, and public health. A basic concern has been the role of cigarette advertising in stimulating demand.[3] Cigarette smoking reached the height of its popularity between the 1950s and the 1970s.[3] Given that reaching the youth market has always been the industry's goal,[4] it is useful to examine the print advertisements that helped to persuade a generation of young Americans to smoke.

From the 1920s to the early 1960s, cigarette companies were lucrative advertising sponsors for student newspapers. Cigarette advertising comprised approximately 40 percent of the national advertising in most campus newspapers. Advertisements played an important role in creating and reinforcing a culture in which smoking was perceived as being glamorous and sophisticated, enjoyable and pleasant, rugged and masculine (or chic and feminine), and symbolic of independent thinking or coming of age.[5]

Brief History of Tobacco Use

Smoking is as old as civilization. Ancient Greeks, Indians, and Arabians all practiced the inhalation of various herbs and other substances for medical and ceremonial purposes.[6] At the turn of the 20th century, cigar smoking was common, but cigarette smoking was seen as somewhat decadent and slightly subversive habit. Cigarette smoking was considered a male custom associated with "rough-and-ready boys, dandies, and improper women."[7] However, by the 1950s, more than one-third of U.S. women smoked.[8] Some estimates state that by the 1950s, the total population of smokers had reached nearly 70 million.[9] This startling shift leads one to question how this habit that was once obscure could have attained such popularity.

EARLY HISTORY

As the use of snuff was declining in the United States, the decade's biggest tobacco news was the emergence of the cigarette as something more than a novelty but less than a socially acceptable habit in most parts of the nation. Many factors contributed to the prevalence of cigarette smoking. In addition to the addictive nature of tobacco, industrialization and mechanization were key factors.

During the 1860s, when Phillip Morris started rolling its first cigarettes, cigarettes started to become a widely recognized form of tobacco consumption. Tobacco played an important role in the Civil War. The South was supported by tobacco revenues and the North by a tax. In 1880 half a billion cigarettes were sold in the United States, and this figure is for manufactured products alone—the roll-your-owns added approximately another one billion to the total.

By the 1880s the cigarette had a small and marginal constituency. For most of the 19th century, tobacco users stuck to chewing tobacco or smoking cigars or pipes. The skill needed to produce cigarettes limited the growth of the industry.[10] However, those who did smoke cigarettes were mostly the poor, new immigrants, or dandies in the large eastern cities. Cigarette smoking was not acceptable among middle-class men. However, some sophisticated upper-class women in large eastern cities occasionally smoked. They primarily smoked Turkish and Russian brands in somewhat the same spirit as middle-aged Americans today might make a deal for a few joints of marijuana. The purchase produced a feeling of guilt and excitement. These women smoked within the privacy of their bedrooms or parlors, often in secrecy.[11]

After the Civil War, a former Confederate solider named Washington Duke converted his family farm into a pipe-tobacco business. However, competition from other brands, specifically the Bull Durham brands, created the need to search for a new niche. Washington Duke's oldest son James Buchanan, "Buck" Duke, saw potential in the cigarette. Though the cigarette market was tiny, the habit was gaining popularity in urban England and New York.[12]

In 1881 Buck Duke returned to Durham to begin the conversion to cigarettes. In 1881 James A. Bonsack of Virginia invented a cigarette-making machine. In 1883, Duke purchased two of the cigarette-producing machines, or Emery machines. The machine could produce more than 200 cigarettes a minute. This was more than 40 times the number of cigarettes that the best skilled workers could roll by hand.[13] The mechanized cigarette producing process increased the volume and decreased the price of producing the product.[14] When Duke turned exclusively to machine production in 1885, he quickly saturated the market in the U.S. In five years' time, Duke's company was selling nearly a billion cigarettes annually, far more than any other producer.[15] Other manufacturers soon followed in Duke's footsteps. The cigarette industry was rapidly becoming a major force in the U.S. economy. Production was no longer an issue; the only task was selling the product to the American public.[16]

Duke believed that there were four facets of the cigarette business: (1) the growing, purchasing, and blending of tobacco, (2) the manufacture and packaging of cigarettes, (3) distribution, and (4) advertising. Unlike other producers, Duke considered cigarettes to be a "cheap smoke" that could capture cigar smokers on the basis of price and advertising. He believed that cigarettes were an entirely new product, and not simply a paper cigar. In addition to revolutionizing the cigarette, Duke showed his understanding of the cigarette market.

Duke understood that Americans were upwardly mobile, and it would be the same with smoking tobacco. Men might begin smoking tobacco with American cigarettes but if they did well they would graduate up to foreign brands and cigars. Therefore, the cheap cigarette had a limited future. The cigarette was destined for the role of the initiator of the young into smoking. Duke would keep them as customers as long as they were not wealthy enough to afford cigars.[17]

Duke's ultimate goal was to dominate the entire tobacco business. First, he planned to engulf the other cigarette firms and take over all forms of tobacco production. Duke started the process by intensifying his advertising and lowering prices. Eventually, retailers earned 50 percent more profit by selling W. Duke Sons than any other competitor's brand. Duke bought out the competition and formed the American Tobacco Company on January 31, 1890. However, the tobacco trust was short lived. The first antitrust action was brought against American Tobacco in April 1890 and the litigation lasted until the Supreme Court dissolved the trust in May 1911.[18]

Cigarette smoking grew in popularity from 1880 onward. By 1890, the use of cigarette tobacco ran even with snuff. The sales of cigarettes grew into the 1890s. However, cigarette use fell from 1900 to 1905 and only equaled snuff sales again in 1911. Cigarettes did not reach the same level as any other tobacco form until the start of the 1920s, when it surpassed cigars, pipe tobacco, and chewing tobacco or plug. Cigarettes comprised more than half of all tobacco use by 1935.[19]

In addition to mass production, marketing played a key role in the spread of the habit. Until World War I, cigarette production in the United States remained relatively stable. Once the United States entered the conflict in 1917, the National Cigarette Service Committee distributed millions of free cigarettes to the troops in France. The cigarettes became such a morale booster that General John Pershing demanded priority for their shipment to the front. The war solidified the habit among the American people. Between 1910 and 1919 cigarette production increased by 633 percent, from less than ten billion annually to nearly 70 billion annually.[20]

CIGARETTE PROMOTION AND ADVERTISING, 1920S AND 1930S

After World War I, tobacco manufacturing had completed its long transition from a laid-back country craft to an aggressive commercial war on a national battlefield. In this fight, advertising was the primary weapon. At the dawn of the 1920s, advertising was repetitious, grating, and emotional. Color advertisements showing movie stars appealing to the audience to try their particular brand promised social approval to youth. Advertising that made cigarette smoking seem sensible, even healthful, stimulated more sales as medical doctors, athletes, and celebrities gladly signed testimonials. The millions spent on advertising were directed at capturing new smokers, fostering brand loyalty, and increasing brand consciousness. Effectively reaching the youth audience was vital to fostering the national smoking habit.[21] New brands were needed to accomplish this goal.

As soldiers returned victorious from the battlefields in Europe, R. J. Reynolds, a former member of the American Tobacco trust, was creating its first nationally marketed cigarette, Camel Cigarettes. Just before the war, the cigarette industry developed a slightly acid blend of burley and Turkish tobaccos. This new blend allowed experienced cigarette smokers to inhale without coughing.[22] The brand rapidly attained market dominance with an upscale smoke that delivered a new tobacco taste.

To compete with Camel, George Washington Hill's American Tobacco Company created a richer, sweeter product, Lucky Strike cigarettes. Hill hired hard-sell expert Albert Lasker of the Lord & Thomas Agency to do whatever was necessary to win the cigarette war. As a result, Lucky Strike broke all previous records. Urged by Lasker, Hill jumped at the chance to reach an untapped audience—women. The Lucky Strike campaign involved several advertising innovations. Hill was concerned that women disliked the green packaging because it clashed with their clothes. To remedy the problem he hired a public relations giant, Edward Bernays, who promoted the color green at the season's fashion show. Hill also used Bernays to help with the necessary social engineering that was needed to persuade women to smoke. They first set out to increase the acceptability of women smoking in public. To achieve this goal, Bernays convinced a group of ten debutantes to smoke cigarettes while strolling with their escorts in Fifth Avenue's Easter parade. The stunt was billed by Bernays as women lighting a "torch of freedom ... to combat the silly prejudice that the cigarette ... is never seen on the sidewalk."[23] Hill also used celebrities from the entertainment world to promote the cigarettes. The new slogan, "Reach for a Lucky instead of a sweet," resonated with the weight-conscious female audience.[24]

Although the new Lucky slogan resonated with women, it did not fare as well with the candy industry. The tobacco-candy fight was a rough one. As a result, the Federal Trade Commission (FTC) became deeply entrenched in the conflict. American Tobacco appropriated $12.3 million for the battle. To accommodate the candy industry, Lucky Strike modified the slogan to "Reach for a Lucky Instead," and ran a "future-shadow" series of advertisements featuring double-chinned and heavy-belted silhouettes behind trim figures. In spite of American Tobacco's efforts, by 1932 the FTC banned the American Tobacco Company from marketing cigarettes as a weight-reducing device, even by suggestion.[25] By establishing a connection between smoking and a slender figure, George Washington Hill and Albert Lasker, of the Lord & Thomas agency, were able to erase some of the negative stigma from cigarette smoking. In fact, they convinced many women that smoking was good for their image. The American Tobacco Company spent more money advertising Lucky Strikes than anyone had ever spent to advertise a single product. Lord & Thomas used this single account to make a place for itself among the major agencies.[26]

Because of the efforts to target women, female smokers became substantial tobacco consumers for the very first time. The new brands intersected with women's liberation. In 1919, *Printer's Ink*, ever on guard for advertising offenses, warned of an insidious campaign to create female smokers. Murad and Helmar cigarette advertisements showed Western-looking women in Turkish harem costumes introducing a daring new habit in an exotic setting.[27]

In spite of the success of cigarette marketing to women, the issue of women and smoking remained controversial. Female smokers found themselves unable to smoke on ships, in railroad diners, and in train station smoking rooms. However, by the mid–1920s, some colleges had established smoking rooms, while railroads and shipping lines relaxed their regulations.[28] Cigarette advertising helped to fuel this cultural revolution. In 1926, the Newell-Emmett agency daringly presented a poster for Chesterfield cigarettes showing a woman perched beside a man in a romantic moonlit seaside scene saying, "Blow some my way." These four words were shocking to many people. Yet Chesterfield persistently continued the campaign, paving the way to the immense women's market.[29] From 1920 to 1928, while the production of pipe tobacco fell by 9 percent and that of cigars by 20 percent, cigarette production increased 123 percent to 106 billion units per year.[30]

During the 1930s, Lucky Strikes and Camels fought to be the leading brand of cigarette. During the Depression years, two new players effectively entered the market. Even though hundreds of companies were trying to enter the domestic cigarette market, only Philip Morris, a small independent producer, and Brown & Williamson, a subsidiary of British-American Tobacco Company, were successful.[31] The tobacco industry was able to maintain profits through the Depression through the use of voluntary health claims and endorsements.

Health claims during the late 1920s and 1930s varied from claims that a particular brand caused less throat irritation and coughing, to aiding digestion and improving concentration and disposition, or even marketing smoking as a remedy for the cold and flu.[32] This time period is unique because of the positive claims that the cigarette industry made regarding health. This uniqueness is partially due to the competitive nature of the cigarette industry at the time[33] and the lack of regulation. For instance, "No one had ever heard of a 'coughless' cigarette before Old Gold came…. No rasping. No coughing … with 'not a cough in the carload' and Lucky Strike appealed to taste and health with their slogan "It's Toasted—No Throat Irritation."[34] However, instead of being reassuring, these health-related appeals were ultimately discontinued because industry research found them to be far more detrimental to the brands than appeals to taste, texture and mildness. Therefore, the health-focused campaigns ended because they reminded smokers about their own fears about smoking.[35]

CIGARETTE ADVERTISING AND PROMOTION, WORLD WAR II–1963

Like World War I, World War II gave cigarette smoking an enormous boost. Cigarettes were sold at military-post exchanges and ship's stores tax-free and virtually at cost. They also were distributed free in the forward areas and were packaged in K rations.[36] Tobacco producers got as much free publicity as they could want during the war. Both Winston Churchill with his cigar and Franklin D. Roosevelt smoking his cigarette helped to promote tobacco.[37] Prior to World War II, it had been socially unacceptable for women to smoke heavily. After the war it became much more widely accepted.[38]

The cigarette business was particularly eager to invest in television commercials. Tobacco was sponsoring prime time programming such as *Arthur Godfrey and His Friends*, *The Chesterfield Supper Club*, *Stop the Music*, and *Your Lucky Strike Theatre*. Rosser Reeves, the chairman of the Ted Bates agency, which was responsible for the hardest of the hard sell in cigarette advertising on television during the 1950s, said that selling cigarettes was "just like wiring the slot machine to keep paying out a perpetual jackpot. My boy, it was just like printing money."[39]

Although cigarette smoking was a popular habit, evidence was rapidly accumulating during the 1950s regarding the potential heath risks of smoking. The press reported on various epidemiological studies providing statistical links between smoking and cancer. While some physicians remained among the doubters, medical opinion began to swing toward the opinion it holds today.[40] The sharp decline in sales that resulted panicked the industry as cigarette manufacturers resumed the health-claims campaigns that most brands had discontinued in the 1930s. The number of health claims in cigarette advertisements peaked in the 1950s, reaching their greatest level of intensity from 1950 to 1955.[41] The negative health claims used to persuade the public often reinforced consumer fears. While these health claims might have benefited the brand, they tended to harm competitors and injure the cigarette industry in general because the "less harmful than" claim suggested that other brands were more harmful.[42] Therefore, health claims were used primarily by upstart or struggling cigarette brands to gain a market edge on the more prominent brands. Health claims quickly declined after the 1955 FTC guidelines restricting health claims.[43]

The cigarette industry responded to the health claims of the 1950s through research and product innovation, which resulted in the introduction of filtered cigarettes. Competition in filtering power became a key marketing strategy.[44] The advertisements for Kent's Micronite filters claimed, "Kent offers the greatest health protection in cigarette history."[45] Micronite was described as "pure, dust-free, completely harmless material that is so safe, so effective, that it is actually used to help filter the air in hospital operating rooms." However, the Kent advertisements did not mention the fact that Micronite is made from asbestos. The campaign was launched just after researchers had linked asbestos to a host of respiratory ailments.[46]

Filters appealed to smokers because they appeared to offer a more healthful alternative. The new brands presented their advertising firms with a formidable challenge. Consequently, cigarette advertising embarked on what has become known as the "filter wars."[47] Rosser Reeves, an advertising industry pioneer, called this rivalry "one of the most vicious running advertising dog fights in our advertising history."[48]

In response to the challenge that the filter wars presented, the industry used several approaches to sell filtered cigarettes. One was to discuss tar and nicotine yield and other explicit health matters. This approach was used until the FTC's 1955 guidelines restricted health claims. In response to the health-related advertising restrictions, the cigarette manufacturers shifted to promoting filters for what they did not do. For instance, they claimed that their filters did not impede taste. In addition, one could advertise filter quality without saying exactly what the filter achieved; for example, "Twice as many filters in the Viceroy Tip."[49] The advertisements never mentioned reducing carcinogens because the filters could not effectively eliminate them. Another issue was that when the filters were most effective, they tended to remove a large portion of the nicotine in the smoke. As nicotine is the addictive ingredient in cigarettes, smokers were unsatisfied and left craving more. Other strategies included using stronger tobaccos and loosening the materials inside the filter tip, making the filtration less effective. However, as a result of their successful marketing, filters made up 20 percent of the market by 1955.[50]

Meanwhile, the non-filtered brands struggled to keep their customers from switching to the filtered brands. The biggest selling point was that by not having filters they continued to deliver "full taste" to their customers. The unfiltered Camels were one of the best selling brands in the pre-filtered days. To avoid losing its prominence, Camel launched a campaign around the question, "Are you smoking more now, but enjoying it less?" But for most other unfiltered brands, including unfiltered Camels, it was a losing battle. Eventually, to meet market demands, the unfiltered brands had to develop filtered versions.[51]

In addition to health-related appeals, many cigarette advertisements used sex appeals. Women's objections to sex-based advertisements and narrow social roles went largely unrecognized during the 1950s. Depicting women as happy homemakers had always worked. Most women of the time did not oppose this portrayal.[52] Many cigarette advertisements reinforced views of women that seem extremely traditional or even sexist to the 21st-century reader. Cigarette advertisements also used celebrities to promote their brand of cigarettes. One early advertisement featured Broadway star Patricia Morison, introduced as "one whose beauty and talent carried her to stardom." Morrison, smoking a cigarette, says, "There is nothing quite like Camels. They taste so good and they are so mild."[53]

Opposition to Cigarettes and Tobacco Use

EARLY OPPOSITION TO SMOKING AND TOBACCO USE

To many, the surgeon general's report in 1964 represents the beginnings of the tobacco and health controversy. However, issues relating to the side effects of tobacco have virtually always followed the industry. King James I of England actively voiced his concerns about the first tobacco crops being grown in colonial Virginia.[54] He stated that tobacco was "loathsome to the eye, hateful to the nose, harmful to the brain" and "dangerous to the lungs."[55] One of tobacco's earliest detractors was published in Britain in 1604, *A Counterblast to Tobacco*. Although originally it was anonymous, the tract now receives considerable attention because historians believe that it was created by James I, who instituted heavy taxes on tobacco as part of a campaign against the product. In 1601, the *Calendar of State Papers (Domestic)* published one of the first records of pathology linked to tobacco use. According to this paper, surgeons attributed the death of a patient to smoking tobacco.[56]

The first anti-tobacco tract was published in the U.S. in 1798 by Dr. Benjamin Rush, a signer of the Declaration of Independence. In Rush's *Observations upon the influence of the Habitual use of Tobacco upon Health, Morals, and Property*, he objects to the use of tobacco on grounds that it had disastrous effects on the stomach, the nerves, and the oral cavity. Many tobacco users, including John Quincy Adams, a connoisseur who had made the cigar respectable, announced that they had shaken the habit with consequent improvement in health.[57]

During the pre–Civil War period, a group of doctors, educators, Clergymen and the great P.T. Barnum formed an alliance to fight the tobacco habit. Some anti-smoking literature also addressed itself to youth. The Reverend George Trask of Boston published a popular tract in 1852 entitled *Thoughts and Stories for American Lads; or Uncle Toby's Anti-Tobacco Advice to his Nephew Billy Bruce*. Likewise, the *Lancet*, a British medical journal, in 1856 and 1857 featured an article entitled "The Great Tobacco Question" in which fifty doctors expressed their opinions on the topic. Doctors described nervous paralysis, loss of intellectual capacity, and vision impairment.[58]

The Civil War increased American cigarette consumption and attracted new smokers in the Midwest and Northeast. In response to the increase in smoking, Midwestern tobacco opponents demanded regulation. Because no major manufacturer of cigarettes existed, and because the government needed money to finance the war, Congress complied by taxing cigarettes arriving from Russia and Turkey.[59]

As cigarettes gained popularity at the turn of the 20th century, the anti-tobacco senti-ments reignited. In 1880, cigarettes constituted 1 percent of tobacco intake, yet they drew regular criticism that increased in intensity as sales grew. The opposition to cigarette smoking took a variety of forms, from verbal criticisms in the form of "epithets associated with death or immortality," such as "coffin nails," "gaspers," and "devil's toothpicks" to more coordinated activities such as attacks from schools, pulpits, and the press.[60]

One of the most outspoken early tobacco opponents was Lucy Page Gaston. Born in 1860 to parents who were active in reform movements, especially abolition and temperance, Gaston could aptly discuss the evils of alcohol and the rewards of clean living as a child. While working as a teacher, Gaston would see young boys sneaking around to the back of the schoolhouse to puff on cigarettes. Invariably, these were her worst students. Gaston organized her Chicago-based campaign modeled on previous anti-alcohol crusades. Children wore pins and sang songs, carried banners, and paraded. Gaston formally organized her cause in 1903, forming the National Anti-Cigarette League. Clergymen, educators, and many busi-nessmen applauded her efforts.[61]

Gaston's zeal was rewarded. Her campaign was effective and, as one could have pre-dicted, it did best in the Midwest. Thanks to her hard work most large cities had clinics that smokers could go to for help if they wanted to quit. Likewise, many new products were being marketed to help tobacco users quit. For instance, the National Anti-Cigarette League intro-duced a mouthwash that was supposed to reduce tobacco cravings.[62]

In addition to Gaston, many other public figures opposed smoking. Boxing champion John L. Sullivan denounced cigarettes as unmanly. Henry Ford and Thomas Edison refused to hire cigarette smokers. A nationwide Committee to Study the Tobacco Problem was established and attracted distinguished men in every field. Anti-cigarette physicians including Surgeon General Rupert Blue condemned cigarettes. In addition, the New England Life Insurance Company found that after investigating the records of policy-holders during a certain period of time that 57 out of 100 nonusers of tobacco died; during the same period, 95 out of 100 cigarette smokers died. By 1909, twelve states and numerous towns created laws restricting tobacco use or sale. However, many of these statutes were never enforced.[63]

There were some within the tobacco industry that made light of the anti-tobacco efforts. However, tobacco sales dropped significantly during the late nineteenth century and early twentieth century. Buck Duke was said to have mixed feelings about the tobacco controversy. For a while, Lucy Gaston's crusade might have harmed American Tobacco, but it almost completely eliminated the company's competitors. At the turn of the century, nine out of every ten packs sold carried the Duke label.

Opposition to Smoking in the 1920s and 1930s

Because of the popularity of cigarettes spurred by World War I and the tax revenue that cigarette sales were earning, much of the opposition died down in the 1920s and 1930s.[64] In fact, throughout the first half of the 20th century doctors largely ignored any negative news about smoking. This is largely because anti-tobacco claims makers usually presented their findings in moral rather than medical terms.[65]

Lucy Gaston remained active in the anti-tobacco cause until her death in 1924. Her goal was to completely abolish cigarette smoking by 1925. However, the thrust of her anti-smoking campaigns during the early 1920s centered on preventing women from smoking. Her anti-tobacco campaign slogan was "Save the Girl." Part of the reason for her change in focus was that she conceded that men would be smokers. The best that she felt that she could do was to help prevent women from taking up the habit.[66]

The Woman's Christian Temperance Union (WCTU) actively opposed the use of cigarettes among women and children. Their 1921 annual report indicated that Iowa's anti-cigarette law had been weakened and North Dakota's had been strengthened. The WCTU lobbied for laws prohibiting smoking at establishments where food was sold. Oregon instituted a law against smoking where food was sold and Minnesota was considering a similar law. By 1927, twenty-one states had laws that prevented smoking where food was being sold. But some legislation was going the other way. In 1927, Kansas repealed a 21-year-old statute by legalizing cigarette sales.[67]

The Anti-Narcotics Department, a federal agency that continues to fight narcotics, also took a stand against tobacco. By 1927, the Anti-Narcotics Department reported that its chapters sponsored 6,699 anti-smoking programs, distributed 580,223 pages of anti-smoking literature, and sponsored nineteen state poster contests. In essay contests, more than 27,000 anti-smoking essays were submitted.[68]

As advertising smoking to women increased in prevalence, there was a backlash from tobacco opponents. For instance, beginning in 1928, American Tobacco Company advertised smoking Luckies as an alternative to eating candy. Chocolate manufacturers feared that women were following American Tobacco's advice and the complaints of the confectioners made news. Both the Cleveland Boy Scouts and the Sioux Falls, South Dakota, City Commission objected to billboards that depicted women smoking. Bills to restrict cigarette advertising were introduced in Illinois, Michigan, and Idaho.[69]

In spite of the growing acceptance of the habit, the consequences of cigarette smoking became evident in the 1920s and 1930s when physicians began to notice cases of a very rare form of cancer, lung cancer, were accumulating at an alarming rate. Dr. John Harvey Kellogg, who gained much of his fame from breakfast cereal, published *Tobaccoism, Or How Tobacco Kills* in 1923. In this publication Kellogg claimed that nine out of ten smokers suffered from mouth and throat cancers. Another physician, Dr. Alton Ochsner, stated in 1936, "All of the afflicted patients were men who smoked heavily and had smoked since World War I...I had the temerity, at that time, to postulate that the probable cause of this new epidemic was cigarette use."[70] A 1932 paper in the *American Journal of Cancer* accurately blamed the tars in cigarettes for the formation of cancer. This was the first major study to make the connection.[71] In a 1936 study, Drs. Aaron Arkin and David Wagner found lung cancer in 90 percent of their patients that were chronic smokers.[72]

In January 1930, the Federal Trade Commission passed some of its first cigarette advertising regulations. These regulations related to testimonials that Lucky Strike created that included testimonials from celebrities who did not smoke. The FTC ruled that American Tobacco Company must stop running advertising that featured the testimonies of endorsers who had never used their product. Further, American Tobacco Company was forced to identify paid testimonials, and the company was told not to claim that smoking cigarettes aids in weight control.[73]

OPPOSITION TO SMOKING, WORLD WAR II–1963

Although a few doctors and scientists continued their research, the issue of smoking and health largely disappeared during World War II. The lack of research was a result of a lack of funding and a feeling that anti-tobaccoism was unpatriotic. The research did not end completely, but it often centered on ways that smokers could continue their habit. For instance, an optimistic study in 1948 found that patients with inactive forms of heart disease could continue to smoke in moderation.[74] In spite of the previous warnings, Americans entered the early 1950s full of enthusiasm and confidence in their smoking habit.[75]

By the early 1950s, however, medical studies began to demonstrate close links between smoking and ill health. Four retrospective studies were published on the smoking habits of lung cancer patients. Research connecting lung cancer with smoking was done by Ernest Wynder and Evart Graham in the *Journal of the American Medical Association* in 1950, by Richard Doll and Bradford Hill in the *British Medical Journal* in 1950 and 1952, by Wynder and Graham with Adele Croninger in *Cancer Research* in 1953, and by Alton Ochsner in 1952, 1953, and 1954.[76] In 1953 investigators at what is now the Sloan-Kettering Institute announced that they had induced cancer in mice by painting their backs with tars from cigarette smoke.[77] This research demonstrated that smoking clearly caused cancer. This incriminating research was a cause for serious concern for the tobacco industry.[78]

At first, the heath research relating tobacco with an increased cancer risk remained in scientific publications. The few articles that did appear in the popular press reassured smokers. For instance, *U.S. News and World Report* ran a two-page spread when Dr. Egon Lorenz of the National Cancer Institute demonstrated that smoking mice lived a normal life span. The article concluded that smoking in moderation would not cause serious health problems.[79] However, by July 1954, when an article in *Reader's Digest* connected general exposure to smoking with health concerns, the general public had been made aware of the smoking-and-health issue.[80]

Initially, the industry responded to the health concerns with denial and buck-passing. In 1952, entertainer and broadcaster Arthur Godfrey reassured his audience by saying, "You hear things all the time that cigarettes are harmful to you… Chesterfields won't harm your nose, throat or accessory organs."[81] A responsible consulting organization had vouched for it. However, industry leaders like American Tobacco Company executive Paul Hahn realized that the every-brand-for-itself campaign was doomed to failure. It would only serve to increase the public awareness of the cancer issues.[82]

In light of all of the negative publicity, it seems that it would have been difficult for cigarette manufacturers to promote their profitable product. However, because of its virtually unlimited funds, the industry was able to purchase the best publicity and advertising that money could buy. And, by doing so, it enticed millions of Americans to begin or continue smoking.

The tobacco industry, assisted by its public relations consultants, won the first battle of the cancer wars. The doubt raising countered, if not deferred, the health anxieties about cigarette smoking. Likewise, the introduction of filtered cigarettes helped to convince the public that there was a healthful alternative to quitting. The tobacco industry's efforts matched their needs perfectly. However, the evidence was beginning to mount and the industry could only argue with the research for so long. In the wake of the landmark reports by the Royal College of Physicians in 1962 and the surgeon general's report in 1964, legislation to limit or ban advertising began to take effect. Likewise, counteradvertising, public service announcements and campaigns by anti-smoking groups began to diminish the consumer base. By the mid–1970s the number of smokers began to plummet.[83] Without advertising, cigarettes struggled to reach the younger markets. When cigarette brands cannot reach young audience members, the number of future smokers is greatly reduced.

2

The Tobacco Industry, the University and the Campus Paper

Tobacco has had a long relationship with the university and intellectualism. Both pipes and cigarettes have been associated with the intellectual elite. However, the strength of influence that the tobacco industry had on university campuses is less well known. The tobacco industry employed an army of campus representatives to promote smoking on campus, sponsored contests to increase product use, fund faculty and student research through tobacco experiment stations, and support student newspapers and other student media through advertising to promote individual brands. The tobacco industry and the university had what some might call a symbiotic relationship. The most visible manifestation of this relationship is seen in the prevalence of tobacco advertising on university campuses.

Tobacco and University Life

Because of their financial dependence on tobacco money, most colleges did very little to discourage smoking from the 1940s to the early 1960s. In fact, Dr. Douglass Thompson, director of student health services at the University of Pittsburgh, felt that colleges and universities actually encouraged smoking. After conducting a pilot survey of 100 health directors at colleges and universities Douglas reported, "I have found that colleges seem to encourage smoking by letting tobacco firms give away free cigarettes at registration and in dining rooms, by sponsoring cigarette contests on campus, and by permitting tobacco advertising in school newspapers."[1] The 1961 survey found that "virtually none" of the physicians responding to the questionnaire denied the existence of a possible relationship between smoking and lung cancer. In addition, there was no relationship between the physicians' smoking habits and their beliefs about the potential adverse health consequences related to smoking. The survey also found that almost every university surveyed accepted cigarette and tobacco advertising.[2]

Although the university was virtually silent on the issue of smoking on campus between 1940 and 1960, there was early opposition to smoking on college and university campuses. However, by the time the FTC helped put an end to the advertising in June 1963, many colleges and universities had become increasingly financially dependent on tobacco and reluctant to criticize the industry that funded its student media, athletics, and some of its faculty's research.

EARLY OPPOSITION TO SMOKING ON
COLLEGE AND UNIVERSITY CAMPUSES

Starting in the late 1920s, smoking on college and university campuses was becoming increasingly prevalent. The idea that men smoked in higher education had been accepted for years. The fact that a growing number of women were smoking on campus was attracting national attention. From the turn of the century to the early 1920s, it was taboo for women to smoke in public places. The issue of female students smoking on college campuses was an especially hot topic because the majority of women attending colleges and universities were being trained in the field of education. The public strongly disapproved of the prospect of elementary school teachers smoking. Therefore, many colleges and universities forbade female students to smoke. However, by the 1930s, the issue had been settled in the minds of most people. Like it or not, women smoked in the institutions of higher learning.[3]

In 1919 Vassar College, in Poughkeepsie, New York, went on record as being opposed to women smoking. The Students' Association voted: "No Vassar student shall smoke while under the jurisdiction of the college, this rule to be enforced under the honor system." However, the rule was changed in 1925 "to lay responsibility on the individual permitting her to smoke inconspicuously."[4] Smoking was prohibited in dormitories and other college buildings. Burgess Johnson, a professor in the English department and director of publicity, stated, "[The college] voted against the proposition; I am told. I have not heard of the students smoking and the students have never asked permission to smoke."[5]

In December of 1921 University of Chicago president Harry Pratt Judson banned smoking in women's dormitories. Accustomed to making their own rules, the dormitory women suddenly were confronted with a notice from the housemothers against the cigarette. No explanation was officially offered, but rumor had it that the dean of women and others on campus protested against what was thought to be excessive smoking by female students.[6]

The New York Times also reported on smoking policies at Radcliffe and Smith.[7] It was front-page news that M.I.T. allowed young women to smoke at dances. Goucher College prohibited students from smoking both on campus and at public places in Baltimore. A study at Bryn Mawr showed that less than half of its female students smoked. Bryn Mawr's self-government association petitioned the college president for a smoking room and the president consented and repealed the previous smoking ban.[8] *The New York Times* editorially endorsed the Bryn Mawr decision in condescending tones. *The Times* said that by allowing cigarettes in certain places, "what once was a feat of defiance becomes rather a bore."[9]

By 1925, one-third of the women at the Ohio State University said that they smoked at least on occasion. And, in 1924, a student leader at Rhode Island State claimed, "practically all girls smoke." The student newspaper at the University of Illinois covered the issue of women smoking often in 1924 and made it clear that progressive students felt that it was perfectly acceptable for students to smoke.[10]

Late in 1929, George W. Stephens, the dean at Washington University in St. Louis, reiterated a long-standing faculty decision that smoking by female students was not permitted at Washington University. This ruling included all university-related social functions. In 1930, a report from Lewisburg, Pennsylvania, stated that 44 out of the 400 women attending Bucknell University were prevented from walking on campus and having dates for the next six months as a result of their admissions that they smoked in their rooms. A self-governing student organization assigned the penalty. Likewise, Charles McKenny, president of Michigan State Normal College in Ypsilanti, told a group of women in 1931 that no woman known to smoke in public places would be allowed to graduate. McKenny believed that Michigan residents would not likely hire schoolteachers that smoked.

However, some schools denied any smoking problems among their female students. James M. Kierman, the president of New York City's Hunter College, maintained that, "Smoking hasn't much of a grip on our girls yet." He also continued by mentioning that the school paper was accepting money from tobacco, but he didn't expect that it would influence the female students' smoking habits. However, the college eventually set up a smoking room for its female students. Many other campuses followed by restricting smoking on campus based on gender.[11]

As late as November 1933, certain schools prohibited cigarette advertising that featured women. For instance, in a letter to the R.J. Reynolds advertising department, the Arkansas State Teacher's College's *Echo*, San Jose State Teacher's College's *College Times*, Drake University's *Times-Delphic*, Holy Cross's *Tomahawk*, and the Tennessee Polytechnic Institute's *Tech Oracle* were listed as campus papers that would not accept cigarette advertising featuring women.[12]

Although women were gradually gaining permission to smoke on campus, many were agitated by the idea of women smoking outside. As late as 1937 a market research firm found that 95 percent of male smokers smoked in the street, but only 28 percent thought that it was right for women to do likewise. Because women felt conspicuous smoking outside, they started smoking inside in places where men had never smoked. For instance, they smoked inside of railroad diners, retail stores, and art galleries. Because of the taboo, colleges and universities established smoking rooms in dormitories. For instance, Smith College announced that smoking was restricted to two fireproof rooms.[13]

By 1937, bans on smoking on campus were the exception rather than the rule. More and more women smoked in public in the United States in general during this period of time. Between 1918 and 1928, American tobacco sales increased fourfold. In 1900 cigarette consumption, as part of the tobacco industry as a whole, was just 2 percent. By 1930 cigarettes accounted for 40 percent of tobacco consumption. Much of that increase was due to the dramatic change in the image of the cigarette as more men switched to cigarette smoking from other forms of tobacco use and more women began to smoke.[14]

Opposition to smoking on college campuses disappeared during the 1940s. One reason is that the tobacco industry shifted its marketing campaign's focus to the armed forces due to the war effort. A second reason is that tobacco is an important American agricultural product. Therefore, cigarette smoking was considered to be a patriotic habit.

CIGARETTE PROMOTION ON CAMPUS 1950–1963

Unlike the 1920s and 1930s, during the 1950s and 1960s cigarettes attained the full acceptance of the college and university community. Young college men and women were both given as much liberty as possible to smoke on campus. And, the tobacco industry was given complete freedom to promote its product.

For instance, among New York State's many colleges and universities, Cortland State

Teachers College was distinguished for its training program for physical education teachers. In 1961, the Cortland Alpha Delta Delta sorority won first place in a contest sponsored by Phillip Morris. For engineering the consumption of 1,520,000 Phillip Morris cigarettes and redeeming the empty packages, the young women of Alpha Delta Delta were awarded a magnificent high-fidelity phonograph.[15]

The women of Alpha Delta Delta paid a high price for their victory. As the deadline for cigarette package collection drew near, the sorority house was immersed with a crisis psychology. The continued smoking of Phillip Morris brands at a breathless pace became a badge of loyalty. One sorority member was compelled to abandon her relatively mild filtered cigarette for the non-filtered Phillip Morris. The reluctant sorority sister daring to venture into the open without smoking a Phillip Morris cigarette risked displeasure or ostracism.[16]

In spite of the difficulties, the Alpha Delta Delta sorority won its phonograph. And, Phillip Morris won the loyalty and gratitude of future physical education teachers whose enthusiasm for teaching the hazards of cigarette smoking might be significantly reduced.[17]

Similarly, a Columbia University student was constructing a replica of the United Nations headquarters from six thousand Marlboro and Parliament boxes. For the collegiate poets, Liggett & Myers held out the lure of eight British Sprite sports cars to be awarded to the best limerick, plus the bottom panels from five Chesterfield, L&M or Oasis packages. And, to the sports-minded students, Brown & Williamson presented cash prizes to those who successfully predicted the outcome of selected football games. The cash prizes ranged from ten to 100 dollars.[18]

The prevalence of college contests was a mere symptom of the umbrella spread by the cigarette companies over every conceivable variety of campus activity. Campus newspapers abounded with cigarette advertisements tailored to their collegiate audience. Tobacco companies typically contributed a staggering 40 percent of all national advertising placed in college newspapers. The undergraduates that developed a taste for the irreverent humor of Max Shulman could find him selling the virtues of Marlboro or Phillip Morris cigarettes in nearly every college publication. Meanwhile, American Tobacco Company's copywriters assured students that the "important things in college life stay the same. Parties. Girls. Luckies." Some advertisements were even more obvious in their approach. Some typical slogans included, "Luckies—the cigarette to start with" and "More college students smoke Luckies—than any other regular cigarette."[19]

Brown & Williamson had at least seventeen salesmen engaging their energies as Viceroy, Kool, and Raleigh Santa Clauses at various colleges during the Christmas season. Likewise, Phillip Morris selected worthy students on 166 college campuses as "campus representatives," paying each $50 a month to spread the good cheer and complimentary Marlboros. No fraternity party, political rally, or tea for international students escaped the presence of the Phillip Morris representatives.[20]

It is possible that after the contests were won, the samples consumed, and the advertising messages burned into the memory of the nation's undergraduates, one or another uncooperative student still declined to smoke. But, the imaginative R.J. Reynolds Tobacco Company established a program with the collegiate-sounding name "The Line-Backer" system. Reynolds recruited college public information officers to ensure that Camels and other company brands advertised in the football programs at many colleges and universities could be seen, admired and purchased in every possible location at the college. By promoting the

Camel brand, the public information officials earned the right to participate in their own contests with foreign cars being the reward for soliciting students.[21]

Student Publications

THE DEVELOPMENT OF THE CAMPUS PRESS IN THE UNITED STATES

Student publications are a long-established feature of college and university life. Established early, likely because of their close relationship with an academic subject, they have persisted in somewhat changing form until the present. Of all student publications, the school newspaper is the most responsive to students needs and expresses their opinions the most clearly. Although the newspaper is more transitory than the yearbook or the handbook, it normally deals with more important issues. Student newspapers are vital because they contribute to students' personal development and enhance school life.

In 1799 the first student newspaper was established at Dartmouth College.[22] *The Dartmouth* was a weekly paper.[23] Established January 28, 1878, the *Yale Daily News* is the nation's first college daily newspaper.[24] Ten years later, in 1883, the *Harvard Crimson*, originally founded in 1856 as a weekly paper named *The Magenta*, also became a daily paper.[25] Dozens of college newspapers existed by the turn of century in a movement that popularized the college press. These publications filled their four to six pages with "news concerning undergraduates and alumni, furnishing persuasive editorials on local affairs, and giving a truthful bulletin of the day's doings sensibly and in small space."[26]

By the late 19th century, the majority of American universities and colleges had at least a weekly newspaper, and many already had dailies. By 1912 there were 400 campus periodicals listed in advertisers annuals.[27] However, the majority of schools did not begin to publish newspapers until after World War I. Thirty-one colleges and universities in the United States published daily newspapers in 1923. And, by 1926, newspapers alone numbered 400 and circulations ranged from 500 to 5,000. *The Daily Illini* was an example of the latter. The newspaper served a community of 30,000 people as the only morning daily. The paper was printed at a university-owned plant valued at $100,000.[28] In 1929, McNeil stated that there were at least four hundred student papers being published at least twice a week. Of this number, 32 were college dailies ranging in size from four to 32 pages.[29] *School and Society* in 1929 summarized the collegiate press as follows:

> Today there are thirty-two college daily newspapers in the country, about half of which use the telegraph service of some nationally known news-gathering organization.... They range in size from four to thirty-two pages.
>
> As was to be expected, the college newspaper has taken the daily newspaper as its model and has written its news stories, its headlines, its editorial, and has adapted its makeup to that of the regular dailies.
>
> In an endeavor to find out to what extent staff members receive compensation, a survey was made and answers received from 230 papers. Academic credit for work on the staff is the exception rather than the rule, according to the reports received for only six dailies, eight semi-weeklies, and forty-eight weeklies reported staff members receiving classroom credit.
>
> When it comes to the question of receiving actual money for work on the staff, either business or editorial, it appears to be the rule that certain members, at least the editor-in-

chief and business manager, receive a definite sum or percentage of the profits...In 40 percent of the cases the amounts given are based on a percentage of the profits that the paper has made during the school year. In other papers where a definite sum is given, the amounts vary from $100 to $800 a year for the head of staff of papers publishing daily.[30]

The first intercollegiate newspaper was created in 1933 among four institutions: Mt. Holyoke, Amherst, Smith, and Massachusetts State College.[31] The first edition included four pages of news and sold for five cents per copy. News was carried in a light style, which was reflected in its headlines, "Smith Has Become Sandwich Conscious" and "Sprinkler System Startles Holyoke."[32] In 1940, *The Minnesota Daily* also achieved a first in the realm of the collegiate press. *The Minnesota Daily* experimented with tabloid journalism much to the dismay of many who complained of the smaller page size. However, the student body voted to keep the unique tabloid format.[33]

As the popularity of higher education grew in the United States during the 20th century, so did the number, size, and frequency of issue of campus newspapers. By 1970, there were more than 1,200 college and university newspapers, and many of them were published daily.[34]

Campus newspapers are a big business. By 1970, more than six million copies were printed every week. Student newspapers are usually partially supported by student-activity fees and distributed to all students. The Intercollegiate Press Association, founded in 1886, was the sole nationwide trade association for student newspapers until 1963 when the U.S. Student Press Association was created. In addition to constituting a large number of newspapers, the campus press also represents an important advertising medium. National advertisers wanting to reach a student audience relied heavily on student newspapers.[35]

The first college and university newspapers usually were independent publications that depended on advertising and circulation for revenue. These early papers were small, had small staffs, and, as a result, did not need much money to survive. As public institutions of higher learning were founded and grew into large enterprises, the funding of student newspapers began to change. The campus publications began to rely more and more on college and university funds and student fees.

Because of the use of university and student funds, colleges and universities created publications boards to oversee the campus papers. Publications boards generally comprised both faculty and students. Usually, the student members were drawn from the publication editors. However, faculty and staff held most of the seats on the publication boards. Board duties ranged from picking student editors to trying to mediate disputes between administration and the newspaper.[36]

In some cases, the student newspaper has been responsible to student government rather than publications boards. In such situations one problem was the amount of control the student governing board wanted to exert over the student newspapers. Sometimes the student board directly imposed its political perspective on the newspaper. Journalism departments or schools often administered student newspapers as laboratories or workshops. In this situation, the newspaper was produced under the direct supervision of the faculty.[37]

By the 1960s, nearly 1,200 campus papers were governed at least in part by their college or university administrations. Most of these student newspapers received funding from student-activity fees or through direct appropriation of university funds. These financial ties with the institution made the colleges or universities the newspaper publishers.[38]

At the same time, the official recognition and support offered by the various colleges and universities involves certain obligations. By informing its readers on matters of interest and importance to members of the college community, the student newspaper plays an important role, particularly in creating a sense of community. It is also useful to the faculty and administration as a sounding board of student attitudes.[39]

With such physical and financial arrangements, it was not a surprise that there was disagreement and confusion over the role of the campus press. For instance, there was a great deal of debate about whether the newspaper was a student publication or if it was an official publication of the college or university. And, given the controversy, there was disagreement about who was ultimately responsible for the contents of the paper, the students or the administrators.

Often, the administrators did not elucidate the situation. Administrators either tried to back away from responsibility for the student paper or else they tried to block the appointment of editors that they perceived to be hostile to what administrators believed to be the institution's best interest.[40]

The campus newspaper is unique because it usually enjoys a monopolistic position on campus. While this alone is not unique in publishing a community newspaper, the importance of monopolistic status is the accompanying subsidy that enables the undergraduate publication to publish daily in large institutions.[41]

CONTROVERSIES OVER THE STUDENT PRESS

The student press was involved in numerous scandals during the 20th century. For instance, during the 1930s student newspapers were involved in controversies involving the military, such as the introduction of compulsory Reserve Officer Training (ROTC) programs on campuses and anti-military and anti-war activities of the time. Another volatile campus issue during the 1930s was the presence of Communist organizations on college campuses. During the 1950s the campus press was unusually silent. This silence reflected the general mood of the time. However this silence was shattered by the civil rights movement of the early 1960s and then by student opposition to the increasingly unpopular Vietnam War.[42]

Neither the Vietnam War nor the civil rights movement in the 1960s caused most of the problems. Instead, the language and the changing mores, including vigorous advocacy and editorial treatment of the news, were at the root of most of the problems. For instance, Pennsylvania state representative Russell J. LaMarca said that he would withhold funding for the University of Pittsburgh if any state funds were used to finance the "obscenities and vulgarities" that he found in student publications. He stated, "I don't feel like sending $36 million to a university that doesn't know what good taste is and doesn't have the guts to inform its students what good taste is."[43] Not only were state legislators discontented with the new boldness of language found in student newspapers, but so were the members of boards of trustees and regents, university presidents, parents, faculty, alumni and editors of general circulation newspapers. However, the controversial language used by college newspapers in the 1960s is now common in newspapers and magazines.[44]

What Is Expected from the Campus Newspaper?

Almost every educational institution has a newspaper. Newspapers resemble the professional press in that they seek to serve a definite group of people with news, opinions, and entertainment. Some campus papers are barely more than a bulletin while others cover local and national news.[45] Further, a college newspaper is a specific publication whose policies, philosophy, ethics, and articles are distinct from those of any other publication. It is an instrument that has a particular and important place in an educational institution. In many ways, the college paper expresses the policies and purposes of the institution, and reflects the effect of the educational process upon its students.[46] In addition to educating students in the newspaper industry, the objectives of the paper also include helping the student and the college or university understand each other and promoting a greater desire to participate in student activities.[47]

One of the basic problems for the student press during turbulent times, like the 1930s, 1940s, and 1960s, is that its various constituents perceived its role differently. For instance, university administrators and members of the boards of trustees and regents generally believed that the campus paper is an arm of the institution that should reflect the members' values of society and institution. These administrators wanted the newspapers to report administrative decisions and policies accurately and fairly. Sometimes this means that the expectation is that the student newspaper will speak favorably about the university administration.[48] The student editors and reporters tended to view themselves as following in the honorable footsteps of the great journalistic crusaders and trust that reporting the news in such a spirit will not always find the trustees and administrators to be in the right.[49]

The newspapers' student audiences turned to the papers for a variety of reasons ranging from an interest in campus issues to current events. Likewise, both students and faculty often saw the paper as a bulletin board for events that lists routine but important meetings that relate to campus life. The faculty and staff of a college or university looked to the newspaper for news that might influence their current jobs, future employment, or working conditions. Faculty members in journalism departments often saw the newspaper as a tool for training students for their future careers in the field of journalism. Critics of the university, both on and off campus, believed that the newspaper was a source of information that could help them fuel their attacks on the institution.[50]

DIFFERENCES AND SIMILARITIES BETWEEN THE GENERAL PRESS AND THE CAMPUS PRESS

Like the general press, the student paper serves a fairly well-defined audience that includes students, faculty, staff and administration as well as the surrounding campus community. A general circulation paper has an established distribution area that usually encompasses a town or metropolitan area. However, some newspapers have a large national or regional audience. Although the audience of the campus press is not as diverse as the general press, it is far from homogeneous. In addition to students, the readers of the student newspapers might also include activists, university sports fans, and editors and reporters for general circulation newspapers. Both general circulation and campus newspapers depend on advertising for a significant portion of their revenue.[51]

However, a number of important differences also exist between campus and general circulation newspapers. The size and circulation of a campus newspaper will never be as large as a general circulation paper in a metropolitan area. Likewise, the student community differs from the general population. While general circulation papers receive the vast majority of their income from advertising, campus papers are financed by advertising and by funds from the college or university that they serve. Another important distinction is that students who are usually much less experienced than the professional journalists that work at general circulation papers produce college and university newspapers.[52]

Further, the creation of a student newspaper differs from that of a general circulation paper in a variety of ways. The student newspaper differs from the general press because there are longer lapses between the writing and the printing of the paper. During the 1930s, the lapses could be up to 24 hours on a college daily and three to four days on some weekly papers. Another key difference was that students usually held a particular staff position for a year, a semester, or a term. No sooner did one staff become competent than its term ended and another staff took over.[53]

Because universities were, in effect, requiring every student to subscribe, they assumed some responsibility for the newspaper's quality. Universities could not force students to purchase daily an inaccurate or inadequate bulletin of essential campus announcements, nor should they force students to purchase an advertising handbill or dodger. The editors, seeking financial support, agreed in effect to publish all official announcements in an accurate and timely fashion. They also agreed that there should be a larger amount of reading material than advertising. The students recognized this obligation and concluded that the advertising space should never occupy more than one-third of the newspaper's total area.[54]

Funding the Campus Newspaper

FINANCING OF STUDENT PUBLICATIONS

During the 1950s and 1960s, some student newspapers were financially secure. For example, *The Cornell University Sun* showed a sizable profit each year. The student newspaper at DePauw was entirely self-supporting, even to owning its own building on campus. Students were charged with full responsibility for the financial and editorial operations of the paper and it received no financial support from the school budget.

The financing of student publications presents a perpetual problem. Campus or university papers can be financed by subscription sales, by subsidy, or by advertising. In decades past it was believed that student newspapers should require subsidies only to get started. Eventually, papers need to be self-supporting. However, funding from subscriptions or student fees is seldom enough to fund the newspaper. Therefore, the question of advertising in student newspapers has always been an important one. Often, the business aspect of the newspaper that is necessary to make the publication financially sound runs against its ethical responsibilities to its audience.[55]

The most remunerative advertisements are normally those that encourage the use of products disapproved by college or university authority. For instance, the stand taken by the *Daily Orange* at Syracuse University in regard to cigarette advertising is particularly poignant. In the Syracuse situation, the faculty and the staff were willing to accept financial difficulty rather than accept advertising that was contrary to the university's principles. The *Daily Orange* was one of the first daily collegiate newspapers not to carry tobacco advertising.[56]

The *Daily Orange* had greater freedom than the majority of undergraduate newspapers of the time. When it decided to reject tobacco advertising in 1932, the *Daily Orange* was thirty years old. In 1921 the student editors and managers of the newspaper found themselves in financial difficulty and appealed to the student body as a whole. In a mass meeting, the student body passed a resolution that every student should be compelled to subscribe to the paper. However, there was no authority behind their action and it was not enforced. A year later the students appealed to the administration, which agreed to assume financial responsibility for the paper and allotted a student fee that paid for the newspaper.[57]

Syracuse University's attitude on tobacco advertising was a logical outcome. The tobacco industry, specifically the cigarette manufacturers, carried on a skillful and vigorous propaganda that had certain definite characteristics in the eyes of the university administration. Its goal was to create an appetite instead of creating a demand. In addition, the advertisements demanded large spaces for pictorial display as well as letter-press.[58]

Opening the pages of Syracuse University's *Daily Orange* to such tobacco displays would make it possible for the student advertising manager to fill the entire area allotted for advertising with cigarette ads. This would essentially eliminate the local merchants from advertising in the newspaper. If the paper were made larger to accommodate both local businesses and tobacco ads, it would be necessary to change the one-third allotment for advertising space.[59] In addition to the *Daily Orange*, Blair Academy, a private college in Blairstown, New Jersey, declined to carry cigarette advertising in its paper. The Blair Academy *Breeze* did not accept any cigarette advertising because of a faculty rule prohibiting such advertising.[60]

Because of the strong opposition to smoking on some university campuses, the campus newspaper's tobacco advertising "would be daily saturating the campus with skillfully prepared propaganda in direct opposition to the athletic and physical education departments' efforts to keep smoking on campus to a minimum." In addition, Syracuse University urged women not to smoke by telling them to "keep kissable" and meditate upon "nature in the raw."[61] Representatives of the tobacco industry were offended by Syracuse University's stand against tobacco, telling them that they belonged with the "ichthyosaurus," the "dodo," and the "great auk."[62]

University policy was not the only factor preventing cigarette advertising in college and university newspapers. Some cigarette manufacturers chose not to advertise in particular newspapers because of high inch rates. For instance, R.J. Reynolds did not advertise in the following newspapers during the 1930s because of high rates: the Loyola College *Greyhound*, the Millsaps College *Purple & White*, the Woodberry Forrest *Oracle*, the Lake Forest *Stentor*, the Upsala College *Gazette*, the Union College *Cardinal & Cream*, the Cumberland University *Collegian*, and the Randolph-Macon *Yellow Jacket*.[63]

Sometimes, cigarette manufacturers withdrew their advertising voluntarily because of low profits or uncooperativeness on the part of the paper. For instance, Chesterfield withdrew its advertising from *The Bardian* in March 1941 because Bard did not comply with Chesterfield's marketing suggestions. Chesterfield requested that *The Bardian* print publicity releases for Chesterfield radio programming. *The Bardian* staff had an issue with the publicity releases because the paper felt they were deceptive. The releases disguised promotional content as newspaper editorial. The letter sent out by the national advertising service stated,

> These publishing orders from Chesterfield advertising are issued your paper on condition that you carry out the agreement in your letter to us which was a reply to our letter of January 29 which asked if, to retain the Chesterfield account you would:
> 1. Run News Releases on Chesterfield four or five times a year.
> 2. Arrange listing of Radio Programs, etc. etc.
> We sincerely trust you will help insure the continuance of this schedule by complying with this agreement for otherwise you risk cancellation. A News Release and Radio Programs Listings are enclosed herewith. Review your letter and make sure you carry out your agreement. It is requested that you publish radio programs in every issue.
> We have been asked to show proof that you have fulfilled your agreement, therefore, do not rely on our chance of finding these articles in checking copies, but- in addition to sending us the usual required checking copies mark one extra copy with red pencil and mail to NAS in an envelope first class mail marked "Attention Chesterfield."[64]

The staff at *The Bardian* felt Chesterfield imposed this requirement because students and faculty at Bard spent only $1,500 on Chesterfields at the campus store that year. Therefore, *The Bardian* editorial staff stated, "'the cigarette that satisfies' was not satisfied with such modest revenue."[65] Ultimately, *The Bardian* staff feared that loss of the Chesterfield account was going to influence the number of issues that could be printed that year.[66]

ADVERTISING AND COMMERCIAL SPEECH

Although journalism is public business, it is still a private industry. Therefore, the newspaper industry had the rights and privileges under the law pursuant to conducting a private business as it applied from the 1920s through the 1960s. During this period, the newspaper could refuse and accept advertising as it saw fit. This right to refuse advertising was tested in the courts. Under the law a newspaper retained the right to determine what it would print. At the same time, the newspaper was legally protected as an entity of public value. The judicial logic behind this principle is as follows: if a newspaper were considered a "common carrier" and required to print every advertisement that it received it would be equally obligated to print all of the news that it received.[67]

The courts agreed that college officials as well as student editors of publications in private colleges could reject any and all advertising at any time for any reason whatsoever. And, the publication was not obligated to provide a reason for rejecting the advertising. However, in public colleges, the courts would not allow college officials the authority to deny access to the advertising columns of college publications. But the courts upheld the right of student editors, who they said were not legally agents of the state, to reject advertising as they see fit. However if the college official rejected the advertisement, it would be an impermissible state action. However, if the student editor rejected the advertising, it would be constitutionally protected.[68]

Advertising, or commercial speech, is part of that class of expression that does not enjoy full protection of the First Amendment. However, in more recent years the courts have been expanding the scope of that protection.[69] When college and student publications accepted advertising, they became responsible for any libelous content in that advertising. However, since *New York Times v. Sullivan* (1964),[70] advertising that advocates ideas, expresses opinions, or is political in nature has enjoyed First Amendment protection. Only product and service advertising was subject to government regulations. And the regulations that apply to the commercial press also apply to the collegiate press.

According to a survey published by James Crimmins in 1968, of the student newspapers stating that they had any restrictions, 52 percent vested this power of decision on the advertising manager. Almost 20 percent vested the power in a university representative, while the remaining 28 percent gave the responsibility to the editor or publications board. Regarding restrictions, 78 percent had restrictions against specific products. However, the restrictions were not spelled out. The restricted products were what one would expect them to be—58 percent had restrictions on liquor advertising, 46 percent had restrictions on tobacco advertising, 8 percent had restrictions on drugs, and 8 percent restricted political advertising. Even though the tobacco industry discontinued its cigarette advertising in 1963, only 46 percent of universities had formal restrictions against tobacco advertisements in 1968.[71]

FUNDING FROM NATIONAL ADVERTISING

For decades, the college market in the United States has been a lucrative target for advertisers. Competition in the college market has been fierce. Lawsuits, confrontations, and squabbles have resulted from this intense competition.[72]

Until the late 1970s, one company, National Educational Advertising Services (NEAS), sold all of the national advertising that appeared in college newspapers. NEAS was a subsidiary of *Reader's Digest*.[73] However, in 1976 the Supreme Court ruled that NEAS held a monopolistic position and was in violation of the Sherman Anti-Trust Act.[74] National Educational Advertising Services sold national advertising space in student newspapers on behalf of the campus papers. NEAS sold space in the newspapers to national advertisers, billed the advertisers or their advertising agencies, deducted a commission for itself, and remitted the remainder to the newspaper.[75] However, student newspapers did have the right to refuse advertising sold by NEAS.

By 1967 NEAS was selling more than $3,000,000 worth of national advertising for college newspapers every year. A 1968 study by James Crimmins reported national advertising revenues in excess of $250,000, or $6,440 per paper. Daily newspapers received a larger portion of the national advertising but it represented a smaller percentage of their total incomes. For example, the average daily paper received $30,000 from NEAS, or 14 percent of its total revenue. The average weekly with advertising revenues of $10,000 or less received more than 86 percent of its total advertising revenues from NEAS. The average newspaper received 24 percent of its advertising income from NEAS.[76]

National advertisers had a large say in the campuses they targeted. The bigger, better-known, and more prestigious institutions received the most national advertising. Among the papers that Crimmins studied, 80 percent of NEAS advertising went to schools that were among the top 201 in the nation as selected by the Associated College Press.[77]

The sale of advertising was necessary to the survival of the student newspaper because the college community was seldom, if ever, willing to subsidize the paper sufficiently so that advertising could be eliminated. In spite of the fact that campus newspapers were often underfunded, next to intercollegiate athletics, the college paper was the largest financial undertaking on most campuses in 1962. However, unlike athletics, the college newspaper derives a large amount of support from the campus community and a variety of advertisers. It is important to mention that not all of student advertising revenue comes from national advertisers. Some local or regional advertisers also purchase space in campus publications.[78]

The sale of advertising in campus newspapers during the 1950s and 1960s was often rather counterproductive. Sometimes the cost of the advertising that seemed to be borne by the advertisers was actually borne by the students. For instance, in some cases, the printing costs for student papers were paid by student fees. These fees needed to increase if additional pages were printed to accommodate larger advertisements or a greater number of advertisements. If a newspaper was mismanaged, the advertising revenue did not cover the cost of the additional pages. In addition, little advertising that was found in student newspapers could be defended as socially productive. For instance, the growth of both cigarette and fashion advertising resulted in an increase in the size of the newspaper. This increase in size usually increased the cost of the production so that relatively little profit was earned from the advertising.[79]

THE IMPORTANCE OF SCHOOL NEWSPAPER ADVERTISING

An understanding of successful school newspaper advertising comes in part from knowing its importance. Before the middle of the 1960s, the importance of student newspaper advertising could be considered in four ways: (1) benefits to the advertiser, the sender of the message; (2) benefits to the consumer, the receiver of the message; (3) benefits to the publication that prints the advertisements; and (4) benefits to the student solicitor, who sells the advertisement.[80]

From the community merchant's perspective, there were six specific purposes of advertising. These goals were (1) to sell goods; (2) to create demands; (3) to introduce styles and customs; (4) to seek goodwill; (5) to keep the product or advertiser's name before the public; and (6) to introduce a new business or announce a change in location. If a given student newspaper advertisement fulfilled one or more of these purposes, then the community merchant benefitted.[81]

There could be many rewards for a school publication advertising program. With additional money from advertising revenue, a journalism program can expand. For example, special extra editions can be published, larger issues can be printed, or the school newspaper can be published more frequently. A more professional publication can be published because of the increase in the size or number of issues could provide more space or give room for fuller coverage of school activities, which in turn can be a determining factor for better school spirit. In addition, students can gain valuable experience by selling advertising in addition to the usual editorial duties.[82]

Conclusion

Cigarette and tobacco promotion have been an important part of the collegiate culture across the nation. However, financial woes have also been an important part of the history of student publications. Because of the desperate need for funding, the campus newspaper's student-centered goal was compromised by its advertising. Unfortunately, the funding from the tobacco companies did little to help the newspaper's financial position.

3

The FTC's Role in Regulating and Ending Cigarette Advertising in Campus Newspapers

Government agencies offered young people little protection from the tobacco industry during the 1950s and early 1960s. During this time numerous college newspapers and some high school newspapers carried cigarette advertisements. By the 1960s, cigarette advertisers were the biggest advertisers on campus by a large margin.[1] In fact, nearly 2,000 college publications, mainly newspapers, received nearly 50 percent of their advertising revenue from the tobacco industry.[2] However, as the body of scientific evidence linking cigarette smoking to cancer was building during the 1950s and 1960s, the Federal Trade Commission (FTC) began to take action against the tobacco industry. And, ultimately, these actions resulted in the voluntary removal of cigarette advertising from student publications in June 1963. This chapter traces the FTC's involvement in tobacco advertising regulation during the 1950s and 1960s that resulted in the end of tobacco advertising in student newspapers.

Cigarette Advertising in Student Papers Faces Criticism

College newspapers and tobacco shared a relationship that spanned more than 40 years. Although most college student newspapers accepted advertising dollars from the tobacco industry without any controversy, some colleges did take action and tried to pull the cigarette advertisements of their own accord. The *Main Events*, the campus newspaper at City College in New York City, and the *Maroon,* the campus newspaper at University of Chicago, were the most well-publicized examples of student newspapers taking the initiative to remove cigarette ads. Both papers dropped cigarette advertisements before the Tobacco Institute, the public relations arm of the tobacco industry, finally pulled the advertising because of pressure from the FTC in 1963. However, attempting to drop cigarette advertising from student newspapers was not a simple matter. It involved contracts, possibly the loss of the school paper, and even lawsuits. For instance, on October 29, 1962, *Main Events* announced that it planned to drop all cigarette advertising. Part of an editorial that underlined the issue stated:

We feel that we are condoning cigarette smoking by allowing placement of advertising space at a time when it is impossible to overlook the facts of cigarette surveys.[3]

Three issues later the newspaper was out of money. It stated that it wished

to express its deep regrets that the financial solvency of this newspaper—and apparently many other school papers across the country—depends, to such a large extent, upon a product which, according to the evidence, contributes so largely to the death of thousands each year.

Because the issue at stake here is not the publication life of a single newspaper, but whether or not the collegiate press must inevitably fold when outside advertising (primarily cigarette) is the basic source of its financial survival.[4]

The Nation printed an editorial on January 26, 1963, titled "Collegians and the Weed":

Apparently *Main Events* is the first college newspaper to discontinue cigarette advertising on the initiative of the staff.... The vaunted editorial independence of the great American press is here being tested, and the fact that the test is on a small and local scale does not alter the principle involved.[5]

Soon after *The Nation's* editorial, *The Catholic Weekly, America,* and the *Medical Tribune,* a national weekly for physicians, devoted space to the story. The public response was immediate—especially from the physicians. The City College school administrators were given the necessary funds to continue their campus paper.[6]

Earle Ubell, the New York *Herald Tribune's* science editor, discussed the issue in a letter to the City College students. The majority of the eight-page issue discussed the controversy. More than 500 of the 6,000 copies that were run were sent to student college newspaper editors with the front-page comment:

We have no wish to point out individuals and tell them not to smoke; what you do is your own business. But especially for the young people who each semester enter the colleges of the nation ... freshmen and seniors alike, whose understanding of this complex story is limited or made lopsided by the continual barrage of advertising through radio-TV, newspaper and magazine, and their own college press, we urge responsible editors of the country to help offset the potentially dangerous effects of smoking by using their good offices to discuss the issue for the benefit of all students.[7]

These comments were issued April 29, 1963—two months before the Tobacco Institute recommended that cigarette advertising be dropped from all college and university publications.

On the same day at the University of Chicago, the American Cancer Society's Illinois division in conjunction with Coccyx, the University of Chicago group organized to eliminate cigarette advertising from the college daily, held a conference attended by editors and editorial assistants from 18 colleges in the metropolitan area. The purpose of the conference was to persuade editors to discontinue cigarette advertising and to enlist them in a drive to write anticigarette material. The presenters at the conference included a surgeon, the editor of the campus newspaper at the University of Chicago, and an advertising executive. The conference presented evidence on smoking and urged editors, if they were convinced that smoking and lung cancer were causally related, to refuse to renew their cigarette advertising contracts for the 1963–1964 academic year. Or, they might publish anticigarette advertisements created by Coccyx, the first series of which was titled "On Campus Cancer" a parody of "On Campus," a column by popular humorist Max Shulman that was first sponsored by Phillip Morris and later Marlboro cigarettes.[8]

However, not everyone on campus was pleased with the decision to pull the advertising from college newspapers. For instance, in 1963 the advertising manager of *Maroon* defended cigarette advertising by stating:

> Cigarette advertisements are highly lucrative and, therefore, highly desirable. Esthetically speaking, cigarette advertisements are generally praiseworthy for their art and good taste.[9]

Although some student newspapers were fighting to remove the cigarette advertising from their pages or keep their lucrative tobacco accounts, a larger battle was taking place to have the advertising forcibly removed from all student publications. As a result of a legal battle between the FTC and the tobacco companies, the advertisements were voluntarily removed from all student publications in June 1963.

Tobacco Litigation and the Formation of the Tobacco Institute

The first lawsuit involving three of the six major cigarette companies and claiming that cigarette smoking caused lung cancer was filed in March 1954. All six manufacturers were involved in litigation based on similar claims. The primary legal issues that the industry faced centered around advertising, antitrust issues and health concerns. These concerns resulted in the creation of various tobacco-related organizations that represented the interests of tobacco manufacturers. These organizations managed the industry's legal, research, and communications issues.

Somewhat surprisingly, the tobacco industry profited from public health concerns for years. Most cigarette makers had, at some time, employed advertising campaigns that suggested health benefits offered by their particular brand, such as "smoother on the throat," "Not a cough in the carload," and "More Doctors smoke Camel," among others. In the early 1950s cigarette producers introduced more filtered cigarette brands to ease consumer fears. For instance, Pall Mall advertised that the unfiltered, yet longer, Pall Mall cigarette successfully filtered the smoke through the tobacco to help "Guard against throat scratch." As the industry capitalized on health fears, they simultaneously worked to disprove the claims that smoking caused serious illness.[10]

Although the tobacco industry had successfully dealt with controversy in the past, it seemed that more significant action was now in order. A December 14, 1953, meeting of the cigarette industry tobacco executives resulted in a call to develop a pro-cigarette public relations entity. The industry felt that the most effective way to face this growing problem was to employ public relations counsel. On December 15, 1953, the tobacco industry hired Hill & Knowlton, a New York-based public relations agency, to create the trade association. Within the month, Hill & Knowlton and the industry collaborated to provide public relations for the industry and, simultaneously, fund research to study the damaging claims being made against its product. The Tobacco Industry Research Committee (TIRC) was officially formed in January 1954.[11]

Providing counterarguments to combat the mounting evidence against the tobacco industry became a primary function of the TIRC. In January 1954 the tobacco industry announced its "Open Question" position in "A Frank Statement to Cigarette Smokers." The four primary elements of this position as it evolved in the 1950s were:

1. It has not been scientifically established that smoking is a cause of disease, particularly lung cancer.
2. The solution lies in more research to which the industry is committed.
3. Scientists have been unable to establish any ingredient as found in cigarette smoke, which has produced lung cancer in animals or human beings.
4. The industry believes that cigarettes are not injurious to health.[12]

In spite of the fact that the tobacco industry claimed in 1954 that the TIRC was formed with the function of sponsoring independent research into smoking and health issues and to resolve the "Open Question" regarding tobacco and health, the actual function of the TIRC was, as the Scientific Advisory Board chairman, Dr. Clarence Cook, stated in 1954, "[T]o build a foundation of research sufficiently strong to arrest continuing or future attacks" on the tobacco industry.[13] Furthermore, one of the TIRC's major activities from 1954 to 1958 and thereafter was to serve as the public relations vehicle for the tobacco industry in interviews, speeches, and testimony before Congress, the FTC, and in court.[14]

In 1955, the FTC issued guidelines to prevent cigarette companies from making direct or indirect health-related claims in their advertising. One effect of this legislation was to prevent the tobacco industry from making any claims that product improvements, such as filtration, had any beneficial health effects. Then, in 1959 the FTC enacted a rule that prevented companies from mentioning tar or nicotine levels in their cigarettes because it could be referred to as a health claim.[15]

In 1958, the tobacco industry created the Tobacco Institute (TI) to replace the TIRC's public relations and legal functions and the Council for Tobacco Research (CTR) to continue the TIRC research functions. The Tobacco Institute's primary objective was to publicize "the industry's position on the smoking and health issue, representing the industry's position to the Congress and the state legislatures and generally stating the industry's position to the public on issues ranging from smoking and health to taxation and all legislation affecting the industry."[16] Led by attorney-based committees (the Committee of Counsel) and Covington and Burling (TI counsel), the Tobacco Institute comprised the tobacco lobby, legislative, public relations, state affairs, and federal affairs branch of the tobacco industry.

The Tobacco Industry, Federal Regulations and the FTC

THE CASE AGAINST TOBACCO

The case against the tobacco industry included charges of conspiracy and misconduct and accusations that its marketing efforts were deceptive and irresponsible. First, as a part of the general corporate "conspiracy/misconduct" case, it was said that statements were being released to the public through advertising with the internal state of awareness of the strength and validity of the connection that was established between smoking and various diseases. For instance, even as the Arthur D. Little Company was replicating, albeit with diminished results, the mouse-painting studies that had previously demonstrated that cigarettes contained carcinogens, Liggett was promoting its L&M filter as "Just What the Doctor Ordered." While the research caused concern about the product, the advertising was clearly created to reassure the public about the product's safety.[17]

Second, the tobacco industry's marketing efforts were said to be irresponsible. Advertising is viewed as the leading factor in smoking initiation with a particular emphasis on youth, young adults, and women, and in smoking continuance in the face of growing public knowledge of increased health risks. For instance, the two themes of safety and glamour appeared repeatedly from 1913 to 1964, with a special emphasis on safety throughout the filter cigarette's introductory era from 1953 to 1955 and the "tar derby" from 1958 to 1960. During this period, celebrity endorsements saturated the advertising media. A powerful component of this argument is the FTC's finding, that was upheld on appeal, that many of these advertisements were deceptive and misleading.[18]

FTC AND GOVERNMENT REGULATION

The FTC had flirted with cigarette advertising regulations since the 1930s, going after manufacturers who made unproven health claims about their products.[19] However, the 1950s and early 1960s are perhaps the most important era in cigarette regulation. Public health concerns drove cigarette manufacturers to compete in rival advertising campaigns promoting their filters (The "Tar Wars" or "Tar Derby"). In the early 1950s, only 2 percent of cigarettes had filter tips. However, by 1960, 50 percent of cigarettes were filter tips.

The reason for this drastic change in cigarette marketing was the publication of the first major study that definitively linked smoking to lung cancer. Mortin Levin's epidemiological survey of Buffalo lung cancer patients between 1938 and 1950 appeared in *The Journal of the American Medical Association*. His controversial and shocking finding: Smokers were statistically twice as likely to develop lung cancer as non-smokers.[20] Because of the scientific research that was beginning to connect smoking with cancer, the FTC started to complain in 1950 that cigarette advertisements that touted the physical benefits of smoking were deceptive.[21] However, the ultimate finding of the FTC's 1950 R.J. Reynolds decision was that cigarettes were not "appreciably harmful" to healthy smokers.[22]

An article in *U.S. News & World Report* stated the FTC's position on cigarettes and cigarette advertising very clearly.

> For smokers, one cigarette is about like another. Cigarettes do not soothe the throat, help digestion, or relieve fatigue according to the findings of the Federal Trade Commission. All cigarettes contain some poison and one brand is no less irritating than any other brand. Cigarette smoking is not good for the individual.[23]

The commission reached these conclusions after an investigation of tobacco industry advertising claims. The findings were based on laboratory tests conducted by the Food and Drug Association and testimonies made by medical professionals.[24]

In proceedings culminating in 1950 with cease and desist orders against every major tobacco company, the FTC found virtually all cigarette advertisements had been false, misleading, and deceptive.[25] For instance, in the proceedings against R.J. Reynolds, manufacturer of Camels, the FTC found that many of the celebrity endorsements were deceptive because either the celebrities did not smoke or they did not smoke Camels exclusively.[26] The Chesterfield "Nose, Throat, and Accessory Organs Not Adversely Affected by Smoking Chesterfields" campaign was also the subject of an FTC investigation that resulted in a cease and desist order entered against Liggett & Myers Tobacco Company.[27]

A statement in an April 5, 1950, press release issued by the FTC explains the commission's response to claims that some cigarettes contain fewer irritating substances than others. The FTC's release of the cease and desist order against Camel and Old Gold reads,

> In any event, it is declared that smoke is an "irritant"—containing as it does the substances carbon dioxide, carbon monoxide, nicotine, ammonia, and various aldehydes, including formaldehyde, tars, and formic acid. The Commission found that the smoke from all the leading brands of cigarettes contains all of these irritating substances "in essentially the same quantities and degree." And, "being an irritant," the Commission pointed out, "the smoke will irritate disordered throats," and "excessive smoking" of any brand will irritate throats even in normal healthy condition.[28]

Regarding R.J. Reynolds' use of celebrity appeals in Camel advertisements, the release said,

> The Reynolds Company is further forbidden to represent that Camels differ in any of those respects from other leading brands of cigarettes, or to use any testimonials which contain any of the prohibited representations or which are not "factually true in all respects."[29]

The FTC decision in the Chesterfield case stated that the advertisement reported the results of a survey of 30 smokers who smoked Chesterfield cigarettes for a six-month period. During this time, a physician examined the research participants every two months. At the end of the six months, the smokers were not adversely affected by smoking Chesterfields. However, the FTC noted that the study extended beyond the initial six months for an additional eighteen months. During this latter period, four of the 30 participants displayed coughing spells that were attributed to smoking.[30]

In 1951, the American Tobacco Company's Lucky Strike Cigarettes received a cease and desist order from the FTC because it was in violation of the Federal Trade Commission's previous rulings and the Federal Trade Commission Act. The American Tobacco Company was ordered to cease and desist from any advertising that:

1. Lucky Strike cigarettes or the smoke therefrom contains less acid than do the cigarettes or the smoke therefrom of any of the leading brands of cigarettes.
2. That Lucky Strike cigarettes or the smoke therefrom is less irritating to the throat than the cigarettes or the smoke therefrom of any of the other leading brands of cigarettes.
3. That Lucky Strike cigarettes or the smoke therefrom contains less nicotine than do the cigarettes or the smoke therefrom of any of the four other leading brands of cigarettes.[31]

The following year, R.J. Reynolds received a modified order to cease and desist from the FTC. On January 17, 1952, the FTC mandated that Camel cigarettes stop implying the following in its advertising:

1. That the smoking of such cigarettes encourages the flow of digestive fluids or increases the alkalinity of the digestive tract or that it aids digestion in any respect.
2. That the smoking of cigarettes relieves fatigue or that it creates, renews, gives or releases body energy.
3. That the smoking of such cigarettes does not affect or impair the "wind" or the physical condition of the athletes.
4 That such cigarettes or the smoke therefrom will never harm or irritate the throat, nor leave an aftertaste.

5. That the smoke from such cigarettes is soothing, restful, or comforting to the nerves, or that it protects against nerve strain.
6. That Camel cigarettes differ in any of the foregoing respects from the other leading brands of cigarettes on the market.
7. That Camel cigarettes or the smoke therefrom contains less nicotine than do the cigarettes or the smoke therefrom of any of the four other largest selling brands of cigarettes.[32]

Later that same year, the FTC was looking into Phillip Morris' claim that their cigarettes were less irritating.[33] On February 5, 1952, the FTC found the following aspects of the Phillip Morris advertising to be false and deceptive and would be banned by Examiner Earl J. Kolb's order.

That by the use of a... hygroscopic agent as a moistener, Phillip Morris cigarettes would be rendered nonirritating or less irritating than those brands in which other hygroscopic agents are employed.[34]

The FTC also prohibited Phillip Morris from stating:

That Phillip Morris cigarettes cause no irritation to the upper respiratory tract and are less irritating to that area than other leading brands.
That they have any value in alleviating or removing irritation of the nose or throat due to smoking.
That they may be smoked as much and as often as one likes without irritation to the throat.
That they give protection from smokers coughs, the effects of inhaling or from throat irritation due to inhaling.
That the leading brands are more irritating than Phillip Morris or that irritation caused by smoking lasts longer when such other brands are used.
That the smoke from Phillip Morris cigarettes will not affect the breath or leave an aftertaste.[35]

In the December 1, 1952, case, *Federal Trade Commission v. Liggett Myers Tobacco Co.*, the FTC found cigarettes definitively not to be a drug. Section 15 (c) of the Federal Trade Commission Act states,[36]

The term "drug" means (1) articles recognized in the official United States Pharmacopoeia, official Homoeopathic Pharmacopoeia of the United States, or official National Formulary, or any supplement to any of them; and (2) articles intended for use in the diagnosis, cure, mitigation, treatment, or prevention of disease in man or other animals; and (3) articles (other than food) intended to affect the structure or any function of the body of man or other animals; and (4) articles intended for use as a component of any article specified in clause (1), (2), or (3); but does not include devices or their components, parts, or accessories.[37]

As a result of this finding, cigarette manufacturers were prohibited from advertising that cigarettes could be smoked without inducing any adverse affects on the nose, throat, and accessory organs.

Because cigarettes were not defined as a drug, jurisdiction was conferred upon the court to issue an injunction against the alleged false advertising under sections 12 and 13(a) of the FTC Act that states that it is unlawful for a person, partnership, or corporation to disseminate false advertising.[38] As a result of this ruling, Liggett & Myers was forced to stop implying that Chesterfield cigarettes were less irritating.[39] The other major cigarette companies such as Lorillard, American Tobacco Company, and R.J. Reynolds were involved in similar legal actions involving the FTC in 1952.

In spite of the FTC's legal actions against the major tobacco companies, many of the brands continued to advertise using the very claims that were just banned. For instance, in 1953 Chesterfield advertised that its cigarettes were "Always milder," "Better tasting," "Cooler smoking," and generally not irritating. In response to Liggett & Myers' continued reluctance to follow the FTC's orders the commission stated,

> This is the second action instituted by the Commission to halt allegedly false and misleading advertising that Chesterfield cigarettes can be smoked without inducing any adverse effect upon nose, throat, and accessory organs of the smoker.... The present complaint alleges that the respondent's advertising represents directly and by implication that Chesterfield cigarettes not only will have no adverse effect on nose and throat and accessory organs, but also (1) that the smoke from Chesterfield cigarettes is milder and cooler and consequently less irritating to the user than other cigarettes, (2) that the smoke from Chesterfield cigarettes will soothe and relax the nerves of smokers irrespective of the physical condition or the smoking habits of the smokers, and (3) that the smoke from Chesterfield cigarettes does *not* leave an unpleasant aftertaste in the mouth. These claims and representations, according to the complaint, are false, misleading, and deceptive.[40]

After chastising Liggett & Myers for not abiding by previous rulings, the FTC complaint mentions that Chesterfield cigarettes are not the only offending brand and that the commission had previously instituted proceedings and issued orders against the American Tobacco Company, R.J. Reynolds Tobacco, P.J. Lorillard Company and Phillip Morris & Company prohibiting the use of a variety of claims, some being of the same general nature as were involved in this complaint.[41] In spite of the FTC's adamant complaints regarding health claims made by tobacco companies, particularly Liggett & Myers' Chesterfield cigarettes, a hearing examiner later dismissed the charges against Liggett & Myers Tobacco Company on the grounds that there was not significant public interest, that such statements were merely "puffing" terms, and that the counsel for the complaint had failed to make a prima facie case.[42] Likewise, the cases against the other companies, including Phillip Morris, were also dismissed.[43]

After nearly four years of frustrating dealings with the tobacco industry, the director of the FTC's Bureau of Consultation, Charles E. Grandey, contacted the presidents of the major tobacco companies urging them to adhere to some proposed industry standards. The FTC defended its desire for further regulation by stating:

> Recent scientific developments with regard to the effects of cigarette smoking have increased the Commission's interest in advertising claims made for such products and have increased its responsibility under the law to prevent the use of false or misleading claims.[44]

The letter continues by stating that the proposed standards are part of a voluntary code and would not modify the provisions of any existing cease and desist order. Grandey also wrote that he believed that the proposed standards were in accordance with the industry's desire to resolve any scientific questions about its product. The letter closed by asking the tobacco industry executives to provide comments and suggestions about the facility of the FTC's proposed standards as well as an indication of whether each particular company would be willing to abide by them.

The FTC's 1954 proposed standards, for instance, prohibited cigarette advertisements from claiming "directly or by implication that cigarette smoking in general or the smoking of any brand of cigarettes is 'not harmful' or 'not irritating.'" The proposed standards also required that advertisements should not imply any medical approval of smoking. Further, the advertisements should not represent directly or indirectly that the smoke of any brand of cigarettes contains any less nicotine, tar or resins than any other brand of ciga-rettes.[45]

The suggested standards for cigarette advertising were:
Cigarette advertisements—
1. Should not represent directly or by implication that cigarette smoking in general or the smoking of any brand of cigarette is beneficial to health in any respect,
2. Should not represent directly or by implication that cigarette smoking in general or the smoking of any brand of cigarettes is (a) not harmful or (b) not irritating,
3. Should not represent directly or by implication, including illustrations, that by virtue of its ingredients, method of manufacture, length, added filter, or for any other reason the smoke of any brand of cigarette contains less nicotine, tar, resins, or other deleterious substances unless such representation is supported by impartial scientific test data, which are current at the time of dissemination of the claim, and which conclusively prove the existence of the claimed differences to a significant degree and the claim is limited to the particular delete-rious substance or substances.
4. Should not refer to (a) the throat, larynx, nose or any other part of the body (b) digestion (c) energy (d) nerves or (e) doctors,
5. Should not use any word, term, illustration or combination thereof, in such a way as to indicate medical approval,
6. Should generally be limited to the subjects of quality, taste, flavor, enjoyment, and other similar matters of opinion,
7. Should make no comparative claims regarding the volume of sales of competitive brands or the purchase of particular types, qualities or grades of tobacco unless such a claim is based on verified current information,
8. Should contain only genuine testimonials that represent the current opinion of the author who currently smokes the brand named. NOTE: By publishing any testimonial the adver-tiser makes all of the direct and implied representations contained therein and all of the standards herein listed apply thereto.
9. Should not contain claims accounting to false disparagement of other cigarette manufac-turers and their products.[46]

The purpose of these 1954 "cigarette advertising guides" was to close the loopholes in its brand specific decrees. Although the guides specifically prohibit all references to "throat, larynx, lungs, nose or other parts of the body," or to "digestion, nerves or doctors," a later press release emphasized that "no advertising should be used which refers to either the pres-ence or absence of any physical effect of smoking."[47] The guides also prohibited all tar and nicotine claims unless definite scientific proof existed that the claims were true. However, the guides specifically allowed the advertising of pleasure and taste.[48]

The tobacco industry appeared to be relatively accepting of the FTC's proposed code. For instance, in American Tobacco Company president Paul M. Hahn's reply to FTC director Charles Grandey's letter, he said that the American Tobacco Company was in full sympathy with the FTC's general objectives in its efforts to eliminate questionable claims and impli-cations from all cigarette advertising. However, Hahn continued by stating the advertising of the American Tobacco Company's brands, Lucky Strike, Pall Mall and Tareyton cigarettes, were completely free from of any questionable claims and implications. Therefore, Hahn stated, the American Tobacco Company should "look with favor upon any process that would provide an effective means of bringing about general adherence to such a policy throughout the cigarette industry."[49] Hahn continued by stating that the American Tobacco Company intended to continue its policy of making no questionable claims or implications in the advertising of its cigarettes. The American Tobacco Company would also be willing to abide by any standards that it deemed fair and proper. To that end, the American Tobacco Company said that it believed that statements made by advertisers should be "truthful, clear, understandable, and warranted by facts."[50]

As a result of the implementation of the code, cigarette advertising changed track within a matter of months. Instead of advertisements that showed dark stains on filters or referred to the heath concerns related to smoking, advertisements featured good taste and pleasure. The cigarette advertising practices that are now condemned, such as the upbeat quality of the advertisements and the alluring portraits of the joys of smoking at work and at play, date from the implementation of the FTC's code in 1955. When it prohibited the mention of doctors and coughs, the FTC removed the most powerful weapons from the small cigarette companies. Even in the face of more convincing cancer research, the sales of cigarettes came back with force in 1955 and continued strongly through the late 1950s and early 1960s.[51]

In 1955, after the hearing examiner dismissed the charges against Liggett & Myers and other tobacco companies on grounds that the advertising claims were puffery, the FTC ordered that the proceedings before a hearing examiner continue to decide if the makers of Chesterfield cigarettes used false advertising when they claimed that their cigarettes were "Milder," "Soothing and Relaxing," and had no "Unpleasant After-Taste." By reversing this decision and remanding the case to the examiner, the FTC stated:

> We do not agree with the examiner's findings that the representations "Milder," "Soothing and Relaxing," and "Unpleasant After-Taste" are laudatory, harmless, or mere "puffing" terms.[52]

Recognizing that misleading representations are difficult to distinguish and that puffing is usually an expression of opinion, the commission stated:

> In our judgment, the questioned representations present sufficient factual issues—as to qualities which Chesterfield cigarettes may or may not possess—to warrant completion of these proceedings.[53]

Although the FTC disagreed with the examiner's general conclusions, the commission agreed with the examiner in dismissing the charges revolving around the use of the word "cooler." The FTC agreed with the examiner's finding that there was "no evidence, certainly no substantial evidence on the issue of coolness." However, the commission wanted the rest of the examiner's decision to be overturned. As further grounds for reversing the hearing examiner's decision, the commission said:

> We also do not agree with the hearing examiner's conclusion that a prima facie case has not been established. There is in the record considerable uncontroverted respectable evidence that is relevant to the issues here involved. Our view is that a prima facie case has been established, by which we do not necessarily mean that on the basis of the present record an order to cease and desist would issue, but rather that there is in the record reliable evidence which, when considered in connection with reasonable inferences which may be drawn therefrom, would probably support an order in the absence of rebutting evidence.[54]

Another series of issues for the FTC were the claims being made about the new filter tip cigarettes that were being advertised. On May 6, 1955, Charles E. Grandey, wrote a letter to

Horace G. Hitchcock of the Manhattan law firm Chadbourne, Parke, Whiteside, Wolff & Brophy, representing the tobacco industry. Grandey wrote,

> In recent weeks there has been a noticeable broadening of claims made for filter tip cigarettes. It is therefore especially requested that your company re-examine its present claims for its products, particularly filter tip cigarettes, in light of proposed Guide No. 2. If, upon reexamination, your company finds that any of its claims are not in harmony with the suggested guides, it is requested that the necessary changes to that end be made.[55]

The new advertisements for the filter tip cigarettes implied that filters made cigarette smoking less harmful. This claim was in clear violation of Guide No. 2 that stated that cigarette advertisements "should not represent directly or by implication that cigarette smoking in general or the smoking of any brand of cigarettes is (a) not harmful or (b) not irritating."

The late 1950s brought more charges against the tobacco industry. After 1955, the fear of cancer persisted but most means for exploiting that fear were prevented. The publicity linking cigarette smoking to cancer took its toll on the industry and smoking began to decline. The industry's response to these events was the aggressive marketing of filtered cigarettes. Filters had been on the market before but had not achieved a significant market share. The market share for filtered brands grew from 10 percent in 1954 to 35 percent in 1957.[56] The reason for this increase was the belief that filters significantly reduced the amount of tar that the smoker ingested. Therefore, filters were marketed with direct appeals to smokers' health concerns. For instance:

> L&M: "This is it. L&M filters are just what the doctor ordered!"
> KENT: "What a priceless difference in PROTECTION a few extra pennies make!"
> VICEROY: "New Health-Guard filter makes Viceroy better for Your Health."
> PARLIAMENT: "Recessed Filter—Maximum Health Protection."[57]

This theme of reassurance surfaced again in the "tar derby," in which many cigarette brands competed to position themselves as being lower in tar and nicotine than the other brands. Finding this competition identical to a new barrage of health claims, the FTC ordered this practice stopped in 1959 and 1960.[58]

In 1957 the FTC began to pursue antitrust action against Phillip Morris, Inc., complaining that Phillip Morris was in violation of the Clayton Act. The FTC complaint stated that Phillip Morris "violated and is now violating the provisions of subsection (d) of Section 2 of the Clayton Act as amended by the Robinson-Patman Act (U.S.C. Title 15 Section 13)."[59] The Robinson-Patman amendment to the Clayton Act requires that if promotional allowances are given, they be made available to all competing customers on proportionally equal terms.[60] The FTC charged that Phillip Morris

1. Paid allowances in varying amounts to some customers, but did not do so or offer to do so, in any amount, to other competing customers.
2. In paying such allowances to competing customers, did so in amounts not equal to the same percentage of such competing customers' net purchases and not proportionately equal by any other test; and did not offer or otherwise accord or make available such allowances to all such competing customers in amounts equal to the largest of such percentages, or proportionately equal by any other test.

3. In paying such allowances to competing customers, required some of them to comply with certain terms and to furnish or make certain reciprocal service or payments, but did not require others to do so in any manner or amount, or required them to do so in a less burdensome manner or in lesser amounts, and did not proportionally equal by any test.

4. In determining allowances to be paid competing customers, did so on the basis of individual negotiations with each such customer, which resulted in proportionately unequal, different, and arbitrary terms.[61]

As an example of this unlawful treatment of customers, the complaint cites a record of payments made in 1956 to various retailers for items such as posters, carton displays, counter displays, and change trays. The complaint continues by listing the amounts paid to various companies selling the Phillip Morris brand through vending machines. Allowances were also granted to customers functioning as tobacco wholesalers. For example, the Metropolitan Tobacco Company of New York City was paid $50,000 in allowances in 1956, yet nothing was offered to any of the other wholesale customers competing with it.[62]

The cigarette market underwent another informational jolt in 1957. Health experts began to argue that reducing the tar content in cigarettes would be likely to reduce the risk of lung cancer as more studies linking smoking and lung cancer were published. Attention quickly focused on the newly popular filter cigarettes, whose tar and nicotine yield had not yet been publicly revealed. Congressional hearings were held on filter cigarette advertising, new tar and nicotine ratings were published in *Consumer Reports,* and a two-part series on cigarette filters appeared in *Reader's Digest.* Each report concluded that filter cigarettes had been so greatly modified to enhance flavor that their tar and nicotine yield was generally no better than that of unfiltered cigarettes.[63]

This news initiated the great "Tar Derby." Notwithstanding the FTC guides, vigorous advertising of tar and nicotine content returned, new filter brands were introduced, and existing filters were improved. And, in a development that the FTC had earlier thought to be technically impossible, the tar and nicotine levels of unfiltered cigarettes were significantly reduced. However, the FTC guides continued to prohibit tar and nicotine claims that were not based on scientific proof. But, with so much noncommercial data on the subject of filters becoming available in technical journals and in the popular press, the "sound scientific data" requirement became another large loophole in the commission's policy.[64]

In July 1957, the Senate introduced a bill that would have required a mandatory warning on cigarette packs. That same month, the House of Representatives introduced a bill that required the disclosure of tar and nicotine levels on cigarette packs. The tobacco industry was in opposition to both bills.[65]

However, during this time when FTC regulation was needed most, the commission was found to be relatively unable to enforce any standards on the tobacco industry. In 1958 the FTC was the subject of hearings conducted by the Subcommittee on Legal and Monetary Affairs, over which Representative John A. Blatnik (D-Minn.) presided. This subcommittee was concerned with FTC efficiency in the field of false and misleading advertising in several areas that included filter-tip cigarettes. The topic of advertising for filter-tip cigarettes was

of concern to the subcommittee because of the health-related claims that the filter-tip cigarette manufactures were making and because filter-tip cigarettes often contained more nicotine than previous unfiltered cigarettes. Many of the advertisements for filter-tip cigarettes
made claims that the tips would remove the elements of smoke that endangered the public's
health. However, the true effectiveness of the filters often came into question. The level of
nicotine and tar in cigarettes also was a cause for concern. For instance, L&M cigarettes produced by Liggett & Myers contained 1.5 milligrams of nicotine and 11 milligrams of tar in
1955. However, two years later there was a 70 percent increase in nicotine and a 33 percent
increase in tar. In 1958 when L&M introduced its filter, the tar content climbed to 17 milligrams. In June 1958, six prominent brands of cigarettes were all advertising the lowest tar
content.[66]

While the FTC failed to protect consumers against these false claims, it is also true
that the FTC lacked the power to do so. The power of the FTC was limited in controlling
tobacco advertising because it did not have the power to ask a court for an injunction when
tobacco was concerned. The FTC had this power when the advertising was related to other
products such as foods, drugs, cosmetics, and devices. Therefore, the FTC needed this power
to effectively govern cigarette advertising.[67]

The Tar Derby's climax came during 1959. All six major manufacturers were in the
process of mounting major advertising campaigns to introduce their new lower tar brands
when the FTC intervened. In December 1959, the Bureau of Consultation at the FTC
started to negotiate secretly with the six companies. First, every claim about levels of nicotine
and tar would be considered an implied claim of positive health effects. Second, epidemiological evidence of the health effects related to cigarette smoking would be mandated for
future claims. Everyone realized that this type of evidence did not exist and could not be
produced for many years.[68]

The furious Tar Derby was still raging in 1960 when the FTC, which previously had
not achieved complete success in trying to get tobacco manufacturers to moderate their
claims about filter cigarettes, put its foot down and announced that no more tar and nicotine
claims would be permitted in cigarette advertising.[69] Early in 1960, the commission
announced it had achieved a significant success from its negotiations with the six companies.
The FTC negotiated a voluntary industry-wide ban that removed nearly all mention of tars
and nicotine instantaneously. For instance, Kent changed its slogan from "significantly less
tars and nicotine than any other filter brand" to "designed with your taste in mind." Likewise,
Lorillard reintroduced the unfiltered king-size version of Old Gold and created a new advertising campaign that would center on the slogan "tender to your taste." Once again the
tobacco industry returned to its traditional and usually successful course—advertising pleasure, flavor and taste against a backdrop of glamour, beauty, and ease. The formula worked,
and its success was proven by all-time highs in sales.[70]

For six years that followed, cigarette advertising was devoid of all references to tar and
nicotine. Likewise, information regarding nicotine and tar nearly disappeared from nearly
all other sources as well. *Consumer Reports* stopped publishing its tar and nicotine ratings
and *Reader's Digest* continued to do so only occasionally. The new advertising regulations
doomed the new low-tar brands. Regarding the FTC intervention, one advertising professional noted: "[Y]ou build a better mousetrap and then they say you can't mention mice or
traps."[71]

A SECOND ATTEMPT AT A VOLUNTARY ADVERTISING CODE

In 1963, the United States Department of Justice in collaboration with the FTC began seeking out ways it could create a "voluntary" advertising code that would define "good advertising practices" and eliminate "undesirable advertising." In a May 20, 1963, letter to Robert L. Wald of Wald, Harkrader & Rockefeller, the legal counsel of P.J. Lorillard Company, Lee Loevinger, the assistant attorney general of the Antitrust Division of the Department of Justice, said undesirable advertising is "advertising that makes an appeal to young persons or which attempts to glamorize smoking by relating it to youth, sex, romance, success, and so forth." The letter continues to state P.J. Lorillard Company was to submit to the Department of Justice an advertising code that might be adopted.[72]

Because of its legal dealings with the FTC and Congress, the tobacco industry considered whether it was advisable to adopt a voluntary advertising code in 1964. In a meeting of Liggett executives and J. Walter Thompson, Liggett President, Zach Thoms, asked the advertising agency to do some exploratory research on a voluntary advertising code. The proposed code included a warning label that was to have read:

This product is intended for the use of adults only. Excessive use may be injurious to health, and in certain cases, even moderate use may be inadvisable.[73]

However, the tobacco industry had some concerns about how a voluntary cigarette advertising code might relate to antitrust laws. For instance, the May 20, 1963, letter to Wald of Lorillard Tobacco Company from the U.S. Department of Justice stated the following in reference to potential antitrust concerns that might arise from following the proposed code: "The Antitrust Division of the Department of Justice has concluded that the Department will not institute criminal proceedings against the tobacco companies and/or their representatives."[74] In a June 19 letter to a Washington, D.C., law firm representing the industry, the Antitrust Division chief, William, H. Orrick, Jr., noted that the Federal Trade Commission was considering standards to regulate cigarette labeling and advertising and that the House Interstate Commerce Committee would be conducting hearings on a number of bills that would establish regulations for tobacco advertising. "Under these circumstances," Mr. Orrick wrote,

it would be inappropriate for us to give any sanction to the permanent establishment of a private organization, setting industry standards until the views of Congress and the Federal Trade Commission have been made known. In the meantime, however, we assure you that no criminal antitrust prosecution will be brought by us as a result of adherence to the code.[75]

If the tobacco industry was not protected from antitrust laws, the code's provisions might raise technical questions of restricting competition through limiting advertising.

Under the terms of the 1964 code, the manufacturers agreed not to advertise on certain television programs and in certain types of periodicals that targeted a younger audience. Specifically, the code's provisions generally banned the use of celebrity endorsements, advertising in college newspapers and other media directed primarily at those under the age of 21, health claims, and the use of models under the age of 25 or who appeared to be under the age of 25. The tobacco industry also agreed not to solicit the trade of persons under 21 years old through the distribution of free cigarette samples.[76] However, the code also discouraged marketing techniques such as trade names for filters (Kent's Micronite name, for example, was banned), further reducing the stock of code phrases used to remind smokers of health fears. In 1966, *Time* magazine observed, "Between the Federal Trade Commission and their own industry's self-imposed Cigarette Advertising Code, cigarette salesmen have just about been reduced to saying that a smoke is a smoke."[77] The authority to enforce the code was given to the code administrator who was empowered to assess up to $100,000 in damages. The first and only code administrator was New Jersey Governor Robert B. Meyner.[78]

Although withdrawing advertising from student newspapers was part of the Cigarette Advertising Code of 1964, the formal decision to withdraw campus advertising was brought before the Tobacco Institute during meeting on June 18, 1963. The minutes from the meeting state,

> Mr. [Robert B.] Walker announced that The American Tobacco Company had already decided to terminate its entire college promotional program and that the decision was effective and being implemented. Mr. [William S.] Smith stated that R.J. Reynolds had already cancelled its advertising in college publications for the coming fall and that the Reynolds company had also decided to terminate its college promotional program.
>   Mr. [Morgan J.] Cramer stated that the Lorillard Company had also already decided to terminate its college advertising and promotion. Mr. [Edwin P.] Finch indicated that Brown & Williamson Corporation had been considering the matter, and that it had decided to terminate its program. Mr. [Zach] Toms said that the Liggett and Myers Tobacco Company's current view was that it was going to terminate its college promotion, with the possible exception of college publication advertising using the same copy as they used in national magazines and newspapers. Mr. Paul Smith said that Phillip Morris had been considering the question of college advertising and promotion, but that Mr. Cullman was out of the country and that Phillip Morris had not reached any decision on its policy.[79]

In addition to their general consensus, with the exception of Phillip Morris, that cigarettes should no longer be advertised in campus newspapers, the major tobacco companies also decided how they were going to publicize the issue. The minutes for June 18, 1963, continued:

> It was the consensus of the group that the Institute should not affirmatively seek to publicize the individual decisions of the various companies to give up college advertising and promotional activities. On the other hand, it was felt that, if Mr. [George V.] Allen [president of the Tobacco Institute] should receive inquiries from the trade press or other areas, it would be proper for him to reemphasize the industry's position that smoking is an adult custom and report the fact that, to avoid any confusion and misunderstanding in the public mind as to this position, a number of the member companies of the Institute had each decided to discontinue college advertising and promotional activities.[80]

On June 19, 1963, the Tobacco Institute's public relations agency, Hill & Knowlton, issued the following statement to the press on the issue of advertising in college newspapers:

> In response to a question from Peter Bart of *The New York Times*,
>   George V. Allen, president of The Tobacco Institute, Inc., today made the following statement:
>   "The tobacco industry's position has always been that smoking is an adult custom. To avoid any confusion or misconception in the public mind as to this position, a number of member companies of the Tobacco Institute, I understand, have each decided to discontinue college advertising and promotional activities."[81]

The next meeting of the Tobacco Institute, held on July 9, 1963, referenced the large amount of publicity that was centering on the decision to discontinue advertising in student newspapers. Nearly every major daily newspaper in the nation covered the decision. The minutes of the meeting stated:

> In view of the amount of publicity and speculation expected to attend any announcement bearing on cigarette advertising or promotion, it was suggested by several members that President Allen's announcement should be the only statement of the Institute's activity and that none of the members should speak to the press with respect to the Institute's decisions. It was of course recognized, however, that any press inquiry relative to the decisions or policies of an individual company was peculiarly a matter for the particular company concerned rather than for the Institute.[82]

Usually pressure from the FTC had been the impetus for self-regulation in the tobacco industry. However, in the case of student newspapers, it seems that the negative publicity that the industry was receiving for advertising on campus motivated the decision, at least in part. The minutes from the July 9, 1963, meeting of the Tobacco Institute also reflect the concern about public opinion. The minutes from the meeting continued by stating,

> There then ensued discussion of the continued appearance in the press of repetitious anti-tobacco charges, and the view was expressed that to many members of the public these repetitions of old charges against tobacco were not recognized as such, but were possibly accepted as new material supporting those who have attacked tobacco. The question was considered whether any steps could be taken by the Institute to correct misconceptions that probably resulted from some of the activities of groups which were attacking the use of tobacco as, for example, the possible use by the Institute of ads in newspapers or other media, which would present facts relating to tobacco and health and correct some of the distortions and misconceptions which may have arisen.[83]

Although public opinion certainly factored into the discontinuation of campus newspaper advertising and the adoption of a new advertising code, the impact of the impending release of the surgeon general's report in January 1964 also influenced the decision-making process. For instance, in September 1963, Liggett & Myers Tobacco Company's Surgeon General's Committee met about the potential consequences of the surgeon general's report and the potential FTC and FDA regulations that might result from the report's findings.

When the 1964 code was enacted, it was heralded as an exercise in "responsible" self-regulation. However, the code proved not to be true regulation at all. First, the office of the code administrator "practically died stillborn." Even though he had the ability to enact some small changes in advertising practices, such as persuading Liggett to discontinue its use of the term "snowy white" to describe its filter, Robert Meyner, the code administrator and former New Jersey governor,[84] found that whenever he endeavored to employ the full scope of his authority, the tobacco industry withdrew from his supervision.[85] For instance, Lorillard withdrew from the code when it was fined for running an unapproved advertisement. All of the cigarette companies except R.J. Reynolds and Phillip Morris followed. However, the judge in the Lorillard case testified that it withdrew from Meyner and the Tobacco Institute because it wanted to promote True cigarette's nicotine and tar levels, a practice forbidden by the code.[86] After resisting its own self-regulation, the industry moved into the comfortable position of regulating each other's compliance with the Advertising Code.[87]

In addition, the code did not significantly impact the Tobacco Industry's historic reliance on the two advertising themes of safety and glamour. Of course, the identifiable film, television and sports stars no longer appeared in the advertisements. However, in their place appeared depictions of happy, healthy, macho, or glamorous models occupied in a range of exotic or enviable social activities. Like the preceding celebrity advertisements, these messages were designed to increase the cigarette market.[88]

Furthermore, the institute's declaration that smoking was "a custom for adults," and thus, presumably not one for non-adults, did have one result that applied on a more general basis than merely the college publication level. In the fall of 1963, the American Tobacco Company began an extensive campaign for Lucky Strike cigarettes in which the advertising copy stated, "smoking is a pleasure meant for adults." This sentiment appeared under a headline spread over two pages that asserted, "Lucky Strike Separates the Men from the Boys... But Not from the Girls." On the left hand side of the page, the first part of the headline was illustrated by a photograph of a helmeted, Lucky Strike-smoking race car driver who was smilingly flourishing a winner's cup as he received the envious glances of youth pressing close behind him. The second part of the headline was illustrated by a shot of the same model— still equipped with his cigarette, smile and cup but without the young male fans. Instead, the driver is being hugged by a female admirer. Therefore, the advertising professionals used the FTC regulation to transform their advertising message to illustrate the theme that cigarettes are not for boys, thus achieving the opposite effect by making the smoking of Lucky Strike the act that turns a boy into a man.[89]

At the time of the 1964 surgeon general's report, the tobacco industry was spending $250 million each year on advertising. The weight of the combined strength of the tobacco industry and its allies was felt in the form of the proposed legislation named the Cigarette Labeling and Advertising Bill of 1965. This legislation appeared to protect smokers by requiring a warning on cigarette packs (Caution: Cigarette Smoking May be Hazardous to Your Health). However, in the end, it would actually constitute a legislative triumph for the tobacco lobby. This piece of legislation was considered a victory for tobacco because it prevented the FTC or any other government agency from mandating that tobacco companies include a health warning in their cigarette advertising for the next four years. The cigarette manufacturers continued merchandising their products with new vigor.[90]

The anticipated surgeon general's report alone did not necessitate the creation of the FTC's code and the removal of the advertisements in the college student newspapers. Nor was it the case that medical findings had no role, because without the release of the medical reports and statements during the 1950s and 1960s, the collegiate community's response as well as the FTC's response to the issue would likely have been even slower. But there were a variety of other factors that influenced how the medical statements and reports were translated into a regulatory strategy, and those factors eventually tipped the balance in the direction of tobacco advertising regulation.

Public Response to the Voluntary Removal of Cigarette Ads from Campus Papers

Although the voluntary removal of all cigarette advertising from student newspapers, magazines, and football programs was a victory for public health advocates on and off campus, the removal of the advertising resulted in a mixed response. Some campuses were fearful that the reduction in funding for the newspaper would adversely affect the quality and reduce the frequency of the publication. Others affirmed the action and implemented more restrictions on campus such as smoking bans and removal of cigarette vending machines.

On many campuses across the United States, the removal of the cigarette advertisements from student newspapers and the forthcoming surgeon general's report inspired anti-cigarette activism on campuses. During an anti-smoking campaign at Auburn Community College in New York, students voted to have cigarette vending machines removed from campus. In addition, students attended lectures where anti-smoking pamphlets were distributed.[91] Other institutions endorsed smoking bans or no smoking zones on campus.[92]

Other institutions were less than happy about the loss of funding. Some of the major institutions in Oklahoma were especially unhappy about the voluntary ban. *The Oklahoma Daily* reported, "The Tobacco Institute evidently took this action in the face of mounting public pressure to step up efforts against teen smoking."[93] Three papers said that the most noticeable effect would be in the revenue cuts they would suffer. For the smallest of the three papers, *The Vista*, the loss of the cigarette accounts represented a 50 percent reduction in advertising revenue. In response to the ban, three of Oklahoma's leading college newspapers, the University of Oklahoma's *Oklahoma Daily*, Oklahoma State University's *Daily O'Collegian*, and Central State College's *The Vista* were polled to see if the cigarette advertising affected teen smoking in any way—except possibly in brand selection. According to the poll, the prevailing opinion was that cigarette ads did not influence nonsmokers to start nor would the absence of ads influence students to stop smoking.[94] Editorially, the *Daily O'Collegian* said, "It's an unrealistic move because of the other contacts students have with cigarettes."[95]

Student papers in Virginia were also concerned about the loss of the tobacco accounts. Virginia Tech said that the advertising loss would demand a decrease in the number of pages. Jenks Robertson, assistant public information officer at Virginia Tech, said, "If *The Virginia Tech* will suffer, papers in smaller college institutes may become feverish."[96] For many college weekly publications in the state of Virginia, cigarette advertising comprised their entire share of national advertising revenue.[97]

Although many papers were adversely affected by the loss of revenue, some student newspapers recovered quickly from the loss. For instance, *The Minnesota Daily,* the largest collegiate daily newspaper in the nation in 1963, reported that it was not suffering any significant economic setbacks due to the loss of the cigarette advertising. Cigarette advertising had accounted for 31 percent of the paper's national advertising revenue. However, the paper planned to increase advertising rates and attract new accounts to make up for the revenue deficit.[98] *The Daily* seemed to feel that the loss of advertising revenue from tobacco companies represented only a temporary setback.

Even into the 1980s, twenty years after the advertising was removed, many struggling college newspapers worked to convince the tobacco industry to advertise in college newspapers. For instance, in a letter dated October 20, 1981, from Ann Shank-Volk, the president of College Newspaper Business Advertising Managers Incorporated (CNBAM) to the Tobacco Institute, the members of CNBAM asked the Tobacco Institute to reconsider their voluntary ban on college newspaper advertising. The letter states,

> We, the members of College Newspaper Business and Advertising Managers Inc. (CNBAM), request that the voluntary ban on advertising in college newspapers be rescinded by the Tobacco Institute. CNBAM is a national organization of over fifty major college newspapers. The college

market itself is a lucrative one, consisting of 12,000,000 full and part-time students. 79 percent of these students read their college newspaper on a regular basis. CNBAM believes that by advertising in college newspapers, your industry would be making an economic, efficient media purchase aimed at the youth market, which has consistently supported the tobacco industry.[99]

In spite of CNBAM's efforts to regain tobacco advertising, the Tobacco Institute did not renew its college newspaper contract.

Conclusion

For many years, cigarette producers claimed that their marketing and advertising efforts endeavored only to convince smokers to switch brands. However, advertising has proven to be an effective method for recruiting young smokers. According to a 1950s article in the *U.S. Tobacco Journal*, "A massive potential exists among women and young adults, cigarette industry leaders agreed, acknowledging that recruitment of these millions of prospective smokers comprises the major objective for the immediate future and on a long term basis as well."[100]

Part II

An Analysis of Cigarette Advertisements Appearing in Campus Papers and Student Media

4

Researching the Campus Paper
Methodology, Evaluation and Implications

Many sources, including industry documents, trade articles, articles in the popular press and even books, discuss the legal and ethical issues related to cigarette advertising. However, very little is written about the ads themselves, their creative strategies, and how often they were published. Virtually nothing has been written about cigarette advertising in the student press since the ads ceased publication in 1963. The tobacco industry had a tremendous advertising budget and supported some of the most sophisticated advertising and marketing efforts of the time.

Media records from both the national media firms and the cigarette companies themselves, Phillip Morris, the American Tobacco Company, and R.J. Reynolds, indicate that almost all of the advertising placed in the student publications resulted from national buys facilitated by NEAS or CASS,[1] the national sales organizations that sold space in student newspapers. For instance, Lucky Strike, the most popular brand, indicated in its 1957 media buying records that 40-inch ads were placed in 400 college and university papers per year for an annual cost of $312,986.72. The expected reach of the advertisements exceeded five million students. However, the media buys were increasingly conservative for Lucky Strike in the 1960s because American Tobacco Company was also advertising its filtered Tareyton brand. In the 1960s, the average media buy cost about 150,000 dollars and the ads were placed in approximately 150 student papers. In the 1960s, the tobacco companies divided their media buys so that they could promote both their filtered and unfiltered brands.[2]

The cigarette advertisements in student newspapers are not remarkable just because of their astounding reach. They are noteworthy because they also represent the state-of-the-art advertising campaigns for the time. The best advertising agencies worked to develop and implement their creative media and marketing plans for the industry. Advertising firms used college and university students to develop and execute creative market research. The American Tobacco Company, Phillip Morris, and Lorillard all enlisted students to support their campaigns.

Student Generated Research and Development: The Case of American Tobacco Company

The advertising industry employed college and university students to both develop and execute creative market research. The American Tobacco Company, Phillip Morris, and

Lorillard all enlisted students to support their campaigns. The extensive research and development that helped to create these campaigns is impressive. The American Tobacco Company, the company producing the most popular brands including Lucky Strike, Pall Mall, and Tareyton, employed the most sophisticated college cigarette marketing campaign. College and university students working for the American Tobacco Company's Student Marketing Institute (SMI) developed taglines, executed market research, facilitated cigarette promotions for athletic events on campus, and assisted with merchandising efforts at campus stores. University faculty members were also recruited to supervise and coordinate the students' work.[3] Many of the cigarette advertisements have uniquely emic elements as they were generated by the audience that they were designed to reach.

The American Tobacco Company's SMI began its work in 1953 and continued until 1962. The students did extensive research to uncover smoking preferences among male, female, black, and white college students during the 1950s and early 1960s. The research consisted of numeric data collected from a survey with closed-ended questions and qualitative data collected from open-ended questions. The survey uncovered patterns in brand preferences, tobacco flavor preferences, smoking habits, and the number of cigarettes smoked.[4] The responses to the questions provided context for the survey responses and generated additional ideas for current and future marketing initiatives. In addition, the research monitored student enrollment to estimate the size of the population that advertising reached. SMI consistently estimated the college audience at over one million students.[5]

The research also showed that the market research and advertising paid off for the American Tobacco Company. American Tobacco brands such as Lucky Strike, Pall Mall, and Tareyton were the most popular on campus by a fairly wide margin during the 1950s and 1960s. For instance, SMI estimated that the American Tobacco Company's brands comprised between 40 percent and 50 percent of the college market from the early 1950s to the early 1960s. The SMI also monitored campus consumption and cooperativeness to make sure that it was advertising to the best possible audiences. For instance, in 1955 SMI suggested that American Tobacco drop its promotional efforts at Boston College, Seton Hall, and Tarleton State due to lack of interest and cooperation. However, SMI felt that Adelphi College, Colgate University, and the University of Santa Clara should be added to the media list.[6]

Although the American Tobacco Company kept meticulous records of its marketing efforts and media buys during the 1950s and 1960s, the archival evidence shows that other tobacco companies such as Lorillard, Phillip Morris, Liggett & Myers, and R.J. Reynolds did not maintain records with the same detail and consistency. Some records do exist but they are sporadic at best. In addition, few student market research records exist for any brands before the 1950s. Therefore, to get a more accurate view of the scope of the advertising, the campus newspapers needed to be surveyed. A variety of newspapers were used to confirm that the same advertising campaigns were placed nationally. Student newspapers from Bard College, Brown University, Fordham University, Indiana University, Ithaca College, Loyola University Chicago, Miami University, MIT, North Dakota State University, Princeton University, San Diego State University, Southern Methodist University, Penn State University, the State University of New York at Buffalo, the University of Iowa, the University of Minnesota, the University of Tennessee, the College of William and Mary, Vassar College, and Xavier University were surveyed to confirm national placement trends. For the most part, the data showed that the same campaigns ran in all of the major campuses across the nation. However, some papers at smaller colleges and universities ran fewer ads and carried ads for a smaller number of brands. However, almost all of the large state institutions carried advertising for all of the major cigarette brands.

Advertising Frequency Information for The Orange and White *from 1920 to 1963*

The University of Tennessee student paper, *The Orange and White*, will be used in future chapters to estimate cigarette advertising frequency in student papers starting in 1920 and ending in 1963. Although a couple of brands, Murad and Fatima, advertised with some frequency in large student papers before the 1920s, most cigarette advertisers initiated their college newspaper campaigns during the 1920s. The cigarette advertising campaigns during the early 1920s were somewhat inconsistent and infrequent. The advertisers varied by year. However, by the late 1920s, the advertisers appeared regularly and frequently.

Some newspapers, such as the *Indiana Daily Student,* did not feature cigarette advertising until the early 1930s when smoking was approved for both sexes. The advertisements increased in size and frequency in all of the papers surveyed until the campaigns ended in the 1960s. After comparing the number of brands advertised in a variety of papers, it appeared that, for the most part, the exact same advertisements appeared in each of the papers surveyed. Therefore, one can assume that advertising information gathered from one campus newspaper at a large state institution is fairly representative of all major colleges and universities. The only advantage that *The Orange and White* would have over other campus papers at major state universities is that the University of Tennessee, like many institutions in the southeast, was home to a tobacco experiment station. Newspapers in the southeast with experiment stations were given more tobacco money than other institutions. Therefore, it is possible that *The Orange and White* has slightly more cigarette advertising than papers in other areas of the nation.

From the 1920–1921 academic year to the 1963–1964 academic year, *The Orange and White* published a total of 2,399 advertisements that promoted the sale of cigarettes. The first cigarette advertisement appeared on February 24, 1921, and the final advertisement appeared on November 26, 1963. The 2,399 cigarette advertisements were published in a total of 1,650 issues of *The Orange and White*. The average number of cigarette advertisements to appear in a single issue of *The Orange and White* from the 1920–1921 academic year to the 1963–1964 academic year equals 1.5 ads.

The Orange and White was published from September until June of each academic year. Because advertising campaigns in student newspapers are generally printed according to the academic year instead of the calendar year, the academic year was used for counting and classifying advertisements. However, in order to save space in the charts and graphs, the academic years are referenced according to the first year of the academic year (for instance, the 1920–1921 academic year is referenced as 1920).

The first graph shows the number of newspapers that were published, by decade, from 1920 to 1963. The second graph provides a comparison of the number of cigarette advertisements that were printed in *The Orange and White* from the 1920–1921 academic year to the 1963–1964 academic year. As the chart shows, the 1920s had the fewest number of adver-

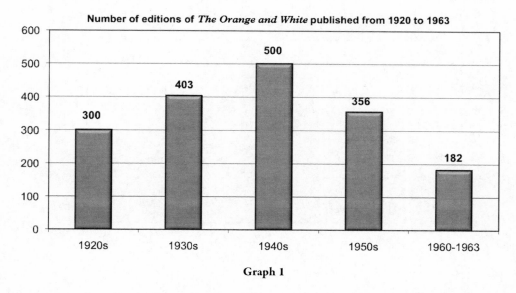

Graph 1

tisements with only 244. The 1950s have the highest advertising frequency with a total of 966 advertisements. If the first and second charts are compared, it becomes evident that the increases in advertisements are not always linked to an increase in newspapers published. For instance, the largest number of editions of *The Orange and White* were published in the 1940s, however, the 1940s had relatively few advertisements for cigarettes. One of the reasons for this disparity is that cigarette marketing moved its focus from the college and university campus to the war front during the 1940s.

Graph three shows the variation in the number of cigarette advertisements printed in *The Orange and White* each decade. The graph clearly shows that even though the 1950s represents the highest frequency of cigarette advertising, other decades surpass or match the

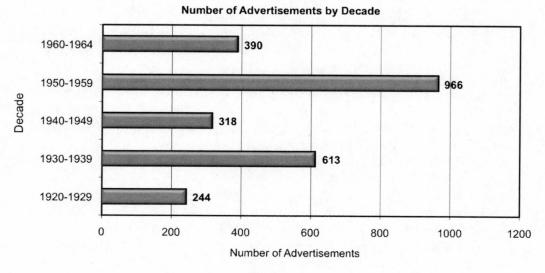

Graph 2

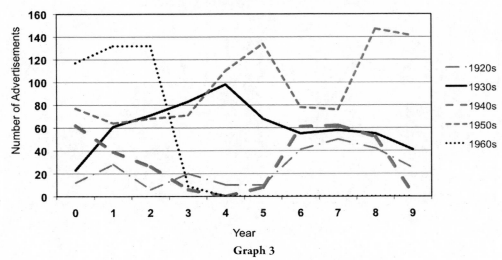

Graph 3

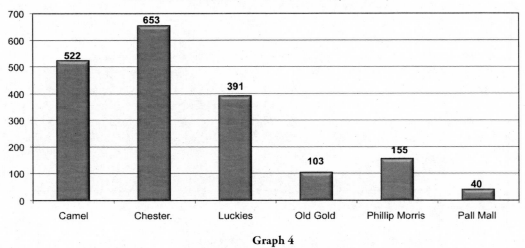

Graph 4

1950s in the number of cigarette advertisements published. For instance, the 1930s and the 1960s surpass the 1950s at times. Likewise, at times, the 1920s nearly matches or surpasses the 1930s, 1940s, and 1960s advertising frequency.

Graph four shows the frequency of advertising as it relates to the six most frequent cigarette advertisers in *The Orange and White*. As the decades progress from the 1920s to the 1960s the number of cigarette advertisers steadily increased. One of the primary reasons for the increase in advertisers is the increase in the number of cigarette brands offered due to the introduction of filtered brands. However, the most popular unfiltered brands—Chesterfield, Camel, and Lucky Strike—advertised consistently until 1963 in spite of the introduction of filters.

Graph four shows the most frequent cigarette advertisers for unfiltered cigarettes. Because filtered brands were not introduced until the 1950s, they are not among the most

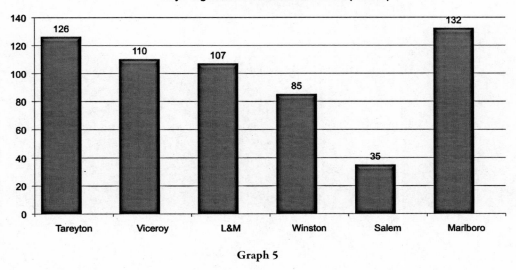

Major Cigarette Advertisers 1920s-1960s (Filtered)

Graph 5

frequent advertisers. This chart represents the most frequent cigarette advertisers in *The Orange and White*. Overall, Camel, Chesterfield, and Lucky Strike (Luckies) are the most frequently promoted brands.

Although their overall numbers are far lower than the unfiltered brands, the major filtered cigarette brands were more prevalent than their unfiltered counterparts from the mid–1950s until the end of cigarette advertising in 1964. The top four filtered advertisers were Tareyton, Marlboro, Viceroy, and L&M or Liggett & Myers. Although a menthol cigarette, Salem could be included because it also advertised its filter.

Evaluation of Message Appeals and Strategy

TAYLOR'S STRATEGY WHEEL

Researchers who study creative and message strategy have recognized the importance of mapping the various strategies in advertising. One model that maps various creative strategies is Taylor's Six-Segment Strategy Wheel.

The first division of the strategy wheel divides the wheel into a "Transmission view" and "Ritual view," based on the work of James Carey. The terms "informational" and "transformational," "claim" and "image," and "rational" and "emotional" have also been used to label this distinction. The wheel identifies six message strategies, three transmission-based strategies and three ritual-based strategies.[7]

The first strategy wheel segment (ego segment) is characterized by the Freudian Psychoanalytic Model. Products that are ego-related fulfill a consumer's emotional needs. These products allow consumers to make a statement about who they are. The role of communication is to show how the product fits within the consumers' definition of who they are. The second strategy wheel segment (social segment) is characterized by the Veblenian Social-Psychological Model. In this segment, products are used to make a statement to others and emotional needs are fulfilled by products that are visible to others. Appeals are directed

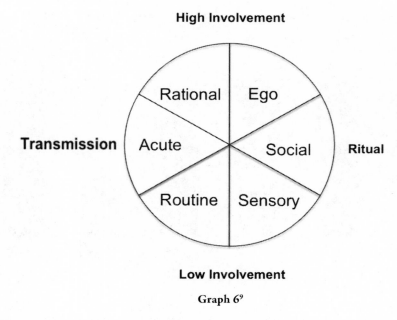

Graph 6[9]

towards being noticed, gaining social approval. The third segment (sensory segment) is based in Cyrenaic philosophy. Products provide consumers with moments of pleasure. Communication transforms the product into a pleasurable moment. The Pavlovian Learning Model characterizes the fourth segment (routine segment). Consumer decisions are motivated by rational buying motives. However, consumers do not invest large amounts of deliberation time and buy according to habit. Urgent needs characterize the fifth segment (acute need). Consumers desire pre-purchase information but time constraints limit the research process. Communication serves to build brand familiarity and recognition so that the brand is known and trusted. The sixth segment (rational segment) is typified by the Marshallian Economic Model. Consumers are assumed to be rational, conscious, and deliberative individuals. The consumers' desire for product-related information is high. Product messages aim to inform and persuade.[8]

The cigarette advertisements were categorized according to which segment represented the dominant strategy in the message. However, many messages use multiple strategies. For the sake of the charts and graphs, only one dominant strategy was selected. If multiple strategies were used in a campaign, they are discussed later in the results section when specific advertisements and campaigns are addressed.

ADVERTISING APPEALS AND TACTICS

The individual tactics and appeals that are used in an advertisement are important elements to examine. Creative strategy is usually thought to be the larger ideas that govern a particular advertising or marketing campaign. Message appeals and tactics are the particular techniques that are used to accomplish the ends of the selected strategy. Therefore, the tactics are the particular persuasive devices that work to help accomplish the advertisement's general persuasive goals. Usually, presenting product-related data and statistics is not enough to alter a consumer's attitude or behavior. Some appeal or incentive needs to be employed to create change. Message appeals include reward appeals and emotional appeals.

Although people experience an array of emotions, appeals to three basic emotions are used most frequently in advertising: fear, humor, and warmth. Within the context of emotional appeals, humor is the emotional appeal that is used most frequently in cigarette advertisements,[10] although many scholars argue that humor does not persuade. However, research has shown that 20 percent to 44 percent of television commercials use humor. Some research-supported guidelines suggest men are more influenced by humor and that humor promotes a positive effect and less counterarguing.[11]

In addition to examining the influence of emotions, one can also examine the influence of the communicator. Traditionally, communication scholars have devoted considerable attention to source credibility, that is, a source perceived to possess high levels of expertise by receivers as trained, experienced, skillful, informed, authoritative, able, and intelligent. Of course, different expert sources are important in different persuasion areas.[12] For instance, some tobacco advertisements made use of experts such as tobacconists and physicians to promote the safety and quality of the product.

On the other hand, sometimes consumers respond to persuasion from sources that are similar to themselves. Examples of similar sources are people with the same problems, the same concerns, who are the same age, and who have the same interests and preferences. In addition, researchers have found that similarity increases message compliance.[13] The similarity or peer appeal has a stronger influence on audience members when the source is a member of the same age group as the consumer.[14] In addition to similarity, physical attractiveness also plays a role in advertising. There is considerable evidence that attractive people are perceived to be more likable, friendly, interesting, poised, affluent, and so forth.[15]

The use of celebrity can be another extremely effective source tactic. Celebrities are most effective when the celebrity is an individual for whom consumers have a strong attachment. Second, children are strongly influenced by celebrities who are currently in or popular among their peer group.[16] Receivers also tend to follow the recommendations of celebrities if doing so helps them adapt to their environment. Another factor that can influence whether a celebrity will effectively endorse a product is the degree of match-up between the product and the celebrity spokesperson.[17]

Another way through which a spokesperson—celebrity, expert or otherwise—might influence consumers is through a power relationship. Individuals in a power relationship can use rewards and punishments when influencing others. According to French social psychologist Bertrand Raven, there are six basic types of social influence: informational, referent, expert, legitimate, reward, and coercive. The primary types of social influence observed in cigarette advertising were referent, reward, expert, and informational.[18] Referent influence stems from the fact that the receiver identifies with the source or influence agent. The term referent is used to parallel the use of the term referent group in sociology. Referent group identification has a strong influence on behavior.[19] When a person is attracted to another, and perceives similarity between them, he or she may comply with a request. Generally, any appeal to similarity or mutual attraction can be called an instance of referent influence. A speaker that has expert influence or power over the receiver if the receiver believes that the source has superior knowledge or ability. Expert influence often influences private behavior or private adoption of beliefs. Reward influence is exerted if the agent can provide a positive incentive to a particular audience member. Sources who reward their audiences often promote more positive interactions between the target audience and the source. Further, agents who reward targets do not necessarily increase the extent to which the target identifies with them. Speakers also can try to influence through the use of information not previously available to receivers, or to employ logic or argument that receivers have not considered. Informational influence includes attempts at influencing others based on the content of the message, a message including facts, evidence, testimony or logical argument. Informational influence results in both a change in overt behavior and in private beliefs.[20]

In addition to coding advertisements according to the six segments of the Strategy Wheel, advertisements were also coded according to the persuasive message appeals that were used. These message appeals are called creative tactics in the charts and figures in this chapter of the paper. The creative tactics listed in the charts and figures include celebrity appeals, referent appeals, informational appeals, humor appeals, reward appeals, and expert appeals. In order to differentiate celebrities and expert appeals from tactics that involve using a similar or attractive source, the term referent is used for non-expert and non-celebrity sources. However, it should be noted that some of the literature does use the term referent to encompass celebrity, expert and similar and attractive sources. The only tactics that were not derived from the literature were those that intended to entertain the audience. This category emerged from the data. For instance, a number of cigarette advertisements used puzzles, games, or riddles to entice their audience to interact with their advertisement and product. Each advertisement was placed into only one category.

Conclusion

Research is essential to advertising. It is important to its development and to its evaluation. Through careful analysis of the cigarette advertisements, the viewer can gain a better understanding of how generations of young educated adults decided to smoke. However, the ads are useful for more than just understanding smoking. Cigarette advertising in the student papers was financed by one of the most important industries in America. Through the microcosm of cigarette advertising, we can see the evolution of the institution of advertising in the United States.

5

The First Page

Cigarette Advertising in Student Newspapers During the 1920s

The 1920s are significant because national cigarette advertising campaigns began to run in the majority of campus newspapers during this period. Before the 1920s, a few advertisements for local tobacconists and pipe tobacco ran in the papers. The occasional cigarette ad could also be found. However, during the 1920s, the tobacco industry started to coordinate campaigns focusing on the college student market that consistently appeared in student papers. Cigarette advertising was slowly working to make cigarette smoking more socially acceptable. Social acceptability was an essential issue for recruiting female smokers.

Advertising Frequency and Strategy During the 1920s

Although cigarette advertising had a rather slow start during the 1920s, by the end of the decade cigarette advertising had a consistent place in most student newspapers. From 1920 to 1929 cigarette advertising in student newspapers evolved from being an occasional presence to an advertising institution. At the start of the decade, advertising was infrequent and not particularly targeted or sophisticated. By the end of the decade, it was clear that the advertising was created for the college market and that the brands had an investment in the college newspaper as a promotional medium.

Between 1920 and 1929, cigarette advertising increased in most student newspapers that carried cigarette advertising. However, the advertising trend did not show consistent growth. Instead, the record shows a series of spikes. During the 1920s, a total of 244 cigarette advertisements were printed in the 300 issues of *The Orange and White* printed from 1920 to 1929. An average of .82 advertisements appeared in each edition of the newspaper. According to graph one, the following academic years had the greatest frequency of cigarette advertisements in *The Orange and White*: 1921–1922, 1926–1927, 1927–1928, and 1928–1929.[1] Graph one also shows that following academic years had the lowest frequency of cigarette advertising: 1920–1921, 1922–1923, 1924–1925, and 1925–1926.

Number of Cigarette Advertisements 1920–1929

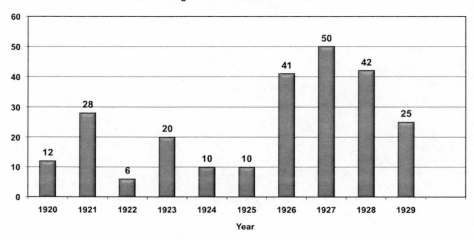

Graph 1[2]

Brands Advertised During the 1920s

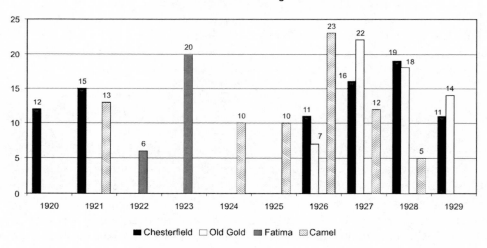

Graph 2

Four cigarette brands, Chesterfield, Old Gold, Fatima, and Camel, launched national advertising campaigns during the 1920s. Chesterfield was the most frequently advertised brand with a total of 84 national advertisements or 34 percent of the total advertising. Camel follows Chesterfield with a total of 73 advertisements or 30 percent of the advertising. Old Gold comes next with 61 advertisements or 25 percent of the advertising. And, Fatima is last with a total of 26 advertisements or 11 percent of the advertising.

Social and rational strategies were the most prevalent approaches used in cigarette advertising in the national campaigns that ran in student papers during the 1920s. Social strategies represented 67 percent of the advertising, or 164 total ads. The second most popular segment was the rational segment with 49 advertisements, or 20 percent, of the total

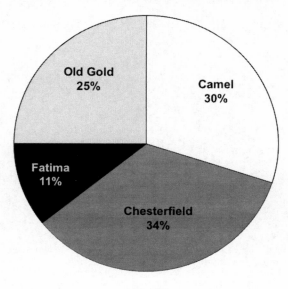

1920s Cigarette Brand Advertisements by Percentage

Old Gold
25%

Camel
30%

Fatima
11%

Chesterfield
34%

Graph 3

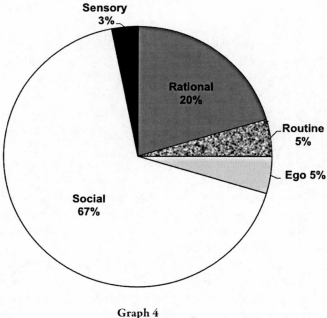

1920s Creative Strategies by Percent

Sensory
3%

Rational
20%

Routine
5%

Ego 5%

Social
67%

Graph 4

number of cigarette advertisements. Both the ego and routine strategies comprised 5 percent of the total cigarette advertisements or 12 advertisements. The sensory approach was used in 7 advertisements or 3 percent of the total advertisements.

During the 1920s, the referent appeal was the most prevalent approach used in cigarette advertising, representing 52 percent of cigarette advertising or 127 advertisements. Humor

1920s Appeals and Tactics Used in Advertisements by Percent

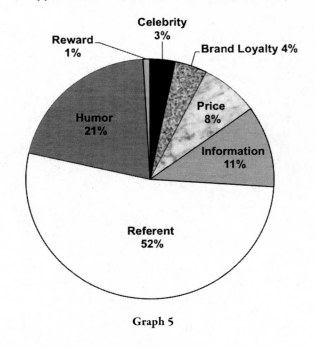

Graph 5

appeals were the second most prevalent tactic used in cigarette advertising representing 21 percent or 51 advertisements. Tactics that served to inform the audience represented 11 percent or 27 advertisements. Appeals that emphasized a particular brand's value or price represented 8 percent or 19 advertisements. Tactics that focused on brand loyalty represented 4 percent of the advertising or 10 advertisements. Celebrity appeals represent 3 percent of cigarette advertising or 7 advertisements. Reward influence comprised 1 percent of cigarette advertising or 3 advertisements.

The need to increase the social acceptability of cigarette smoking was one of the primary reasons that the referent appeal and social strategy seemed to dominate advertising campaigns during the 1920s. During the 1920–1921 academic year, the vast majority, 12 of the 13 total cigarette advertisements, featured only men. The one advertisement that featured a woman did not depict her as a smoker. Chesterfield was the only advertiser during this academic year. No people were featured in the cigarette advertising campaign during the 1921–1922 academic year. Fatima was the only brand advertised. During the 1922–1923 academic year, 15 of the 16 total advertisements featured only men and the one advertisement that depicted both sexes did not show either person smoking. Fatima was the only brand promoted. Only Camel cigarette advertisements appeared in *The Orange and White* during the 1924–1925 academic year. Cigarette advertising featured men only during the 1925–1926 academic year. Camel was the only advertiser.

However, starting in 1926, advertising began to change. For the first time, during the 1926–1927 academic year, more than one cigarette advertiser bought advertising space in student newspapers. Chesterfield, Old Gold, and Camel advertised using primarily men in the 41 advertisements that appeared in *The Orange and White*. A few ads featured women and three

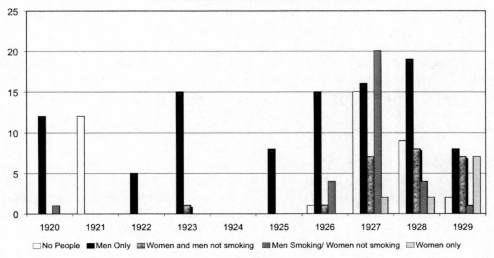

1920 to 1929 Men and Women in Advertisements

Legend: □ No People ■ Men Only ▨ Women and men not smoking ▤ Men Smoking/ Women not smoking □ Women only

Graph 6

advertisements depicted women smoking. During the 1927–1928 academic year, Chesterfield, Camel, and Old Gold continued to advertise and the number of women in advertisements continued to increase. Of the 50 advertisements printed, 35 featured women and eight of the 35 showed women as smokers. More than half of the advertisements featured women. In the 1928–1929 academic year, 20 of the 42 advertisements featured women in some capacity. Again, about half of the advertisements included women. And, Chesterfield, Camel, and Old Gold continued to be the primary advertisers. During the 1929–1930 academic year the number of cigarette advertisements fell to 25 and Old Gold and Chesterfield were the only advertisers. However, 15 advertisements, nearly two-thirds of the total, featured women.

College Advertising Campaigns in the 1920s

Cigarette advertising in the 1920s was somewhat sporadic and inconsistent. Most campaigns did not consistently appear in the student newspaper until the late 1920s. The issue of women and cigarettes further complicated matters. Many coed campuses either did not allow women to be featured in cigarette advertising or featured smoking in cigarette advertising because they were not permitted to smoke on campus. Therefore, some advertisers had to develop various versions of advertising campaigns to adhere to rules on various college and university campuses. Another issue was the novelty of the medium. Cigarette advertisers were unsure of the effectiveness of advertising in student papers. Consequently, there was an initial lack of commitment to the medium.

OLD GOLD

Some of the most exceptional and innovative creative work of the 1920s promoted Lorillard's Old Gold brand. Old Gold employed the most prominent illustrators and celebrities to promote its cigarettes. Old Gold pioneered the newspaper advertorial targeting college students. Advertorial techniques draw readers by mimicking popular editorial content such as syndicated comic strips and editorial columns. Advertorials often feature humorists who develop a comic strip or a column.

Old Gold began advertising during the 1926–1927 academic year with the "Something Always takes the Joy out of Life" comic strip campaign. This comic strip was the first comic strip sponsored by a cigarette brand to appear in student papers. A renowned cartoonist named Clare Briggs created the comic. Briggs was a featured cartoonist during the peak of American newspapering, which spanned from 1900 to 1930. Briggs was born in Reedsburg, Wisconsin, in 1875 and lived there until 1884 when he and his parents moved to Dixon, Illinois. Brigg's cartoons were syndicated across the country and, by the 1920s, he was one of the most highly paid illustrators in the United States. In addition to his newspaper work, Briggs also published a number of books of cartoons, *Skin-nay, The Days of Real Sport, Ain't It a Grand and Glorious Feeling,* and *When a Feller Needs a Friend,* that reached a large audience.[3] Many of the comic strips printed in student papers featured the titles of his books of cartoons such as "Ain't It a Grand and Glorious Feeling" and "When a Feller Needs a Friend." The comic strip combined a social strategy that emphasized the social acceptability of smoking, and the importance of smoking Old Gold in particular, with humor tactics. Many advertisements emphasize the necessity of smoking Old Gold to make a good impression on others. The fact that Old Gold does not irritate the throat is of particular importance. In each execution, the advertisement concludes with Old Gold's slogan "Not a Cough in the Carload."

Like many other cigarette advertisers by the end of the 1920s, Old Gold was also eager to prove that cigarette smoking was socially acceptable. Old Gold's 1927–1928 campaign featured various prominent people who attested that Old Gold cigarettes were the best. It was the first cigarette campaign to use celebrity tactics in *The Orange and White.* For instance, heiress Gloria Laura Mercedes Morgan-Vanderbilt selected Old Gold as her cigarette of choice in a blind taste test. Using an image of Gloria Morgan-Vanderbilt to promote smoking suggested that women of the elite class found cigarettes to be socially acceptable. Babe Ruth and Charlie Chaplin also participated in Old Gold's blind taste test campaign. This advertising campaign combined a sensory strategy with a celebrity testimonial tactic to help persuade men and women to start smoking.

During the 1928–1929 academic year, Old Gold continued to target women. Instead of using a taste test, this campaign again focused on persuading the audience that smoking Old Gold cigarettes does not cause coughing. This sensory strategy promotes what the cigarettes do not do. In addition to the sensory strategy, the campaign uses a celebrity testimonial tactic. Actress Madge Bellamy praises Old Gold for being easy on her throat. The campaign also included the testimonial of the famous artist and illustrator James Montgomery Flagg.[4]

In addition to celebrity testimonials, Old Gold also published statements from local tobacconists that were popular with college students in their advertisements. This innovative approach used local endorsements instead of celebrities. For instance, Gray Piper Drug Co., located at 1506 West Cumberland, Knoxville, Tennessee, said,

> The growth of OLD GOLD Cigarettes' popularity here has been amazing to me, but what interests me most is the way students stick to the brand after they start smoking it. OLD GOLD smokers don't switch.[5]

"Somebody is Always Taking the Joy Out of Life"—by Briggs. Old Gold comic strip/advertorial combining a social strategy with humor tactics. Printed with permission of Fordham University's Special Collections and Archives. Old Gold, Fordham University Digital Collections, *The Ram,* January 20, 1928.

Another leading tobacconist that served college students, J. Blaufeld & Son, 516 Gay Street, Knoxville, Tennessee, said,

> OLD GOLD is easily the fastest-growing cigarette in this locality, and I shouldn't be surprised before long to find it the most popular cigarette on the campus. The boys sure do like its smoothness."[6]

Similar ads were published across the country using various tobacconists' testimonials.

Because of the tobacco industry's large budget, cigarette advertisers often could hire famous artists and designers to create their advertising. Few artists define an age as completely as John Held, Jr. In many ways, he defines the Roaring Twenties. Seldom have two generations experienced the same gap as the young adults of the 1920s and their parents. Mothers who grew up with petticoats and hoopskirts had daughters who wore short shirts and straight dresses in the popular flapper fashion. Popular magazines like *Vanity Fair, Harper's Bazaar,*

Old Gold *hits a homer for* Babe Ruth
in Blindfold *cigarette test*

"Yes, I am well over 21 . . . so I could see no reason why I shouldn't make the blindfold test. As I tried the four leading cigarettes I kept this 'box score' on the results:

No. 1 . . . . out at first
No. 2 . . this one 'fanned'
No. 3 . . out on a pop fly
No. 4 (OLD GOLD) *a home run hit!*

"OLD GOLD'S mildness and smoothness marked it 'right off the bat' as the best."

Babe Ruth

The idol of the baseball world . . . "The King of Swat"

. . . .

BABE RUTH . . . making the test in the dressing room at the Yankee Stadium. He was asked to smoke each of the four leading brands, clearing his taste with black coffee between smokes. Only one question was asked: "Which one do you like best?"

On a non-stop flight to the bleachers! . . .

THE TREASURE OF THEM ALL
© P. Lorillard Co., Est. 1760

Why *do they choose* OLD GOLD . . . *even in the dark?*

What is this superiority that wins so many famous people? It's simply *honey-like smoothness* . . . the new and delightful quality that OLD GOLD has added to cigarettes. And it comes from the *heart-leaves* of the tobacco plant . . . *the finest tobacco that grows.* That's why you can pick OLD GOLDS with your eyes closed.

Made from the *heart-leaves* of the *tobacco plant*

SMOOTHER AND *BETTER*—"NOT A COUGH IN A CARLOAD"

Advertorial featuring Babe Ruth for Old Gold using a Social and Sensory strategy combined with a celebrity appeal. Printed with permission of SUNY-Buffalo Special Collections and Archives, Old Gold, UB Digital Collections, *The Bee,* State University of New York at Buffalo, October 5 1928, http://digital.lib.buffalo.edu/utils/getarticleclippings/collection/LIB-UA007/id/325/articleId/DIVL260/compObjId/328/dmtext/.

not a cough in a campus-ful!
(and of course, "not a cough in a carload")

And still another leading tobacconist in Buffalo, N. Y., says:

"The rapid growth in the popularity of OLD GOLD Cigarettes among the students is remarkable. Never in my experience have I seen a new cigarette catch on so quickly with the boys on the campus."

James J. Murphy
Cigar Store
3225 Main Street

AT LEADING COLLEGES.. *This is an Old Gold year*

For a most refreshing change:
"Follow your friends and switch to this smoother and better cigarette"

© P. Lorillard Co., Est. 1760

Old Gold
CIGARETTES
THE TREASURE OF THEM ALL

"Not a cough in a campus-ful!" Old Gold advertisement featuring college campuses across the nation using a social strategy. Printed with permission of State University of New York at Buffalo Special Collections and Archives. Old Gold, UB Digital Collections, *The Bee*, State University of New York at Buffalo, May 15, 1928. http://digital.lib.buffalo.edu/cdm/compoundobject/collection/LIB-UA 007/id/348/rec/2

Comic advertorial for Old Gold by John Held, Jr. using a social strategy and humor tactics. Printed with permission of the University of Tennessee Special Collections. Old Gold advertisement printed October 1, 1927, Archives of *The Orange and White*, University of Tennessee Libraries, Knoxville.

and *Redbook*, Held's images of Betty Coed and Joe College were placed weekly before an adoring public of parents who longed to see some humor in the situation and the teenaged and college crowd who looked to them as role and style models. The skirts were never quite that short, nor were the sheiks quite so pencil-necked, but everyone wanted to believe that they were. Held's images confirmed their delusions.[7]

Old Gold's use of Held's creative abilities helped the brand resonate with a college audience during the 1920s. The Old Gold campaign's humor does indeed make fun of the Gay Nineties. The creative strategy is primarily social because it reinforces the idea that smoking cigarettes is a modern way to distinguish oneself from the previous generation.

Old Gold concluded the decade with advertisements that promoted an Old Gold premium that was being offered with the purchase of Old Gold cigarettes. The premium is an Old Gold velour cigarette box. This advertising approach combines a rational strategy with reward tactics. Again, from the advertisement itself and the design of the cigarette box, it seems that Old Gold is targeting female smokers.

CHESTERFIELD

Chesterfield's first college campaign was launched in 1921. The advertisements employed a social strategy that marked occasions for smoking cigarettes. For instance, the example provided in the text centers on a sitting for a portrait. The man being photographed is nervous but the photographer makes him smile by showing him a package of Chesterfield ciga-

Advertisement for Chesterfield using a social and rational strategy. Printed with permission of Fordham University's Special Collections and Archives, Chesterfield, Fordham University Digital Collections, *The Ram*, February 17, 1928.

rettes. Therefore, this soft-sell approach shows that cigarettes can be used to put someone at ease. The primary tactic that is used is humor. The headline reads, "I smiled—and he shot me." This initially shocking statement is further explained through the text. The text reads:

> **"I smiled—and he shot me."**
> AFTER MONTHS and months,
> MY WIFE persuaded me.
> SO I went around
> TO THE photographer,
> AND GOT mugged.
> WHEN THE pictures came,
> I SHOWED them to a gang,
> OF AMATEUR art critics,
> AND PROFESSIONAL crabs,
> DISGUISED as friends
> WHO FAVORED me.
> WITH SUCH remarks as
> "DOESN'T HE look natural?"
> "HAS IT got a tail?"
> "A GREAT resemblance."
> AND THAT last one
> MADE ME sore.
> SO WHEN friend wife
> ADDED HER howl
> I TRIED again.
> THIS TIME they were great.
> FOR HERE'S what happened.
> THE PHOTOGRAPHER said,
> "LOOK THIS way please"
> AND HELD up something
> AS HE pushed the button,
> AND NO one could help
> BUT LOOK pleasant.
> FOR WHAT he held up
> WAS A nice full pack
> OF THE cigarettes
> THAT SATISFY.

Other similar advertisements in this campaign were titled "Every man in class knew the answer," "The tale of a dog—with a moral," and "Transfer? A fat chance!" Each of the advertisements appealed to college-aged men.

Humor appeals are used throughout the Chesterfield campaign in the description of the situations and the double meanings of the words that are used. Humor complemented the social strategy because humor plays an important role in social situations. Although the social strategy is the primary method used to help persuade the audience, a sensory strategy is also employed. The man being photographed smiles because Chesterfield cigarettes satisfy.

Because the question of women smoking was controversial on college campuses, this first advertising campaign focuses on male characters. Only one advertisement features a woman, and she is not a smoking character. This first Chesterfield campaign lasted until June 2, 1921. Another important feature of this advertising campaign is that it appears to have been developed especially for college students. Several of the advertisements mention the collegiate environment or professors.

After several years without making an appearance in student papers, Chesterfield appeared again during the 1926–1927 academic year. Again, Chesterfield used a social strategy. The advertisement shows men at a nightclub purchasing cigarettes from a cigarette girl. The text reads, "The natural choice—Out of the whole lot men pick Chesterfield for its genuine tobacco character–its natural good taste." The text and the image reinforce the popularity of Chesterfield. The copy also suggests that smoking is a habit for men, pacifying universities that opposed women smoking.

By the 1928–1929 academic year, Chesterfield marketed to both men and women. The text of the advertisements no longer suggested that cigarette smoking was a practice for men alone. Women became active participants in the storyline plots and it was even suggested that they might smoke. To encourage the idea that smoking might be acceptable for women, a social strategy was used to promote the place of women within a smoking culture. In addition, many of the Chesterfield ads simply promoted the fact that Chesterfield was a popular brand and supported the idea that smoking was socially acceptable. However, by using statistics that proved that Chesterfield was a popular cigarette and that 13 million smokers preferred Chesterfield, there was an element of rational argument within the social strategy.

CAMEL

In 1921, Camel's campaigns began to appear in *The Orange and White*. Instead of using a soft-sell approach like the Chesterfield and Old Gold advertisements, Camel used a rational approach that focused on product quality. The advertisements describe the packaging that keeps the tobacco air-tight. Informational tactics reinforce the rational approach by persuading the consumer by providing privileged facts. Further, the advertisement states that Camels are for "men who think for themselves." This approach complements both the rational strategy and the fact that smoking was not appropriate for college women. Camel's advertising was conforming to the social mores of the time. A secondary strategy that is present in this advertisement is the sensory strategy. The primary objective of the special cigarette packaging is to preserve taste. This campaign ran for the entire 1921–1922 academic year.

Camel did not run its campaigns again until the 1925–1926 academic year. That campaign used a sensory strategy that positioned smoking Camels as a reward and also suggested a romantic setting. The headline reads, "When silvery moonlight falls on town and field— and the long, joyous tour home is ready to begin—have a Camel!" The advertisement features a couple in a car enjoying the evening scenery. The advertisement also emphasizes the affluence of cigarette smokers by depicting an aspirational lifestyle. The advertisement features a luxury vehicle and a wealthy couple enjoying an evening drive. However, neither person is shown with a cigarette.

During the 1926–1927 academic year, Camel continued to combine a sensory strategy with referent appeals. Instead of evening drives and other romantic excursions, this time the advertisements centered on formal social gatherings. The headline reads, "Some call it mellowness..." and the text continues by describing the high-quality tobacco used in Camel cigarettes. The image in the advertisement shows a party where men smoke and women are shown in the background dancing. In another advertisement in the same campaign, cigarette

When old grads drop in—and around the fire experiences of then are fondly retold —have a Camel!

WHEN famed men return. And by dancing firelight they relate their stories of old — have a Camel!

For Camel helps all men who rise proudly to rise higher and more jauntily. Camels never harm or tire your taste, no matter how plentifully you smoke them. You'll never find more friendly flavor than you get in Camels.

So this night when those from long ago return to think of the roads that join. As you see in their past your future unfold, then restfully taste the smoke that's prized by the world's experienced.

Have a Camel!

Into the making of this one cigarette goes all of the ability of the world's largest organization of expert tobacco men. Nothing is too good for Camels. The choicest Turkish and Domestic tobaccos. The most skilful blending. The most scientific package. No other cigarette made is like Camels. No better cigarette can be made. Camels are the overwhelming choice of experienced smokers.

Our highest wish, if you do not yet know Camel quality, is that you try them. We invite you to compare Camels with any cigarette made at any price.
R. J. Reynolds Tobacco Company
Winston-Salem, N. C.

© 1926

Advertisement for Camel using a social strategy. Printed with permission of Fordham University's Special Collections and Archives, Camel, Fordham University Digital Collections, *The Ram*, March 12, 1926.

smoking is depicted as a memorable rite of passage for male college students. The advertisements show young male students socializing with alumni. The advertisement suggests that cigarette smoking will help future college alumni reminisce about their college experience.

Camel returned to a rational strategy that focused on product-related information during the 1928–1929 academic year. A secondary strategy that comes into play is the sensory strategy. The advertisements communicate that Camel is particular about its product quality because of its desire to make enjoyable cigarettes.

FATIMA

In its first college advertising campaign during the 1922–1923 academic year, Fatima made use of a popular advertising figure during the early 20th century, the bellhop. Bellhops or bellboys were frequently called upon to perform services for hotel guests. These errands could include delivering necessary items. And, one such item could be a pack of cigarettes. The turn-of-the-century bellhop is also a recognizable symbol of the hospitality industry. Hoteliers take pride in the services they provide. The bellhop's image is that of a helpful, friendly individual, someone you can turn to for assistance or information. The use of the bellhop also communicated luxury because expensive hotels frequently used bellboys. The Fatima campaign strategy combines an ego strategy with a routine strategy. The headline "Day in and day out!" suggests the cigarette can be depended upon to satisfy. The large fluted Doric columns and the use of the bellhop suggests the luxury of the hotel and implies that the cigarette is high quality through association. Although the bellhop is an appealing figure, it is not an image that is exclusive to the college scene. Therefore, it seems that the campaign was designed for a mass audience.

Fatima changed its campaign for the 1923–1924 academic year. Instead of using the bellhop and a luxury hotel to communicate quality, Fatima used an exotic social scene. The headline, "What a difference just a few cents make!" accompanied by a scene from a downhill skiing resort, suggests that Fatima is a luxury or ego brand. Thus, Fatima continued with the same ego-based approach but used the appeal of an aspirational social group to execute the strategy. Unlike previous advertisements, this campaign used women prominently in the advertisements. However, the women were not depicted as smokers. Again, the advertising campaign appeared to be a national campaign instead of a campaign designed for the college market.

Conclusion

During the 1920s cigarette advertising in college and university papers increased in its frequency and in the number of brands being advertised. In addition to increasing in its regularity, cigarette advertising also became more sophisticated in its message appeals. By the end of the decade, advertisements were using complex social strategies that associated cigarette smoking with high social status. This approach helped to make smoking more socially acceptable for women. Cigarette advertising also seemed to reflect the progressive attitudes and optimism of the time. Smoking seemed to be a way to celebrate the financial prosperity and innovation of the 1920s.

6

Cigarette Advertising Becomes an Institution on Campus

Cigarette Advertising in Student Newspapers During the 1930s

By the 1930s, cigarette smoking had become an established habit among both male and female college students. Cigarette advertising helped win the battle to gain social acceptance for the habit for both genders on college campuses. The college market was becoming increasingly important. Advertising frequency steadily increased into the 1930s. Cigarette advertising in most student newspapers more than doubled.

The 1930s began with a change in the basic approach that cigarette advertisers used. More advertisements were using a sensory strategy instead of a social strategy, perhaps because public opinion of cigarette smoking had changed. In addition to gaining social acceptance for smoking, cigarette advertisers promoted smoking as a glamorous and sophisticated habit that was embraced by both celebrities and socialites.

Advertising Frequency, Strategy and Sophistication During the 1930s

From the 1930–1931 academic year to the 1939–1940 academic year, nearly half of the cigarette advertisements that ran in larger student papers promoted Chesterfield cigarettes. In *The Orange and White*, Chesterfield's campaigns comprised 305 of the 613 cigarette ads. In smaller papers, like Bard College's newspaper, *The Bardian,* Chesterfield sponsored the only national cigarette advertising campaign that appeared during the 1930s. Camel also maintained a regular advertising frequency in many larger papers with 174 advertisements appearing in *The Orange and White*. Lucky Strike also began to print regular advertisements in student papers during the 1930s. On the other hand, Old Gold reduced its college presence. Numbers remained quite low for Old Gold when compared to the other brands. Old Gold advertised only in 1931 and 1934.

Both the frequency of cigarette advertisements being published in student newspapers and number campus newspapers printing cigarette advertisements increased during the 1930s. For instance, during the 1920s, 244 cigarette advertisements ran in the University of Ten-

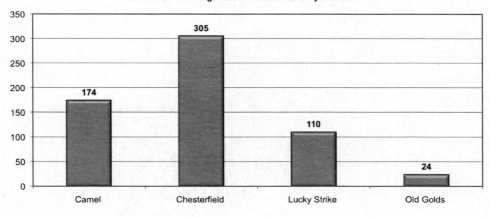

Graph 1

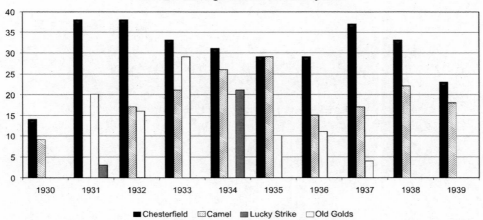

Graph 2

nessee's *Orange and White*; 613 cigarette advertisements ran in the 403 editions of *The Orange and White* that were published from the 1930–1931 academic year to the 1939–1940 academic year. Although the increase in the number of advertisements is large, the advertising frequency per edition did not change as much as one might imagine. The University of Tennessee already published more cigarette advertisements than most student papers. And, the paper increased its printing schedule to become a bi-weekly. For instance, during the 1920s an average of .82 advertisements ran in each edition of *The Orange and White*. By the 1930s, the average increased to 1.52 advertisements per edition.

During the 1930s, the sensory strategy dominated creative strategy with 251 advertisements, or 41 percent of the total advertising, using this approach. The sensory strategy was the prominent approach in the 1930–1931, 1935–1936, 1936–1937, 1937–1938, 1938–1939 and 1939–1940 academic years. Although the sensory approach was the most frequently used approach, the social strategy was not far behind with 234 advertisements or 38 percent

1930–1939 Creative Strategies

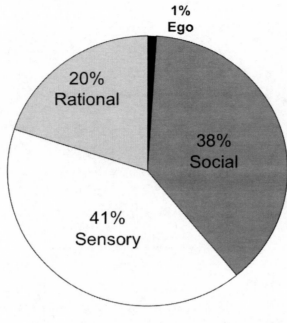

Graph 3

1930–1939 Advertising Tactics by Percent

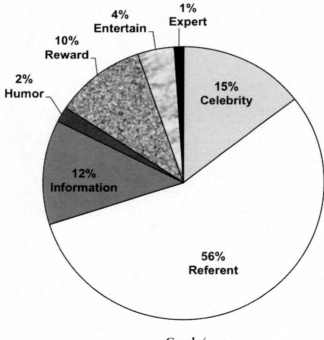

Graph 4

of the total advertising. In fact, the social strategy dominated from 1931 to 1934. A large number of advertisements, 20 percent of the total or 123 advertisements, used a rational approach. The ego strategy was the least frequently used with only 1 percent or 6 advertisements falling into this category.

Although a social advertising message strategy no longer dominated cigarette advertising in *The Orange and White*, from a tactical perspective, the use of a socially desirable referent or celebrity was prevalent; for instance, 71 percent or 435 advertisements used this type of approach. An informational approach was fairly common; this approach was used in 74 advertisements or 12 percent of the total. Using a reward tactic was also used occasionally; 61 advertisements or 10 percent of the ads employed this tactical approach. Relatively few advertisements endeavored to entertain their audience. Only 4 percent or 25 advertisements used this approach. Few advertisements used humor to sell their product. Just 2 percent or 12 advertisements used this tactic. Using an expert was even more rare with only 1 percent of the total or 6 advertisements using this approach.

Similar advertising trends were observed in a variety of papers. The University of Minnesota's *Minnesota Daily* increased its advertising frequency and printed the same campaigns as *The Orange and White*. The University of Indiana's *Daily Student* began printing national cigarette advertising campaigns in the 1930s. It also carried the majority of the national campaigns. Cigarette advertising also began appearing in smaller campus papers. This trend could even be seen at small papers printed by women's colleges, such as Bard College's *The Bardian* and the *Vassar Miscellany News*. Chesterfield published its campaigns in the smaller student papers with the greatest frequency. Camel, Lucky Strike, and Old Gold usually bought space in larger papers. However, even these brands occasionally appeared in smaller papers.

1930s Cigarette Advertising Campaigns in Student Newspapers

During the 1930s, cigarette advertisers established their presence in the student newspapers through annual advertising campaigns. Popular brands such as Chesterfield, Camel, Lucky Strike and Old Gold published weekly ads. Many of the campaigns were praised by the advertising industry for their high quality and aesthetics. In addition, many student papers came to depend on the revenue that the campaigns generated.

CHESTERFIELD

During the 1930s, Chesterfield cigarettes dominated college cigarette promotions. In 1930 Chesterfield used a sensory strategy that focused on Chesterfield's fine tobacco and taste. The headlines state, "milder and better taste." The text follows, "'Promises fill no sack'—it is TASTE and not words you enjoy in a smoke." The purely sensory approach is complemented by the image of a burning cigarette.

Chesterfield changed its strategy from a sensory to a rational strategy in January 1931. Chesterfield's rational strategy compares the rationale required to select a cigarette brand with the strategies used to figure out puzzles or optical illusions. Therefore, the objective of the advertisement is to communicate the idea that the taste or quality of a cigarette is easy to determine. From the analogy, it should be easy to determine that Chesterfield is the superior brand.

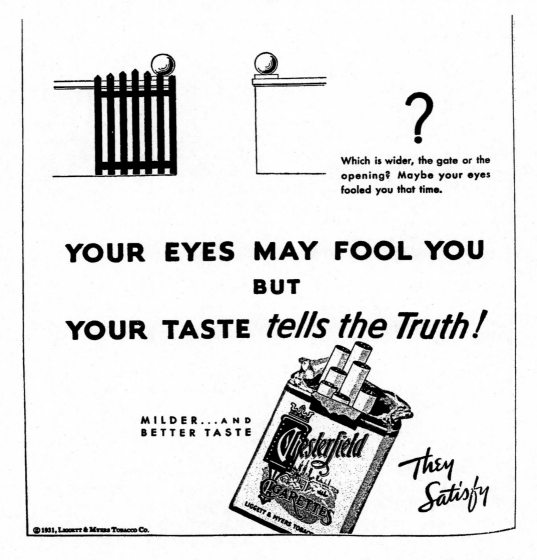

Chesterfield advertisement using a rational strategy. Printed with permission from Southern Methodist University Chesterfield, SMU University Archives, *The Semi-Weekly Campus*, March 11, 1931.

In addition to using product characteristics such as tobacco taste and quality, Chesterfield also used the fact that it used Turkish tobacco to sell cigarettes. An advertising headline reads, "Let's all go to Turkey." Featuring exotic Eastern destinations such as Cavalla, Smyrna, and Samsoun as suppliers of their tobacco adds to the allure of cigarette smoking. For instance, the familiar image of the Hagia Sophia, a monument that is widely associated with travel to Turkey, also adds to the exotic feel of the advertisement. Therefore the major strategies at play in this advertisement are rational and ego-related. The use of information is the primary persuasive appeal.

Chesterfield changed its strategy again during the 1931–1932 academic year. Instead of focusing on the product itself, the advertising centers on the greater social context or meaning

"I was afraid Grandfather would be Shocked ..

HE'S rather a bossy old darling, and I didn't know how he'd like the idea of my smoking.

"The first time I lit a Chesterfield in front of him, he sniffed like an old war-horse...and I braced myself for trouble. But all he said was, 'That's good tobacco, Chickabiddy.'

"You know Grandfather raised tobacco in his younger days, so he knows what's what. I don't, of course —but I *do* know that Chesterfields are milder. It's wonderful to be able to smoke whenever you want, with no fear you'll smoke too many.

"And it doesn't take a tobacco expert to prove that Chesterfield tobaccos are better. They *taste* better... that's proof enough. Never too sweet. No matter when I smoke them...or how many I smoke... they always taste exactly right.

"They must be absolutely pure... even to the paper which doesn't taste at all. In fact...as the ads say...'They Satisfy!'"

● Wrapped in Du Pont Number 300 Moisture-proof Cellophane...the best and most expensive made!

© 1932, LIGGETT & MYERS TOBACCO CO.

CHESTERFIELD'S RADIO PROGRAM
Nat Shilkret's Orchestra and Alex Gray, well-known soloist, will entertain you over the Columbia Coast-to-Coast Network every night, except Sunday, at 10:30 E.S.T.

THEY'RE MILDER • • THEY'RE PURE • • THEY TASTE BETTER • • *They Satisfy*

Chesterfield advertisement using a social strategy. Printed with permission of the University of Tennessee Special Collections. Chesterfield advertisement, printed February 19, 1932, Archives of *The Orange and White,* University of Tennessee Libraries, Knoxville.

of the product. For instance, one recurring theme is that the smoking habit is universally accepted—even stodgy grandfathers approve of smoking. However, societal acceptance of cigarette smoking is dependent upon smoking the right brand of cigarettes. And that brand was Chesterfield.

For the 1932–1933 academic year, Chesterfield used a more sophisticated approach for advertising cigarettes. The primary strategy in this campaign is social. For instance, the women in one advertisement seductively inquires, "Tell me something ... what makes a cigarette taste better?" Presumably, she is speaking to a male smoker who is ready and wil-

Chesterfield advertisement using a social strategy. Printed with permission from Bard College Archives & Special Collections. Chesterfield advertisement, *The Bardian*, printed March 18, 1936.

ling to answer her request. In addition to the primary social strategy, a secondary sensory approach is also being used through the implication that Chesterfields are the best tasting cigarettes.

Chesterfield used a social strategy to promote its brand during the 1934–1935 academic year. Again, Chesterfield uses a social strategy to imply that the approval of others depends upon smoking its brand. For instance, in an advertisement from the campaign printed in *The Daily Princetonian*, the justice of the peace agrees to marry a young couple because they smoke Chesterfields.[1] During the 1935–1936 academic year Chesterfield continued to promote its brand by implying social approval. However, some of its ads used sensory strategy instead of social approval or combined a sensory approach with social approval. Chesterfield copy during 1935–1936 often reads, "I wouldn't give that for a cigarette that doesn't Satisfy ... that doesn't give me what I want in a smoke." However, an element of peer approval is also present. The use of a similar or familiar source reinforces the social aspects of smoking. For instance, in Chesterfield ad that ran in *The Bardian*, a professor is convincing a young coed sipping a bottle of milk to smoke by saying, "I venture to say that by 1937 all the girls will be smoking them." Therefore, smoking is used as a way to connect with others on campus and to conform with campus culture. In addition to referencing campus life, Chesterfield advertisements often poked fun at college students' grandparents' generation. In an advertisement that combines a social approach with humor tactics, two elderly women smoke Chesterfields. The headline reads, "I'm not saying a word." Smoking is shown to be a slightly taboo habit that is appealing even to elderly women.

During the 1937–1938 academic year, Chesterfield continued to use a social strategy by focusing on occasions when one should smoke. One advertisement focusing on use occasion reads, "First a handshake ... then 'Have a Chesterfield.'" This social strategy helps establish a social routine of smoking or offering a cigarette when you meet someone. In addition to promoting smoking, Chesterfield advertising in student papers began promoting the radio programming that it sponsored. The performers that were used in the programming were also featured as spokespeople in print advertisements for the particular cigarette brand. This use of cross promotion was a fairly sophisticated technique during the 1930s. In most student newspapers, Chesterfield was the only brand employing this marketing technique. Sensory-focused advertising for Chesterfield also appeared during the 1938–1939 academic year. However, even the sensory-based advertisements that focused on smoking pleasure promoted local radio programming sponsored by Chesterfield.

Although Chesterfield's advertising appealed to young adults, it was not always clear whether the ads were directed at a college audience. Some advertisements featured college students and professors while other ads simply featured young people. However, Chesterfield advertisements still demonstrated a high level of sophistication in their cross promotion across media vehicles and in the execution of their creative strategies.

CAMEL

When the 1930s began, Camel promoted its brand in campus papers using relatively generic advertisements that were not exclusively for a collegiate audience. However, by the end of the decade, Camel's campaigns became increasingly sophisticated and targeted. These campaigns spoke to a collegiate audience specifically and addressed smoking benefits from the student perspective.

During the 1930–1931 academic year, Camel advertised its new humidor packaging. The term humidor refers to a special airtight container that was normally used to keep expensive cigars moist. As cigars are typically thought of as being a premier or high-end tobacco product, the use of the term humidor implies quality. Therefore, the primary strategy that is used in this campaign is a rational strategy that is supplemented by informational appeal. A sensory strategy is a secondary approach in this campaign. The goal of the special humidor packaging is to preserve the freshness of the tobacco and to enhance the taste. To support this message, the copy reads, "Smoke a *fresh* cigarette." In addition to promoting Camel's superior quality, R.J. Reynolds also financed contests rewarding its customers for smoking its brand. For instance, the Camel advertisements publicized the $50,000 awards distributed in contests in the previous year.

During the 1933–1934 academic year, Camel cigarettes ran an advertorial campaign that mimicked the appearance of syndicated comics. The campaign focused on explaining the trickery involved in various illusions and magic acts. The campaign makes the connection that smokers should resist being tricked by other cigarette brands that do

Camel ad using a rational strategy with sensory elements. Printed with permission from Vassar College Special Collections & Archives. Camel advertisement, Vassar College Special Collections & Archives, *Vassar Miscellany News,* **January 23, 1935.**

not adhere to the same standards as Camel. The advertising uses a rational strategy to try to persuade students to smoke Camel. However, the tactics used in the advertisement entertain the audience member by revealing the secrets to various magic acts. In the advertisement provided, Camel provides the reader with the secrets behind the famous magician Harry Houdini's milk can escape. Other tricks that were revealed included Hardeen's packing case escape,[2] the Japanese thumb tie illusion,[3] and the cut rope made whole again trick.[4]

For the first time, in 1934 Camel developed a campaign targeting college students specifically. In this series of advertisements cigarettes are prescribed as a remedy for various nervous habits. Through these ads, cigarettes are recommended as a way to counteract negative or undesirable sensations. Therefore, the campaign's primary strategy is sensory. The

Promo advertisement for Camel's "Jack Oakie's College." Printed with permission from Vassar College Special Collections & Archives. Camel advertisement, Vassar College Special Collections & Archives, *Vassar Miscellany News,* January 20, 1937.

campaign seems to be intended for college students that may be experiencing stress. Camel claims to alleviate other habits such as newspaper crackling,[5] doodling,[6] forehead wrinkling,[7] and hair mussing.[8]

In 1934, instead of prescribing Camels for nerves, this advertising campaign promotes tobacco as a stimulant, stating, "After Concentrating...Get A Lift with a Camel." Again, Camel uses a rational strategy by focusing on promoting the product benefits but also features a secondary sensory message by describing the lift that students get from smoking. The use of students' testimonials provides referent tactics that help to reinforce the rational strategy. This campaign includes students from a variety of majors including pre-med,[9] law,[10] architecture,[11] agriculture,[12] and history.[13] In addition to featuring students in various majors, it also featured people pursuing various career paths such as pilots, rodeo riders, engineers, firemen, and explorers.[14]

Camel continued to target college students by offering cash incentives for smoking its brand. Camel also invited college students to try a pack of Camels, and if they were not satisfied they could return it for a cash rebate. This rational advertising strategy is combined with referent tactics. The young woman in the campaign presenting the offer looks much like a typical 1930s college student.

In addition to college students, Camel also used athletes to promote its cigarettes. However, in spite of the change in spokesperson, the strategy remained the same. Both campaigns use a rational approach to persuasion. In this case professional athletes attest that Camels "Don't get your Wind" or impede athletic performance. This campaign featured Lou Gehrig, first baseman for the Yankees; Betty Bailey, a champion diver; George Barker, a track star; Bruce Barnes, tennis champion; and Tommy Armour, champion golfer.[15]

From 1937 to 1940 Camel continued promoting the fact that Camel cigarettes "never get on your nerves." Each of the advertisements used a sensory strategy that described the medicinal properties of Camel and used the testimonials of various celebrities and athletes to support this claim. Like Chesterfield, Camel ads also promoted its sponsored radio programming. *Jack Oakie's College* was a popular radio program among students that was sponsored by R.J. Reynolds and Camel cigarettes.

Lucky Strike

Lucky Strike first advertised in *The Orange and White* on October 13, 1931. The brand's first campaigns were product-oriented and was not specifically targeting college students. The campaign's primary message strategy was rational and centered on product information. For instance, the advertisement focused on the moisture-proof cellophane packaging. Like the Camel advertisements, Lucky Strike compared its packaging to a humidor. Although every execution is different, the rational strategy remains the same. By focusing on taste and packing, the campaign combines a rational strategy with a sensory strategy. Lucky Strike tastes good because of its packaging.

Lucky Strike also used celebrity endorsement tactics to promote its product. The celebrities also benefitted from the publicity. For instance, an advertisement that features Jean Harlow endorsing Lucky Strike also promotes her current film. In addition to Jean Harlow, the campaign used other female celebrities such as aviatrix Sally Eilers[16] and actress Dorothy Mackaill.[17] Each of the endorsements included a statement that the celebrity was not compensated for her testimonial and that Lucky Strike actually is her cigarette of choice.

During the 1932–1933 academic year, Lucky Strike's advertising used sensory strategy in metaphors that communicated the taste of its product. By using wild animals and Native Americans or other exotic people in its campaign, Lucky Strike compared uncured tobacco to uncivilized animals or humans by stating, "Nature in the *Raw* is seldom *Mild*." Lucky Strike made a drastic change from a sensory to a social strategy during the 1933–1934 academic year. This campaign focuses its attention on a female audience by featuring a fashionable young woman. The headline, "The Height of Good Taste" suggests both a social and sensory strategy. Therefore, the campaign suggests that women should smoke because it's pleasurable and communicates high social status.

Again, during the 1934–1935 academic year, Lucky Strike combined sensory and social strategies. However, instead of capturing a purely aspirational lifestyle, the advertisement idealizes the ordinary—picnics, outings in nature, gathering with friends, and other everyday occurrences. This approach makes the idealized lifestyles depicted in the advertisement seem much more attainable than in the previous campaigns. During the 1934–1935 academic year, Lucky Strike continued using a social strategy. However, this time the strategy appears to be used within the context of a dating situation instead of a social context. Cigarettes are presented as a way to cope with awkward social situations. One advertisement plays upon the fact that many people have had disagreements with their significant others. Smoking is promoted as a way to make amends.

During the 1936–1937 academic year Lucky Strike used celebrity testimonials to attest that Lucky Strike cigarettes are easy on the throat. For instance, Margaret Sullavan said that "Luckies are the answer for her throat." In addition, the campaign included celebrities such as actress Claudette Colbert,[18] actress Carole Lombard,[19] actor Cary Grant,[20] U.S. senator Gerald P. Nye,[21] and radioman Boake Carter.[22] This campaign combines sensory-focused copy with a celebrity appeal.

Although Lucky Strike began its collegiate campaign in a fairly generic and neutral manner, by the end of the decade Lucky Strike's campaigns increased significantly in sophistication. These changes made the brand more appealing to young people. However, the campaigns still lacked the sophistication of Camel's and Chesterfield's marketing. The advertisements were not as highly targeted and Lucky Strike did not cross-promote its brand across media vehicles.

OLD GOLD

During the 1930s, Old Gold significantly reduced its advertising presence in student newspapers. In the 1920s, Old Gold was a top advertiser. In the 1930s, its campaigns appeared infrequently. At the start of the 1930s, Old Gold's college campaign focused on keeping kissable. The campaign used a sensory strategy and a referent approach to suggest that Old Gold cigarettes are not as offensive as other cigarettes and will not diminish attractiveness. The woman featured in the advertisement appears to be a typical college student.

Later during the 1934–1935 academic year, Old Gold maintains the same sensory strategy that it used during the 1932–1933 academic year. However, the campaign changes its approach to focus on "throat ease" instead of "keeping kissable." In addition, the tactics change from using a referent to a celebrity appeal. For instance, singer and actor Bing Crosby said, "My throat is my fortune ... that's why I smoke Old Gold's." Old Gold also featured other celebrities such as actress Mae West,[23] actor James Cagney,[24] actress Claudette Colbert,[25] and actress Carole Lombard.[26]

While Lucky Strike, Camel, and Chesterfield worked to increase the strength of their advertising campaigns, Old Gold was slowly leaving the college scene. Old Gold stopped advertising consistently and its advertisements became less focused on the college market. During the 1930s, Old Gold was losing its edge in the youth market.

Conclusion

In spite of the Great Depression and the increased stress and pessimism that the economic downturn caused, cigarette advertising campaigns in student newspapers continued to increase in frequency and size. Like the motion picture industry, cigarette advertising during the Great Depression focused on escape and fantasy. In fact, the tobacco industry recruited many top film stars to appear in advertising campaigns during the 1930s. In addition to featuring glamorous film stars, cigarette advertising also started to position cigarettes as a practical way to start one's career path during a time when economic depression and high unemployment rates were serious concerns. The industry maintained its efforts to target women by featuring women of high social standing and by continuing to demonstrate social approval through advertising. In addition, the advertisements began to promote the habit as a way to manage stress and relax. R.J. Reynolds' Camel brand used highly targeted advertisements that used college students to promote the effectiveness of its brand. Although the number of campaigns featuring college students and targeting the college audience increased, some brands simply targeted young people and were not specific to the college audience.

7

Targeting the Efforts
to the War Front

Cigarette Advertising in College
Newspapers During the 1940s

Cigarette advertising in college newspapers during the 1940s was sporadic because of the outbreak of the Second World War. Because of the number of young people leaving to serve the war effort, the college campus was no longer the home of the younger market. In response to the changing market dynamics created by the war, cigarette manufacturers focused the majority of their marketing efforts on promotions that collaborated with the war effort, such as supplying troops with cigarettes in their K-rations. Although cigarette advertising in the campus paper was reduced, it didn't completely stop. Because the nation was at war, many of the advertisements that appeared in the papers made cigarette smoking seem patriotic. In fact, campaigns used the testimonies of servicemen and women to promote their product. Although the total number of cigarette advertisements dropped during the 1940s, the number of brands being advertised increased. New brands such as Phillip Morris and Raleigh began to advertise in student papers during the 1940s. However, longstanding brands such as Chesterfield and Camel continued to have a strong and consistent presence in student media.

Cigarette Advertising and Frequency and World War II

World War II changed cigarette marketing and advertising. These changes were evident in the student paper as the tobacco industry refocused its efforts on the war effort. Virtually every student newspaper from *The Daily Iowan* to *The Flat Hat* at the College of William and Mary saw a reduction in cigarette advertising. The campaigns were fairly inconsistent and sporadic. Many lost their focus on the student audience and focused on patriotism and the war effort. Like most student newspapers across the nation, the University of Tennessee paper, *The Orange and White*,[1] continued its operations during the war. From the 1940–1941 academic year to the 1949–1950 academic year *The Orange and White* published 500 editions. A total of 346 cigarette advertisements appeared, averaging .69 cigarette advertisements per newspaper. Many student newspapers, especially the dailies,

1940–1949 Frequency of Cigarette Advertising by Brand

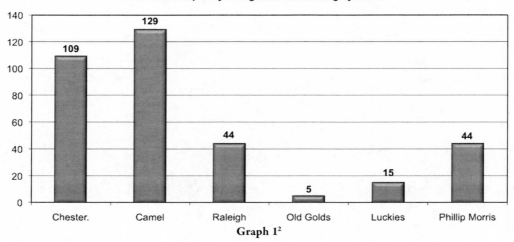

Graph 1[2]

no longer printed cigarette advertising in every edition of the paper. Although the number of cigarette advertisements dropped during the 1940s, the number of brands being advertised increased. In addition to Chesterfield, Camel, Old Gold and Lucky Strike, Phillip Morris, and Raleigh also advertised during the 1940s. As the graphs show, Chesterfield and Camel were the most advertised cigarette brands, and Old Gold and Lucky Strike were the least advertised brands in *The Orange and White* during the 1940s. Chesterfield and Camel were the most heavily advertised brands from the 1940–1941 to the 1942–1943 academic years.

However, due to the war effort, advertising either stopped completely or nearly stopped from the 1943–1944 to the 1945–1946 academic years. In addition, the editorial content published in *The Orange and White* also was significantly decreased. Cigarette advertising in *The Orange and White* made a healthy comeback from the 1946–1947 to the 1948–1949 academic years. However, cigarette advertising dropped in *The Orange and White* in 1949 for an unknown reason.

During the 1940s, the sensory strategy dominated cigarette advertising in *The Orange and White* with 59 percent of all advertisements using a sensory approach. The social strategy was the second most common with 27 percent of the advertisements falling into this category. The third most popular strategy was the rational approach with 12 percent of all advertisements using reason to reach consumers. During the 1940s, ego, acute need, and routine strategies were not widely used in cigarette advertisements.

Overall, tactics using celebrities were the most popular advertising approach during the 1940s. Forty-seven percent of the cigarette advertisements in *The Orange and White* used celebrity tactics. The referent approach was the second most popular tactic with 36 percent of the advertisements using this approach. Although the referent appeal was the most popular during the first half of the decade, celebrity appeals dominated the latter years during the 1940s. If combined, 83 percent of all the advertisements used an aspirational individual to promote cigarettes. The informational approach also was somewhat popular with 12 percent of advertising using information as the primary tactic. Few advertisements used reward, expert or humor tactics during the 1940s.

1940–1949 Advertising Strategy by Percent

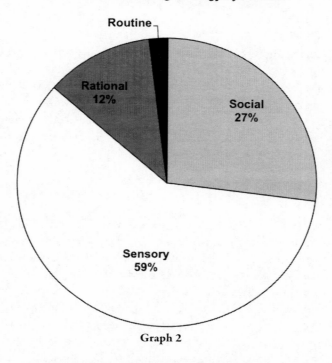

Graph 2

1940–1949 Advertising Tactics by Percent

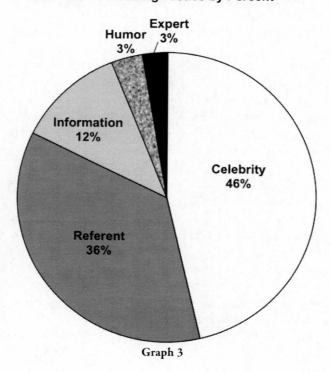

Graph 3

Advertisements Published in Student Newspapers during the 1940s

Cigarette advertising in campus papers fundamentally changed during the 1940s. Instead of featuring the idyllic life of young adults on campus, cigarette advertising promoted the tobacco industry's war efforts. Much of the advertising printed during the war was created for a mass audience instead of college students. As the nation united for war, Americans shared the same patriotic spirit. Therefore, the use of universal advertising campaigns promoting patriotism might have been more effective than highly targeted campaigns featuring happy college students.

CAMEL

During the 1940s, Camel was the most popular brand advertised in most college newspapers. Camel continued the student-focused campaigns that it started during the 1930s during the early part of the decade. However, because of the war, servicemen and patriots were also featured in the campaigns. During the 1940–1941 academic year, the war was absent from the Camel campaign. The attack on Pearl Harbor did not occur until December 1941 so the reality of World War II had not hit home for most Americans. The first Camel campaign of the 1940s employed a social approach that focused on men who had succeeded in their particular career paths. The campaign is a continuation of the approach used in the late 1930s. For instance, in one advertisement an air traffic controller relates the keys to his career path and tips for picking a good cigarette. Therefore, cigarette smoking is implicitly positioned as a way to fit into the business world. Camel also uses referent tactics. These tactics are made clear in the fact that the careers featured in the advertisements are both appealing and glamorous.

During the following year, Camel began to use rational strategy combined with a social strategy to promote its brand. Its advertisements combined celebrity with product information. A celebrity spokesperson promotes the virtues of smoking Camel cigarettes. The advertisement also promotes the fact that Camel cigarettes contain 28 percent less nicotine than the other four largest selling brands. Lower nicotine is promoted as a product benefit, but the advertisement does not give the reader any reason why lower levels of nicotine are better.

For the 1941–1942 academic year, Camel used the same approach by promoting the product using a spokesperson and product-related information. However, because of the attack on Pearl Harbor and the start of American involvement in the war, the spokesperson was a member of the armed forces. It is important to note that this military-based approach was used even before Pearl Harbor Day, which officially involved the United States in the escalating global conflict. Using the armed forces in Camel advertisements continued into the 1942–1943 academic year. In this campaign, Camel used jargon or slang from the various branches of the armed forces to build rapport with its patriotic audience and establish the fact that its brand has a close relationship with the armed services. One headline reads, "In the Air Force they say—'Dodo' for the new flying recruit, 'Kite' for airplane, 'hit the silk' for taking to parachute, 'Camel' for their favorite cigarette." Therefore, this social strategy

Curtiss Test Pilot Bill Ward endorsing Camel cigarettes using a social and sensory strategy. Printed with permission of the University of Iowa, *The Daily Iowan.* **Camel Advertisement,** *The Daily Iowan,* **January 30, 1942.**

is combined with the powerful referent appeal of a member of the air corps. In addition, the Camel campaign featured war heroes such as test pilots, whose service combined heroism with glamour. In addition to the air corps, this advertising campaign featured servicemen from the other branches of the military such as the army and navy.

After a three-year break, Camel resumed advertising in student papers during 1947. The war had ended; therefore, the brand returned to its pre-war marketing and advertising strategies. The primary message in this series of advertisements was, "More people are smoking Camels than ever before." In addition to the social strategy implied in promoting the popularity of the cigarette, big band singer Beryl Davis[3] was the celebrity spokesperson for the brand. Davis was born in England, the daughter of famous bandleader Harry Davis. Davis spent her formative years on tour with her father's orchestra, eventually becoming the act's featured vocalist. In 1944, Davis was recruited to join Glenn Miller's Army Air

Test Pilot Andy McDonough endorsing Camel cigarettes using a social and sensory strategy. Printed with permission from Vassar College Special Collections & Archives. Camel advertisement, Vassar College Special Collections & Archives, *Vassar Miscellany News,* **January 17, 1942.**

Force Orchestra. Other featured musicians and singers included "Skitch" Henderson,[4] Patty Andrews,[5] Al Nevins,[6] and Desi Arnaz.[7]

During the 1948–1949 academic year Camel began to use a rational appeal in its college advertising. In this campaign, Camel urges students to give its cigarette a 30-day test for mildness. Although the primary appeal is a rational appeal, the secondary appeal is sensory because the smokers are testing the cigarette for mildness.[8]

Although Camel advertised consistently in student newspapers during the 1940s, it was clear that the college market was not the primary target. When compared with the 1930s, the advertising from the 1940s lacked the high level of targeting. Most of the advertising appearing in the student papers was designed for a broader audience instead of college students. None of the advertisements referenced college students or life on campus. However, many of the approaches that were used would have still appealed to college students. College students, like most Americans, were interested in the war effort and celebrities. So, it appears that the advertising was probably effective even though it was more generic in nature.

CHESTERFIELD

During the 1940–1941 pre-war academic year, Chesterfield created advertisements that focused on the social acceptability of smoking. Using a referent appeal, one advertisement features a woman conversing with her father about smoking. The headline reads, "Right Dad ... it's the one cigarette that really satisfies." In addition to the referent appeal, the advertisement promotes the satisfaction that one gets from smoking.

By the 1941–1942 academic year, like the other brands, the Chesterfield campaign strategy changed to a patriotic effort that supported World War II and used a sensory message. The headlines read, "The Order of the Day is Chesterfield Milder, Cooler...Better-Tasting" or "More Pleasure for You." In addition to promoting cigarettes, Chesterfield publicized its financial support of the war effort and added a secondary social element through its use of patriotism.

During the 1942–1943 academic year, Chesterfield switched to using a patriotic appeal. The brand used an army medic to attest to the quality of Chesterfield brand cigarettes to implicitly suggest that smoking is not detrimental to one's health while supporting the war effort. Therefore, this rational appeal combines the expertise of a physician with a product-focused argument. The following academic year, Chesterfield continued to use advertising that related to the war effort. In this advertisement, the social strategy implies that popular people, like Chesterfield's hotshot World War II pilot spokescharacter "Tailgun Smitty," smoked Chesterfields. And, if you want the serviceperson that you care about to be popular like "Tailgun Smitty," you ought to send him plenty of Chesterfields. However, the advertisement also makes use of a sensory approach instead of focusing on product qualities.

During the 1945–1946 academic year, Chesterfield used a referent approach to promote its brand in *The Orange and White*. The beautiful women featured in the campaign promoted Chesterfield's ABC slogan that stands for "Always Buy Chesterfields." The headline implies brand loyalty and suggests a routine strategy.

Chesterfield's tactics changed during the 1947–1948 academic year. Instead of using a referent appeal, the tactics changed to a celebrity appeal. Although the celebrity, Lauren Bacall, is the primary feature in the advertisement, the strategy is based in the sensory segment because the focus is on enjoyment that smoking cigarettes provides. In addition to promoting Chesterfield, the advertisement also mentions that Lauren Bacall will star in the film *Dark Passage*. Therefore, the advertisement promotes smoking and Bacall's upcoming film. Other featured celebrities included actor James Stewart,[9] actress Loretta Young,[10] actress Claudette Colbert,[11] and actor Ronald Reagan.[12]

Chesterfield returned to the routine strategy during the 1948–1949 academic year by featuring the ABC "Always Buy Chesterfield" slogan. Again, Chesterfield combined the ABC slogan with a celebrity appeal. As in the previous campaign, the spokesperson, in this case Rita Hayworth, is promoting her new film, *The Loves of Carmen*. In addition to Rita Hayworth's testimonial, Chesterfield includes the testimonial of a college student from the University of Colorado. Chesterfield advertisements also included actress Betty Grable,[13] singer Perry Como,[14] actress Jane Wyman,[15] and actor Gary Cooper.[16]

Like Camel, Chesterfield didn't develop a highly targeted campaign for the college audience during most of the 1940s. Instead, the advertisements appealed to a mass audience.

Chesterfield advertisement featuring servicemen endorsements using a sensory strategy. Printed with permission of the University of Iowa, *The Daily Iowan*. Chesterfield Advertisement, *The Daily Iowan*, January 30, 1942.

Chesterfield advertisement featuring Tailgun Smitty endorsements using a social strategy. Printed with permission of the University of Iowa, *The Daily Iowan*. Chesterfield Advertisement, *The Daily Iowan*, January 30, 1942.

PHILLIP MORRIS

In its college campaign for the 1943–1944 academic year, Phillip Morris featured Johnny Roventini, the famous Phillip Morris bellboy. Alfred E. Lyon, Philip Morris' vice president for sales, and Milton Biow, the president of Milton Biow advertising, who managed the

Philip Morris Inc. account, discovered Johnny Roventini in the Hotel New Yorker lobby during an April evening in 1933. Roventini served as one of the Hotel New Yorker's corporate images. The hotel had been featuring the Brooklyn born, 48-inch youngster on its souvenir post cards as "the smallest bellboy in the world." The corporate executives along with their bellhop took a little-known cigarette brand and moved it to number four in national sales in five years' time.[17] Therefore, to *The Orange and White* audience, the Phillip Morris bellhop was a well-known figure.

Roventini reappeared during the 1948–1949 Phillip Morris campaign. In this series of advertisements, Roventini is featured in his own comic strip called "Campus Capers" that targeted college students. The comic strip is a social drama where Phillip Morris cigarettes save the day by eliminating cigarette hangover and by building students' vocabularies. The overall strategy is social but the tactic is entertaining college students.[18]

Unlike most of the other cigarette advertisers, Phillip Morris, a newcomer, created a highly targeted campaign for college students. The comic strip advertorial was unique in its use of a social appeal and humor tactics.

RALEIGH

Like Old Gold, Raleigh advertised in *The Orange and White* for only one year. During the 1947–1948 academic year, Raleigh used a sensory strategy and celebrity tactics to sell its brand. For instance, Tyrone Power, an American film actor who appeared in numerous of films from the 1930s to the 1950s, often as a swashbuckler or romantic lead, promoted the brand. The primary product feature advertised is that the cigarette is moisturized to minimize throat irritation and increase enjoyment. Other celebrity spokespeople included actress Joan Crawford,[19] actor and decorated naval officer Douglas Fairbanks, Jr.,[20] and actress Gene Tierney.[21] Raleigh's celebrity tactics and a general mass appeal made it blend with most of the other cigarette campaigns being printed at the same time.

OLD GOLD

Old Gold continued to reduce its presence on campus during the 1940s. Old Gold advertised during the 1946–1947 academic year only. The campaign was simple and rational. The Lorillard Tobacco Company emphasized the fact that the company is made of tobacco men and that the only thing that they attest about their product is that it is made for enjoyment. This advertisement works on a sensory and rational level. The generic appeal of the campaign suggests that it was not designed exclusively for the college market. The lack of targeted advertising and presence on campus makes it clear that Old Gold was no longer trying to be major player in the college market.

Opposite: **Phillip Morris "Campus Capers" comic advertorial featuring "Johnny." Printed with permission of the University of Tennessee Libraries and Special Collections. Phillip Morris advertisement,** *The Orange and White,* **October 8, 1948.**

Conclusion

Cigarette advertising in the campus newspaper during the 1940s was influenced by the outbreak of the Second World War. The war influenced cigarette advertising in two ways: (1) The frequency of advertising was reduced in the 1940s due to a shift in marketing efforts due to the war, and (2) The advertisements present in newspapers often used patriotic themes to promote cigarette smoking. In addition to the new marketing strategies instigated by the war, many of the advertisements used the same strategies and tactics as before. Common approaches included social approval, celebrity appeals, and rational strategies. Although throat irritation and coughing had been referred to before in advertisements, during the 1940s advertisements began to refer to the healthfulness of particular brands as well as nicotine content for the first time. In addition, most brands ran generic campaigns instead of creating ads that were particular to the college market.

8

An Advertising Boom

Cigarette Advertising in Student Newspapers During the 1950s

During the 1950s, more cigarette advertisements appeared in student newspapers than ever before. After a brief hiatus in the 1940s to focus on the war effort, the student newspaper once again became a primary promotional vehicle for cigarette advertisers. In many ways, the 1950s was the most fruitful decade for cigarette advertisers. College students in particular held tremendous market potential for the industry during the 1950s. James Bowling, Phillip Morris' public relations director, stated, "Research and experience proved that the consumer at this age and experience level, is more susceptible to change, has far-reaching influence and value, and is apt to retain brand habits for a longer period of time than the average consumer reached in the general market. Therefore, though the average cost per thousand is relatively high, the actual expenditure can be a great deal more efficient."[1] Cigarette advertisers ran consistent campaigns that included some of the best creative strategies that the decade had to offer. The advertisements featured serial comics, college contests, puzzles and games, and iconic taglines, while introducing new brands and product categories.

In the 1950s, the American Tobacco Company targeted colleges and universities with its largest ever Lucky Strike campaign. The integrated campaign included extensive newspaper advertising placement, campus radio stations, football programs, and extensive campus tie-in promotions and sampling. Other brands also initiated extensive college and university campaigns. A research firm specializing in young people reported that cigarette brands were spending approximately five million dollars per year on college and university promotions during the 1950s.[2] However, it is noted that many of these college and university students had started their smoking habits before entering college. And, "continual exposure to advertising to adults through different media has its effects on young people."[3]

Because of the increase in expenditures and the tobacco industry's intensified focus on the college market, the number of cigarette advertisements appearing in the campus press during the 1950s surpassed any previous decade. One reason for the increase was the introduction of new varieties of cigarettes. Tobacco companies began promoting filtered brands and menthol-flavored cigarettes in addition to their traditional unfiltered brands. From the 1950–1951 academic year to the 1954–1955 academic year, unfiltered cigarettes were the most popular products advertised. Starting with the 1955–1956 academic year and ending with the 1958–1959 academic year, filtered and unfiltered cigarettes were advertised with a similar frequency. However, cigarette advertising in general began to dip from 1955–1956 academic year to the 1957–1958 academic year. By the 1959–1960 academic year, the frequency of filtered cigarette advertising surpassed the pre–1955–1956 levels for advertising unfiltered cigarettes. Menthol cigarette advertising fell behind both the filtered and unfiltered brands. But, during the 1959–1960 academic year the frequency of advertising among the menthol brands surpassed that of the unfiltered brands.

Cigarette Advertising Frequency and Strategy During the 1950s

During the 1940s, cigarette marketers focused their promotional campaigns on the war effort. However, during the 1950s cigarette marketers took back the college audience in a

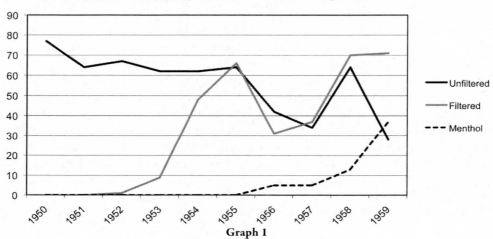

Graph 1

way that exceeded their efforts before the war. Cigarette marketers nearly doubled their efforts to reach the young adult audience. Cigarette advertisements increased in frequency, size, and sophistication. For instance, a total of 966 cigarette advertisements appeared in 355 editions of *The Orange and White*. On average, 2.72 advertisements appeared in each issue of the newspaper in the 1950s. This total is nearly twice the 1930s average of 1.52 advertisements per edition with a total of 613 ads for the decade. A number of factors influenced the large number of advertisements in the newspaper. In general, cigarette smoking was a socially acceptable habit during the 1950s. The tobacco industry also recruited students and faculty to assist with research. For instance, the American Tobacco Company created the Student Marketing Institute[4] in 1953 to generate student insights to generate ideas for creative strategies and evaluate the effectiveness of their campus campaigns. In addition, new brands and varieties of cigarettes were introduced into the cigarette market. The filter wars played an important role in advertising frequency. Many tobacco companies were producing filtered brands that competed with their original unfiltered brands. Therefore, many companies needed to advertise twice as much.

The filter wars profoundly impacted advertising during the 1950s. However, most of

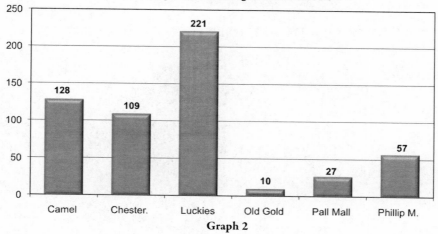

1950s Major Unfiltered Cigarette Advertisers

Graph 2

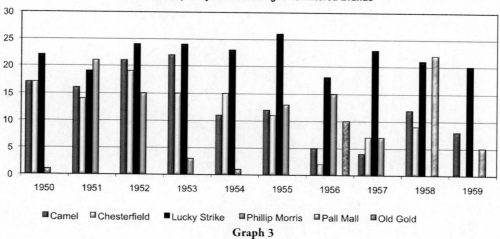

1950s Frequency of Advertising for Unfiltered Brands

Graph 3

the brands advertised in student papers were still unfiltered. In total, 552 of the 966 cigarette advertisements in *The Orange and White* promoted unfiltered brands. Unfiltered cigarette advertisements represented 57 percent of the total cigarette advertisements that appeared. Lucky Strike was consistently the most frequent advertiser with 221 advertisements. Camel and Chesterfield also were major advertisers with over 100 advertisements each. Phillip Morris, Old Gold and Pall Mall also advertised in *The Orange and White*. And, although they were not consistent advertisers, they did have a significant presence during certain years. For instance, Pall Mall was the most frequent advertiser in the unfiltered segment during the 1958–1959 academic year. But, it did not advertise in *The Orange and White* from the 1950–1951 to the 1957–1958 academic year.

During the 1950s, 255 of the 966 advertisements printed in *The Orange and White* promoted filtered cigarettes. In total, 26 percent of the cigarette advertisements in *The Orange and White* related to filtered cigarettes. Filtered cigarette advertising steadily increased from the 1952–1953 academic year to the 1955–1956 academic year. Cigarette advertising dropped during the 1956–1957 and the 1957–1958 academic years. However, the advertising frequency

1950s Creative Strategy by Percentage

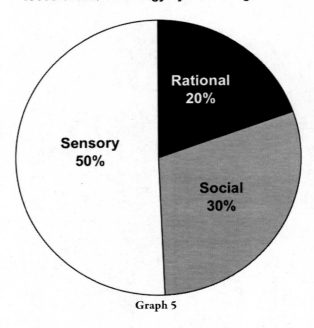

Graph 5

1950s Creative Tactics by Percent

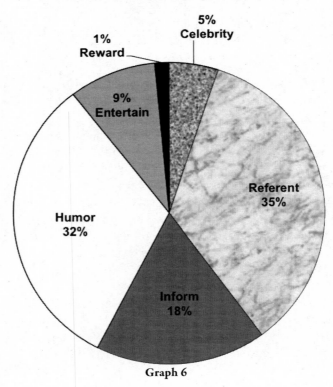

Graph 6

resumed during the 1958–1959 and the 1959–1960 academic years. With a total of 77 advertisements, Tareyton was the most frequently advertised brand. Viceroy's advertising rates were nearly the same as Tareyton with a total of 75 advertisements. Marlboro, Winston, and L&M also were frequent advertisers with more than 55 advertisements each.

Three primary strategies dominated cigarette advertising in *The Orange and White* during the 1950s. These three strategies were the rational, social, and sensory strategies. The sensory dominated with 50 percent of the advertising falling into this category. Although the sensory strategy dominated, it was the primary strategy during the 1950–1951, 1955–1956, 1956–1957, 1958–1959, and 1959–1960 academic years. However, the social and rational strategies also dominated creative strategies certain years. During the 1951–1952 and the 1952–1953 academic years the social approach dominated. Likewise, the rational approach dominated the 1954–1955 academic year, which was the year after the *Reader's Digest* article was published warning the American public about the harms of smoking.

During the 1950s, the referent tactic was the most popular in cigarette advertising in most student papers. In *The Orange and White,* 35 percent of the advertising fell into this category. The referent approach was the most prevalent approach during the 1950–1951, 1951–1952, 1952–1953, and the 1955–1956 academic years. The humor approach was the second most popular tactic with 32 percent of the advertising using this appeal; it was the most frequent appeal during the 1953–1954, 1954–1955, 1956–1957, and the 1958–1959 academic years. Information was another tactic that was fairly prevalent with 18 percent of cigarette advertisements printed using this approach. In spite of the fact that using entertainment was not one of the most popular tactics, it was the most popular appeal during the 1959–1960 academic year. Celebrity tactics and reward appeals were also occasionally employed.

Unfiltered Brands Advertised During the 1950s

At the beginning of the 1950s, the unfiltered brands had a clear marketing edge on campus. Filters were not yet popular among young people. The unfiltered brands were also the most recognizable and established on campus. The campaigns for the filtered brands were specifically designed for the college market and involved contests and other promotions to engage students.

LUCKY STRIKE

During the 1950s, Lucky Strike created the most highly targeted and integrated advertising campaign on college campuses. At the start of the 1950–1951 academic year, Lucky Strike advertised using a series of contests that would reach nearly every college campus in the U.S. In the first series of contests, Lucky Strike challenged students to write "Happy-Go-Lucky" jingles about Lucky Strike. Lucky Strike offered $25 cash prizes for winning jingles. For instance, a winning entry from Brooklyn College reads, "In art class we may disagree, if Goya beats Van Dyke. But one thing is unanimous, We all pick Lucky Strike." The campaign's appeal is social because it reinforces the idea that cigarette smoking is popular among college

Advertisement for Lucky Strike "Jingles Contest" using a social strategy with humor tactics. Printed with permission from Vassar College Special Collections & Archives. Camel advertisement, Vassar College Special Collections & Archives, *Vassar Miscellany News,* January 16, 1952.

students. Every edition of *The Orange and White* would feature winning jingle submissions from around the nation. The jingles were intended to be humorous and entertaining. The jingle contest ran until the 1952–1953 academic year.

During the 1954–1955 academic year, Lucky Strike changed its contest from jingles to droodles. Droodles were humorous picture puzzles that related to smoking Lucky Strike. Like the previous contests, a $25 reward was offered for featured droodles. Again, the primary tactic used is humor. However, the strategy is social. During the 1956–1957 and 1957–1958 academic years, Lucky Strike changed its contest from droodles to sticklers—jokes or riddles that rhyme. For instance, one example reads, "What do you call a dirty bird? ...a murky turkey." The humorous approach was used to entertain students. Both the droodles and sticklers have a format that resembles the "Happy-Go-Lucky" jingles. Like the jingles, the other contests that ran throughout the 1950s demonstrated Lucky Strike's popularity across college campuses.

CAMEL

Like Lucky Strike, Camel created campaigns to connect specifically with college students. However, instead of using contests, Camel used humor appeals and comics to reach young smokers. Camel began a series of cartoons called "Campus Interviews on Cigarette Tests" during the 1950–1951 academic year. This humorous approach profiled various animals and proved that in spite of their idiosyncratic traits, they agree that Camel is the best cigarette. For instance, even though the "Long-Wattled Umbrella Bird" lacks the common sense to get out of the rain, he still knows that Camel is the best cigarette. The advertisement continues by stating that "More People Smoke Camels than any other cigarette!" and that students should give the brand a 30-day trial. Therefore, this series of advertisements combines humor with a social strategy. This cartoon continued through the 1951–1952 academic year. Other featured cartoon characters included "The Blow Fish,"[5] "The Flicker,"[6] and "The Common Loon."[7]

In 1952, Camel changed from the "Campus Interviews on Cigarette Tests" cartoon to the "...But Only Time Will Tell" cartoon. The objective of the cartoon is to convince college students to try smoking and to give the habit time before they decide. For instance, the cartoon shows a fraternity house and fraternity brothers testing out a new cat to see if it is a good mouser. But, just because the cat doesn't catch a mouse immediately doesn't mean that it cannot catch mice. In the same way, students should give smoking a fair try. Camel provides a rational argument for trying smoking that is complemented with humor tactics.

During the following academic year, Camel advertised using a celebrity approach that used a social strategy. The campaign slogan was, "Camels Agree with More People" and focused on "how the stars got started." Dick Powell was the celebrity spokesperson. In addition to providing his testimonial on cigarettes, he also gives the story of how he got his start in the music industry by singing with a choral group at Little Rock College. Powell was a famous singer, actor, and director. Other Camel spokespeople included baseball player Mickey Mantle,[8] actress Lisbeth Scott,[9] actress Maureen O'Sullivan,[10] actor Tyrone Power,[11] and actor William Holden.[12]

The 1955–1956 Camel campaign focuses on smoking as a reward and a way to celebrate. The primary strategy is sensory—smoking is a sensory treat for holidays and a reward for a job well done. The text in one advertisement reads, "When you've worked pretty late, And the issue looks great...Why not celebrate! Have a CAMEL!"

Camel continued to use a social approach during the 1956–1957 academic year. However, instead of addressing the pleasure of smoking directly, Camel promotes its cigarette as the "real cigarette." The headline reads, "Have A *Real* Cigarette ... have a Camel!" This headline, accompanied by a photograph of a documentary film cameraman, implies that Camels are for real men.

Camel ended the 1950s by returning to the cartoon approach that it used at the begin-

Camel "Campus Interviews on Cigarette Tests" using a social strategy and humor tactics. Printed with permission of The University of Iowa, *The Daily Iowan*. Camel Advertisement, *The Daily Iowan*, October 5, 1950.

ning of the decade. The cartoons used a humor appeal, but the overriding strategy is sensory because both the caption of the cartoon and the headline relate to the product's quality and taste.

CHESTERFIELD

Like Lucky Strike and Camel, Chesterfield created advertising campaigns that would appeal to college students rather than running more general ads. However, the Chesterfield ads focused more on the quality and popularity of the cigarette than using contests or humor. To start off the 1950s, Chesterfield used a cigarette-smoking test to appeal to college students on a rational level. The headline reads, "Open 'Em, Smell 'Em, Smoke 'Em—Easiest Test In The Book." Then, the student is challenged to compare Chesterfield with any other cigarette.

During the 1951–1952 academic year, Chesterfield's advertisements featured various national and Ivy League universities to show that their brand is the most popular among the most accomplished college students. For instance, the advertisements featured Rice,[13] Northwestern,[14] Princeton,[15] Cornell,[16] University of Virginia,[17] M.I.T.[18] and many others. Because the campaign focuses on the popularity of the brand and the fact that many college students, like themselves, smoke Chesterfield, the primary strategy is social. In an alternate campaign that ran the same year, Chesterfield advertisements featured famous people who graduated from various well-known colleges and universities such as Jane Wyatt, who graduated from Northwestern University,[19] Pat O'Brien from Marquette University,[20] and Bing Crosby from Gonzaga.[21]

As health concerns regarding smoking began to surface in the popular press, Chesterfield changed its campaign strategy to a more rational approach during the 1952–1953 academic year. Therefore, Chesterfield presents its own scientific evidence that proves that the "Nose, Throat, and Accessory Organs" are not harmed by smoking Chesterfield. In addition, Chesterfield claims that its report is the first published about a cigarette. In fact, the report even claims that it studied heavy smokers that smoked up to 40 cigarettes a day. Most of these health-related advertisements appear to be part of a national campaign to counteract fears about smoking. They do not seem to be specifically targeting college students.

Like Camel, Chesterfield also used celebrity tactics to appeal to college students during the 1953–1954 academic year. However, Chesterfield combined the appeal of a celebrity with ordinary college students. The appeal of the advertisement is primarily social as it shows Chesterfield to be a popular cigarette. In one particular situation, Ray Anthony is the celebrity. Anthony is an American songwriter, trumpeter, bandleader, and actor. He is known for "The Bunny Hop" and the "Hokey Pokey." In addition, the advertisement features two female college students who also provide their testimonials.

During the 1955–1956 academic year, Chesterfield changed its strategy from a social strategy to a sensory strategy. The headline reads, "Packs More Pleasure because it's *More Perfectly Packed*!" The change in strategy is evident because of the focus on pleasure. The tactics used to execute the strategy also changed. Instead of using celebrity or source similarity tactics, the Chesterfield advertisement used source attractiveness to promote its brand. The use of a sex appeal complements the use of an attractive source. Both the image of a beautiful

Jane Wyatt endorsing Chesterfield using a social strategy. Printed with permission of North Dakota State University Archives and Special Collections. Chesterfield advertisement, *The Spectrum*, April 7, 1950.

University of Virginia endorsing Chesterfield using a social strategy. Printed with permission of SUNY-Buffalo Special Collections and Archives. Old Gold, UB Digital Collections, *The Bee,* State University of New York at Buffalo, October 19, 1951.

model reclining with a cigarette and the tone of the copy seems more sexual in nature than previous advertisements.

Like Camel's campaign from the previous year, Chesterfield also tries to position its cigarette as the masculine cigarette. One advertisement reads, "Men of America: The Test-Driver. Nothing satisfies like the BIG CLEAN *TASTE OF TOP-TOBACCO.*" Other featured professionals included a law enforcement officer,[22] uranium geologist,[23] highway architect,[24] and a U.S. Air Force pilot.[25] Although the tactics are based in a referent appeal and there are social elements of the advertisement, the primary strategy is sensory because the product focus is on enjoying the tobacco. Chesterfield ran the "Men of America" campaign during the 1957–1958 and 1958–1959 academic years.

PHILLIP MORRIS

Phillip Morris started out the 1950s with its popular Johnny the bellhop campaign ads that appeared to be targeted toward a general audience of smokers. However, by the end of the decade, Phillip Morris created a college campaign like the other major brands. Like Chesterfield, Phillip Morris started out its 1950–1951 college campaign with a rational appeal that challenged students to test the quality of Phillip Morris cigarettes. This particular advertisement features a woman and reads, "Believe in Yourself! Don't test one brand alone—compare them all!" This advertisement seems to work toward empowering women and would resonate with female college students for this reason. Like the Phillip Morris advertisements that appeared in the 1940s, this advertisement includes the slogan "Call for Phillip Morris" and features the bellhop Johnny.

In 1951, Phillip Morris changed from a rational strategy to a sensory strategy that focused on celebrity testimonials. In this case, Desi Arnaz and Lucille Ball attest that Phillip Morris does not cause throat irritation. In addition to providing their testimonial, they also promote the new *I Love Lucy* show on CBS. Again, the bellhop Johnny and the slogan "Call for Phillip Morris" appear at the bottom of the advertisement.

From 1954–1957, Phillip Morris cigarettes sponsored the Max Shulman column that specifically targeted college students. The column was created by Leo Burnett Company, Inc.[26] Shulman was an American writer best known for his television and short story character Dobie Gillis. His writing usually centered on young people, particularly in the college setting. After his success with the Gillis character, Shulman continued to write. His humor column, "On Campus," was syndicated in more than 350 collegiate newspapers.

OLD GOLD

During the 1956–1957 academic year, Old Gold resumed advertising in *The Orange and White*. Like Lucky Strike, Old Gold also used a college contest called Tangle Schools. The headline of the advertisement suggests a sensory approach by stating, "No Other Cigarette Can Match The Taste of Today's Old Gold's." To enter the contest, students needed to untangle the names of well-known schools and send them in to the address listed on the advertisements. Because the advertisement involves a puzzle, entertainment is the primary tactic in this campaign. Old Gold's approach, although targeted, did not demonstrate a heavy investment in the college market. The ads were small and ran for only one year. By the 1950s, most people regarded Old Gold as a cigarette for an older demographic.

PALL MALL

Pall Mall began advertising in *The Orange and White* during the 1958–1959 academic year. The strategy for the campaign was purely sensory. With the headline, "So *friendly* to your taste!"[27] the campaign compares the experience of smoking cigarettes with eating fine foods such as various fruits and vegetables and shrimp. The imagery makes it obvious that the advertisements are capitalizing on the pleasure associated with smoking. However, the campaign does not seem to appeal to college students specifically. Instead, the ads appear to be intended for publication in a variety of print media.

Filtered Brands Advertised During the 1950s

Filtered cigarettes began advertising in student papers in 1952. At first, the advertising was not specific to the college audience or the young adult market. Instead, the general audience advertising focused on tar and filtration. FTC legislation helped the filtered brands become popular. By forcing the filtered brands to stop advertising tar levels and filter effectiveness, by the end of the 1950s, the advertisers had to start promoting the brands using the same humor, sensory, and image-based appeals that they used for their unfiltered brands. Although sensory appeals were popular across cigarette brands, they were particularly popular among filtered brands. Filtered brands needed to assure smokers that their brand provided the same flavor as their unfiltered counterparts. Although initially unpopular, by the end of the 1950s, several cigarette brands emerged that are still popular today, including Winston and Marlboro. Other filtered brands included Tareyton, Viceroy, and L&M.

WINSTON

R.J. Reynolds introduced its new filtered brand, Winston, to the college student market in 1955–1956 academic year. Winston started its first college campaign year with its famous "Winston Tastes Good! Like a Cigarette Should!" slogan. The advertisements' primary strategy was sensory. The headlines read, "Winston sets a new tradition of flavor!" However, the

Winston advertisement using a social and sensory strategy. Printed with permission from Vassar College Special Collections & Archives. Camel advertisement, Vassar College Special Collections & Archives, *Vassar Miscellany News*, October 12, 1955.

copy also has significant social undertones such as, "You'll both go for this cigarette."[28] Again, smoking is shown as a way to start relationships, especially with members of the opposite sex. The characters in the advertisements appear to be college students. The background also appears to be a college or university campus. The copy directly refers to college students: "College students know why Winston changed America's mind about filter smoking."

During the 1957–1958 academic year, Winston changed tactics from a referent approach that focused on relationships to a humor approach that reinforced the overall sensory strategy. The campaign mimicked a comic strip with the characters ending the strip with the slogan, "Winston tastes good ... like a cigarette should." In one example that was a satire of Arthurian legend, Sir Gollyhad, a knight, befriended a dragon that terrorized the citizens of Camelot by offering the beast cigarettes. The dragon was satisfied and Sir Gollyhad won the lady. Other comics included "Mopy Dick," a spoof on Herman Melville's *Moby-Dick*,[29] "In The Soup,"[30] a parody of the antics of burglars, and a comic featuring the ghost "Luke the Spook."[31]

L&M

In addition to advertising the taste and pleasure that filtered cigarettes provided, some filtered cigarettes promoted their brand based on the effectiveness of the filter. Eventually, FTC forced advertisers to stop making these kinds of claims. Liggett & Myers introduced

L&M advertisement using social and sensory strategies. Printed with permission of The University of Iowa, *The Daily Iowan*. L&M advertisement, *The Daily Iowan*, October 17, 1958.

its L&M brand on campus by promoting its low tar levels and the effectiveness of its filter. For instance, a popular L&M headline stated, "No filter compares with L&M's Miracle Tip." This focus on the filter properties implies a rational strategy. However, the advertisements also mentioned flavor in their subheads. Therefore, the sensory strategy is a secondary strategy in this advertisement. In addition, the advertisements used socialites and businessmen referents to promote the social status of the brand.

L&M launched a similar campaign the following academic year, 1956–1957. The focus remained on the cigarette filter and the strategy remained rational. However, the photograph and text related more directly to the college audience. The photograph used a similarity-based referent appeal as the man and the woman appear to be interacting or starting a conversation thanks to their mutual smoking habit. Therefore, the campaign combined social and sensory elements.

L&M continued to use the same social and referent approach during the 1957–1958 academic year. However, the focus is on the flavor. But, the similar referent approach remained the same. The college students in the advertisement say that L&M "Smokes Cleaner" and "Tastes Better" or "Less Tars, More Taste."[32]

VICEROY

Like L&M, Viceroy's advertising often focused on the filter. Viceroy's campaigns combined a rational and sensory strategy. The taste of the cigarette and the construction of the filter are important components but it seems that the construction of the filter and the reasoning behind the smoothness of the taste are paramount. This campaign also appears to be directed at college students. The headlines read, "On Every Campus College Men and Women are discussing why Viceroys are Smoother." During the 1958–1959 academic year, Viceroy continued to use a rational strategy to advertise the effectiveness and healthfulness of its filter by stating, "The Viceroy Filter Is Made From A Pure Natural Material Found In Fruit."

TAREYTON

During the 1955–1956 academic year, the American Tobacco Company introduced its filtered brand, Tareyton. Like other filtered brands, Tareyton advertises that "*All* the pleasure comes thru...The *Taste* is great!" in its headline. Therefore, like other filtered brands, the sensory strategy is dominant. However, the advertisement also mentions that the cigarette has a dual filter. The description of the double filter seems to suggest a more rational approach is also in play.

As in the previous campaign, Tareyton used a sensory strategy. One headline states, "Gives you *more to enjoy*—the *taste* is great!" And, like the other filtered brands ads, this campaign sells smoking as a way to facilitate relationships. However, the effectiveness of the filter remained as a rational element of the advertising strategy.

In a campaign that ran during the 1959–1960 academic year, Tareyton used a rational strategy to explain how its dual filter works. The campaign features the two layers that filter the cigarette smoke and the band that shows the division between the two separate filters. The sensory strategy is secondary as the advertisement focused on the filters filtering for flavor.

MARLBORO

Phillip Morris began advertising its filtered brand, Marlboro, during the 1955–1956 academic year. Marlboro's functional slogan, "You get a lot to like—filter, flavor, flip-top-box" suggests a rational approach. Yet, the image in the advertisement portrayed a rugged-looking man with a tattoo on his hand, lending the brand a rather hardened or rebellious image. The campaign seems to imply that this filtered brand is not a brand for sissies.

During the 1957–1958 academic year, Phillip Morris decided to change its sponsor of the "On Campus" column from its unfiltered Phillip Morris brand to its filtered Marlboro brand. This switch represents a change in the college market's preference. College students were starting to prefer filtered brands. In spite of the change in sponsor, the column remained the same. Max Shulman continued to make humorous observations about campus life. Using Shulman as a spokesperson for Marlboro demonstrates that the brand was working to become more of a mainstream brand on college campuses instead of appealing to a more rebellious crowd.

Menthol Brands Advertised During the 1950s

When compared to the filtered and unfiltered brands, the mentholated cigarettes represent a less significant portion of the college cigarette market. Only two menthol brands were advertised in student papers during the 1950s, Kool and Salem. Because of the unique flavor of mentholated cigarettes, the primary strategy is sensory. Salem advertised frequently during the 1957–1958 academic year. For its campaign, the headline read, "A *new idea* in smoking...Salem refreshes your taste." In addition, the brand advertised the social aspect of smoking through the use of a referent appeal. One typical Salem photograph depicts a young couple smoking in a park. Salem consistently advertised using romantic and natural settings. The advertising did not seem to target the college market specifically, but it was appealing to young adults—particularly women.

Kool advertised using the same sensory strategy as Salem during the 1958–1959 and 1959–1960 academic years. However, Kool used a different tactical approach. The headline reads, "Switch from the Hots to Snow Fresh Filter Kools." But, the Kool Krossword puzzle occupies the majority of the advertising space. Therefore, the entertainment tactic is a significant part of the advertisement.

Conclusion

The 1950s were marked by innovations both in the cigarettes themselves and the techniques used to market the new brands. During the 1950s, more brands targeted college students more directly in their advertising. Lucky Strike, Camel, Chesterfield, Tareyton, Winston, Kool, Old Gold, L&M and Viceroy all created advertisements that directly targeted a collegiate audience. Relating directly to college students became more popular than the celebrity and status appeals that were popular in the past. However, relating cigarette smoking to career success remained a popular approach. The primary innovations in cigarette production were the introduction of menthol and filtered cigarettes, which resulted in the introduction of several new brands. Filtered cigarettes initially used a rational approach to market their brands by focusing on the healthfulness of the brand and the effectiveness of the filter. However, by the end of the decade, the rational approach to promoting the filtered brands was replaced by social and sensory strategies.

9

The End of the Campaign

Cigarette Advertising in Student Newspapers from 1960 to 1964

During the early 1960s, for the first time, the number of advertisements for filtered cigarettes consistently surpassed those for unfiltered cigarettes. In fact, filtered cigarette advertising reached its peak during the 1962–1963 academic year, the final year that cigarettes were advertised in student media. However, the frequency of advertising for other varieties of cigarettes, including unfiltered and menthol cigarettes, generally dropped during the early 1960s. Detailed explanations of the effectiveness of filters virtually disappeared as social and sensory strategies dominated cigarette advertising. Cigarette advertising tactics became increasingly image-based and humorous. If filters were mentioned in advertisements, they were promoted based on what they did not do (i.e. impede flavor) instead of their actual perceived function of filtering cigarette smoke. This change in message content adhered to the FTC's voluntary code enacted in 1960 that prohibited the mention of nicotine or tar. In addition, the code discouraged any type of health claim or the use of celebrity endorsements.

In spite of the increases in regulation, the Student Marketing Institute estimated that cigarette brands' promotional efforts to reach college and university students doubled in the five years leading up to the advertisements' removal from student publications in 1963. During those years, promotional tactics for the 20 cigarette brands that were active on campus included free cigarette samples distributed by student representatives who worked for the various cigarette brands. For instance, Brown & Williamson employed 17 salesmen on college campuses; Phillip Morris paid 166 campus representatives $50 a month to distribute free cigarettes at colleges and universities. However, student newspapers were the major promotional venue for the cigarette manufacturers. In total, the 850 college newspapers participating in the national advertising service received 40 percent of their income from cigarette advertising.[1]

Cigarette Advertising Frequency and Strategy During the 1960s

Although the filtered brands clearly were gaining an edge in the college market, filtered and unfiltered cigarettes continued to battle for new smokers. The number of cigarette adver-

120

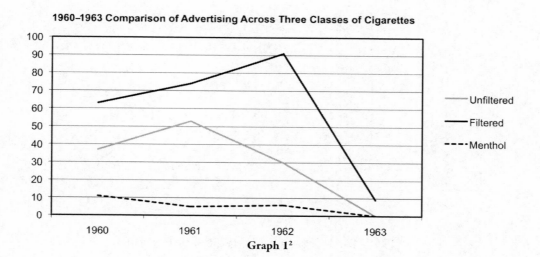

Graph 1[2]

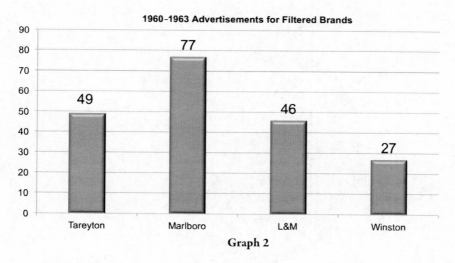

Graph 2

tisements published in campus newspapers continued to increase. From 1960 to 1963, 182 editions of *The Orange and White* were published. During these three years, 390 cigarette advertisements were printed, averaging 2.14 in each edition. This number is less than the average of 2.72 cigarette advertisements published during the 1950s. However, only nine advertisements, all advertorials sponsored by Marlboro, were published during the 1963–1964 academic year, and all of them were published before January 1964. If only the academic years that span 1960–1961 to 1962–1963 are counted, the average number of cigarette advertisements published during this time period surpasses the 1950s average at 2.93 advertisements printed in each edition of *The Orange and White*.

During the early 1960s, Chesterfield was the most frequently advertised unfiltered cigarette brand. Chesterfield was the dominant unfiltered brand during the 1961–1962 and the 1962–1963 academic years. Lucky Strike was a close second; it was the prominent unfiltered brand in the 1960–1961 academic year. Camel was the third most frequent advertiser. Old

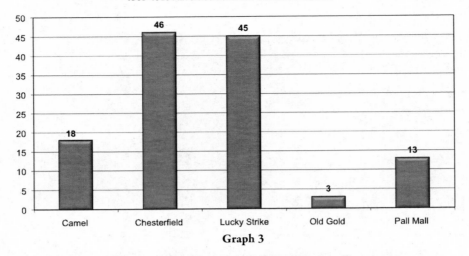

1960–1963 Advertisements for Unfiltered Brands

Graph 3

1960–1963 Creative Strategies by Percent

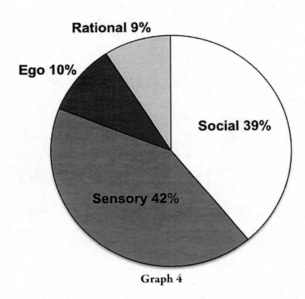

Graph 4

Gold and Pall Mall also advertised in student newspapers but their advertising was relatively infrequent.

During the early 1960s, the filtered cigarettes were advertised more than any other variety. The prominent brand of filtered cigarettes advertised was Marlboro with 77 advertisements published in *The Orange and White*. And, Marlboro was the most popular brand advertised from the 1960–1961 academic year to the 1962–1963 academic year. The second most frequent advertiser was Tareyton with a total of 48 advertisements. L&M was third with 46 advertisements printed, in *The Orange and White*.

The dominant creative strategy during the early 1960s was a sensory strategy with 42 percent of the cigarette advertisements in *The Orange and White* using this approach. The second most popular strategy was the social strategy with 39 percent of the advertisements

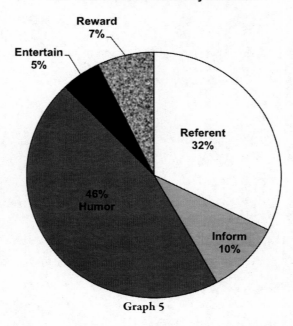

1960–1963 Creative Tactics by Percent

Graph 5

falling into this category. The least popular strategies used were the ego strategy, featured in 10 percent of advertisements, and the rational strategy, employed in 9 percent of the advertisements.

During the 1960s, the humor approach was the most popular tactic used by cigarette advertisers with 47 percent of advertisements printed in *The Orange and White* employing this tactic. The second most prevalent approach was the referent or user image tactic with 32 percent of advertisements falling into this category. The tactics of entertainment, reward, and information were used between 5 percent and 10 percent of appeals falling into this category.

Unfiltered Brands Advertised During the 1960s

During the late 1950s and early 1960s, the unfiltered brands entered a slow decline as cigarette marketers began to respond to college students' preference for the filtered variety. Many of the most popular unfiltered brands either adopted filters, reduced the size and frequency of the ads, ran general audience advertising instead of campaigns focused on the college market, or simply disappeared from the student papers. A popular rebranding strategy for unfiltered cigarettes was to reposition them as cigarettes for "tough guys" who are too manly for a filtered brand. Camel, Chesterfield and Lucky Strike took this approach at the very end of their college campaigns.

CHESTERFIELD

Although Chesterfield still published advertising geared toward the student market, the size and frequency of the ads were greatly reduced during the 1960s. During the 1961–

LUCKY STRIKE PRESENTS:

DEAR DR. FROOD:

DR. FROOD'S THOUGHT FOR THE DAY: *A little learning can be a dangerous thing—especially in a multiple-choice exam.*

DEAR DR. FROOD: I have calculated that if the population explosion continues at its present rate, there will be a person for every square foot of earth by the year 2088. What do you think of that?

Statistics Major

DEAR STATISTICS: Well, one thing's sure, that will finish off the hula hoopers—once and for all.

DEAR DR. FROOD: I have been training our college mascot, a goat. He has learned how to open a pack of Luckies, take out a cigarette, light up and smoke. Do you think I can get him on a TV show?

Animal Husbandry Major

DEAR ANIMAL: I'm afraid not. To make TV nowadays, you've got to have an act that's really different. After all, there are millions of Lucky smokers.

DEAR DR. FROOD: I am a full professor—and yet I stay awake nights worrying about my ability to teach today's bright young college students. They ask questions I can't answer. They write essays I don't understand. They use complicated words that I've never heard before. How can I possibly hope to win the respect of students who are more learned than I am?

Professor

DEAR PROFESSOR: I always maintain that nothing impresses a troublesome student like the sharp slap of a ruler across his outstretched palm.

DEAR DR. FROOD: You can tell your readers for me that college is a waste of time. My friends who didn't go to college are making good money now. And me, with my new diploma? I'm making peanuts!

Angry Grad

DEAR ANGRY: Yes, but how many of your friends can do what you can do—instantly satisfy that overpowering craving for a peanut.

DEAR DR. FROOD: Could you give a word of advice to a poor girl who, after four years at college, has failed to get herself invited on a single date?

Miss Miserable

DEAR MISS: Mask?

THE RECRUITERS ARE COMING! THE RECRUITERS ARE COMING! And here's Frood to tell you just how to handle them: These representatives of big business are, on the whole, alert fellows. They may be aware that college students smoke more Luckies than any other regular. Let them know that you know what's up—offer them a Lucky, then tap your cranium knowingly. Remember—today's Lucky smoker could be tomorrow's Chairman of the Board.

CHANGE TO LUCKIES and get some <u>taste</u> for a change!

© A. T. Co.   *Product of The American Tobacco Company — "Tobacco is our middle name"*

Lucky Strike advertisement featuring Dr. Frood using humor and a social strategy. Printed with permission of Fordham University's Special Collections and Archives. Lucky Strike advertisement, Fordham University Digital Collections, *The Ram,* **April 20, 1961.**

Lucky Strike "Lucky Puffers" advertorial comic strip using humor and a social strategy. Lucky Strike advertisement, printed November 2, 1961, Archives of *The Orange and White,* University of Tennessee Libraries, Knoxville.

1962 academic year, Chesterfield ran a series of advertisements called Sic Flics. This campaign used images from silent films dating from 1920s or perhaps earlier. However, the headlines made the images seem like they were taken at college frat parties. One headline states, "Every Fraternity Needs Some Kind of Mascot."[3] The ad features a flapper in a short skirt being carried by a group of gentlemen.

During the 1962–1963 academic year, Chesterfield changed its approach to a sensory strategy that positioned the brand as a masculine brand. Instead of promoting the standard Chesterfield cigarettes, the Chesterfield King brand is advertised. The headlines reflect the sensory strategy by stating, "Tastes Great because the tobaccos are!" In addition, a young man is shown enjoying a cigarette. Unlike its previous campaigns, this final campaign seemed to appeal to a mass audience of young men instead of college students.

LUCKY STRIKE

During the 1960s, Lucky Strike struggled to connect with its college audience. Instead of keeping a consistent campaign featuring young co-eds and contests like the brand did in the 1950s, Lucky Strike changed its campaign approach each year. This lack of continuity demonstrates that the brand was struggling as more and more students switched to filtered brands.

In 1960, Lucky Strike introduced a character named Dr. Frood to promote its brand. Dr. Frood was an eccentric character that offers advice and clever observations to college students. Usually, the advice was intended to be humorous in nature and focused on the social aspects of campus life such as dating, academic success, school spirit, and, of course, smoking. Other ads parodied typical cigarette contests and premiums. For instance, one advertisement threatens to deliver a life-sized portrait of Dr. Frood to students' dorms if they do not smoke Lucky Strike. The Dr. Frood advertisements employ a social strategy and humor tactics.

In 1961, Lucky Strike changed its campaign again by replacing Dr. Frood with Lucky Puffers, a comic strip that personified cigarettes and cast them into various campus roles. The Lucky Puffers spoofed campus athletics, Greek life, and undergraduate romance. This approach combines a social strategy with humor tactics to entice college students to smoke their brand.

During the 1962–1963 academic year Lucky Strike changed its campaign strategy for its final college campaign to a social strategy that positioned its brand as a young man's cigarette. This brand positioning is similar to the approach that Camel and Chesterfield were using. In addition, Lucky Strike works to persuade its smokers to keep smoking Lucky Strike after graduation. The headline reads, "Get Lucky—the taste to start with ... the taste to stay with."

PALL MALL

Pall Mall resumed advertising in *The Orange and White* during the 1961–1962 academic year. Pall Mall began advertising by publishing the "Girl Watchers Guide" serial comic. Part of the social strategy of the "Girl Watchers Guide" involves joining "The American Society of Girl Watchers," a club sponsored by Pall Mall. This advertising serial used a humorous spoof on girl watching to attract new male smokers.

The following academic year, Pall Mall ran a similar campaign for its final appearance in the student papers. However, in this case, the focus was on identifying the various types of girls on campus. As in the previous campaign, there is an implicit comparison between bird watching and girl watching. In one example, the campus type described is a "White-Coated Lab-Loon." Men on campus were advised not to be intimidated by her and are assured that this variety of female students doesn't really want to compete with the male students. The copy says that she really has marriage on her mind just like other coeds. Again, the advertisement combines a social strategy with humorous tactics.

Girl Watcher's Guide

Presented by Pall Mall Famous Cigarettes

Well-Preserved Forty plus

LESSON 4 - Why men watch girls

Men watch girls for various reasons. Personally, we need no better reason than the reason men climb mountains. *They are there*. We have heard old men say they watch girls because it makes them feel younger and young men because it makes them feel older (see above). While investigating the reasons why men watch girls we picked up a clue from, of all things, a bird watcher. He told us that he formerly had been a flower watcher. Then one day a Speckle-Breasted Jackdaw happened to land in his garden as he was watching a calla lily and he noticed that the bird *moved*. He switched to birds on the spot. Girl watchers have discovered that girls enjoy this same advantage (movement) over calla lilies. (Speaking of advantages, how about Pall Mall's natural mildness!)

**WHY BE AN AMATEUR?
JOIN THE AMERICAN SOCIETY
OF GIRL WATCHERS NOW!**

FREE MEMBERSHIP CARD. Visit the editorial office of this publication for a free membership card in the world's only society devoted to discreet, but relentless, girl watching. Constitution of the society on reverse side of card.

This ad based on the book, "The Girl Watcher's Guide." Text: Copyright by Donald J. Sauers. Drawings: Copyright by Eldon Dedini. Reprinted by permission of Harper & Brothers.

PALL MALL
FAMOUS CIGARETTES

WHEREVER PARTICULAR
PEOPLE CONGREGATE

Pall Mall's
<u>natural</u> mildness
is so good
to your taste !

So smooth, so satisfying,
so downright smokeable!

ᴾᴬᴸ Co *Product of The American Tobacco Company "Tobacco is our middle name"*

Pall Mall cartoon advertorial "Girl Watchers Guide" using humor and a social strategy. Printed with permission of the University of Iowa, *The Daily Iowan*. Pall Mall Advertisement, *The Daily Iowan*, November 14, 1961.

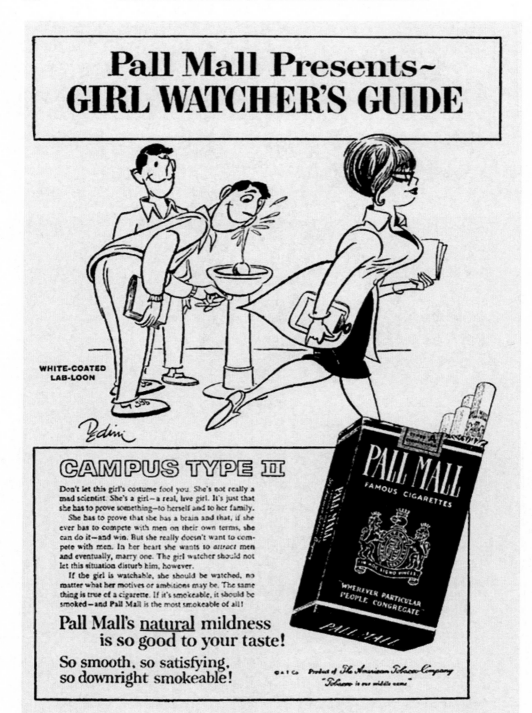

Pall Mall cartoon advertorial "Girl Watchers Guide—The Campus Type" using humor and a social strategy. Pall Mall advertisement, printed October 2, 1962, Archives of *The Orange and White,* University of Tennessee Libraries, Knoxville.

CAMEL

At the start of the 1960s, Camel continued to promote its brand as a masculine cigarette. The campaign featured successful professionals, thrill seekers, and athletes as referents. The use of male referents reinforces the brand's masculine image and reinforces an aspirational lifestyle. This technique complements the campaign's combination of an ego and social strategy. The headline reads, "Have a *real* cigarette—have a Camel." This statement implies that Camel is stronger or better than other brands. Other advertisements featured athletes,[4] sailplane enthusiasts,[5] and a helicopter pilot.[6] However, some advertisements from the campaign were printed in papers at women's colleges such as the *Vassar Miscellany News*. The

Camel advertisement featuring the endorsement of Jack and Mary Lambie using a sensory and social strategy. Camel advertisement, Vassar College Special Collections & Archives, *Vassar Miscellany News,* **January 13, 1960.**

advertisements in the women's papers often featured women as the adventurers. One such advertisement featured a female sailplane enthusiast. The inclusion of a female in the predominantly male campaign probably resulted from the advertisement's placement at an all women's school.

During its final campaign, Camel continued to position its brand as a masculine cigarette. A series of advertisements called "Career Clues" featured high-level executives relaying their advice on how they succeeded in their particular fields while endorsing Camel cigarettes. Therefore, the primary goal of this campaign was to create a relationship between smoking cigarettes and career success. The campaign combined elements of ego and social strategies by providing male students with clues about how to rise into a higher social caste by succeeding professionally. Featured spokesmen included bankers, company presidents and entrepreneurs.

Filtered Brands Advertised During the 1960s

After the FTC's voluntary code was passed in 1960, filtered brands were advertised in much the same way as the unfiltered brands were in previous years. Although filters were an important selling feature, they were not as important as user image, humor, or social status. As the most popular brands on campus, the filtered brands were advertised in the most highly targeted campaigns and with the greatest frequency. In addition, the majority of the advertorials, cartoons, and contests on campus were now sponsored by filtered brands.

TAREYTON

During the 1960–1961 academic year, Tareyton combined a rational and sensory approach to promote its brand. The headline reads, "Filters for flavor—*finest flavor by far!*" This combination of strategies in the headline promises the safety of a filter without impeding flavor.

During the 1961–1962 academic year, Tareyton combined a social and a sensory strategy to promote its brand. Tareyton sponsored a Greco-Roman cartoon serial and advertising copy inspired by the classics and the Latin language tap into the Greek social scene on campus. The advertising copy also complements this theme while communicating product benefits.

> "Tareyton's Dual Filter is duas partes divisa est!" says Sextus (Crazy Legs) Cato, Bacchus Cup winner. "There are lots of filtered cigarettes around," says Crazy Legs, "but e pluribus unum stands out—Dual Filter Tareyton. For the best taste of the best tobaccos, try Tareyton—one filter cigarette that really delivers de gustibus!"[7]

The headline reads, "Tareyton delivers the flavor—DVAL[8] FILTER DOES IT!"[9]

WINSTON

During the 1960–1961 academic year Winston advertised using a rational strategy supported by a social strategy. The headline read, "It's what's up front that counts!" with an image showing the cigarette's filter below. In addition to informing the audience about Winston's filter, the advertisement also uses the dating context to promote its brand. Cigarette smoking is presented as a way to "break the ice." The advertisement included the famous Winston slogan, "WINSTON TASTES GOOD *like a cigarette should.*"

L&M promotional quiz using humor. L&M advertisement, printed October 2, 1962, Archives of *The Orange and White,* University of Tennessee Libraries, Knoxville.

L&M

During the 1961–1962 academic year L&M began to publish quizzes that related to relationships, careers, politics, and dating. In addition to providing the quiz, L&M tells how 1,383 students at 138 colleges responded to the items. The primary advertising strategy is social because the advertisement emphasizes the relationship between college life and the L&M brand.

The following year L&M and Chesterfield sponsored a sweepstakes called the "L&M Grand Prix" that targeted college students. The sweepstakes promised to award 50 Pontiac Tempests to students. The campaign uses a rational strategy and reward tactics to promote the Chesterfield and L&M brands.

Viceroy

For its final campaigns, Viceroy used contests to promote its brand. During the 1961–1962 academic year, Viceroy sponsored a college football contest. Every week, students were to guess the winners of the next series of big football games. The $100 prizewinner from a previous list also had his picture published in the advertisement. The names of the winners of the $10 prizes were also published in the advertisement. Therefore, this campaign used a social strategy combined with tactics that entertained the collegiate target audience. The next year, Viceroy changed to a social strategy that also focused on the sensory aspects of smoking. The advertising images focus on the college social life while the text centers on taste.

Marlboro

The Marlboro Man made his first appearance in student newspapers during the 1962–1963 academic year. The primary strategy in this advertisement is ego related. The Marlboro Man is an individual that represents the ideal American cowboy. During the 1950s and early 1960s the American public tuned in to a variety of popular television westerns, including *Bonanza, Davy Crockett, Gunsmoke, The Lone Ranger, The Virginian,* and *Zorro.* The strong cultural identification with the western and the cowboy makes the Marlboro Man a powerful referent figure. Although the advertisements featuring the Marlboro Man create a strong cultural identification, they do not appeal specifically to college students.

From 1960–1963 Max Shulman continued to publish his "On Campus" column for the Phillip Morris' Marlboro brand. The Max Shulman column stands in stark contrast when compared to the advertisements that feature the stoic Marlboro Man. The column continued to focus on Shulman's humorous observations of campus life. One column celebrating the column's popularity and Shulman's ninth year as the syndicated writer for "On Campus" was titled "Another Year, Another Dollar." The "On Campus" column was the last series of cigarette advertisements printed in *The Orange and White.* The final column that Marlboro sponsored was printed on November 26, 1963. All of the other brands ended their campaigns in June 1963. Not surprisingly, "On Campus" resumed publication starting in 1965 with new sponsors. Burma Shave and Persona Injection Blades took the place of Marlboro as Shulman's financial sponsor.

Menthol Brands Advertised from 1960 to 1963

Like the unfiltered brands, advertising for the menthol brands was becoming less frequent in the student papers. In 1960, Kool discontinued its Kool Krossword and began to advertise using a sensory strategy. The campaign suggested Kool menthol cigarettes as an alternative to students who are tired of filter cigarettes and other menthol cigarettes, as the reader is urged to "Come up...All The Way Up to the MENTHOL MAGIC of KOOL!" The primary image in the advertisement is a young man who looks as if he is college-aged. Therefore, the advertisement combines a sensory strategy with referent tactics. Although targeted at a younger market, the last Kool campaign does not seem to target college students specifically.

Until the ads were removed, the Salem campaign continued with the same romantic and natural theme that was used during the late 1950s. In the early 1960s, the campaign combined a sensory strategy with referent tactics. The primary image in advertisements featured a couple enjoying some time in a park. The headline reads, "Salem refreshes your taste—'air-softens' every puff." Therefore, the sensation of smoking is compared with the feeling of fresh air. Like previous campaigns for Salem, the advertisements seem to appeal to young adults, especially women, instead of college students specifically. Therefore, the ads appeared to be designed for a national audience.

Conclusion

During the early 1960s cigarette advertising continued its dominating presence in student newspapers. The cigarette advertising was the most formidable promotional force on campus until it was removed in June 1963. Advertising for filtered brands was more prevalent than the non-filtered brands and the filtered brands had larger advertisements than their non-filtered counterparts. Many brands used humorous advertorials such as cigarette-sponsored comics or the humorous text of the Max Shulman column. Detailed explanations of the effectiveness of filters virtually disappeared as social and sensory strategies dominated cigarette advertising. Although filters were mentioned in the ads, the copy did not detail any information about the filter. This change reflects the tobacco industry's adherence to the 1960 voluntary code that required cigarettes to avoid health related messages and any references to nicotine or tar.

10

Support Media

Campus Cigarette Advertising in Broadcast and Sports Programs

Although advertising in the student newspaper often served as the most direct way to reach the college student population, other profitable advertising opportunities also existed on campus. Industry documents show that the cigarette manufacturers utilized a variety of media on campus to support the advertising campaigns that frequently appeared in the student newspapers. In addition to the campus paper, tobacco advertisers also used promotional opportunities available through college and university athletic programs to reach their audience. Cigarette advertisers promoted their products by sponsoring athletic tournaments, advertising during broadcasts of athletic events, sponsoring booths or featuring a product at athletic events, or by printing advertising in the game program. In addition to athletics, tobacco brands also provided premiums in their cigarette packs or by mail with a purchase that related to college and university athletics.

Because higher education has generally refused to bring athletics under the academic model and support teams with the general college or university budget, funding for athletics has always had to come from outside sources. Therefore, athletics has been traditionally more vulnerable to commercial interests than any other area of college or university life. Although collegiate sports are often considered to be peripheral to the educational goals of colleges and universities, they produce both positive and negative stereotypes of institutions of higher learning. Athletics programs help inspire school spirit, foster a connection with local communities, and offer valuable publicity. However, the party atmosphere that often accompanies sporting events can damage a school's credibility and reputation.

Early Campus Promotions: Cigarette Cards and Premiums

Some of the earliest and most popular forms of advertising premiums were cigarette cards. Originally, cigarette cards were included in packages of cigarettes to protect the products from damage during shipping or storage. Each pack would have contained five cigarettes. However, as the cards became more extravagant and popular, smokers would send away for the cards as advertising premiums and they would arrive to the customer by mail. The cards were usually issued in numbered series of twenty-five, fifty, or larger runs to be collected, spurring subsequent purchases of the same brand. Typically, these small cards feature illustrations on one side with related information and advertising text on the other. From the late 19th century to the mid-twentieth century, colorful cigarette and tobacco cards became an ideal way to advertise the use of tobacco, and collecting these cards became an increasingly popular hobby. The height of cigarette card popularity occurred in the early decades of the 20th century, when tobacco companies around the world issued card sets in an encyclopedic range of subjects. After a slump during World War I, the cards' popularity resumed, with new emphasis on movie stars, college sports, and military topics, such as a popular series on the Civil War.

The earliest cards using single images dated from 1877. As the popularity of cigarette cards escalated, series of images were produced to promote the sale of cards to collectors and traders. The early success of cigarette cards led many companies, such as chewing gum brands, to adopt this new advertising method. A variety of series of cigarette cards related to collegiate themes including college sports. Murad cards featured collegiate themes starting in the early 1900s. However, Murad's first edition of college cards, titled "Murad Cigarettes College Series," was released in 1910 and featured a large collection of colleges and universities, a significant aspect of the school, and the college or university seal. Murad's collegiate card series were released through the 1920s.[1] For instance, Murad's 1914 college cigarette card campaign (series 51–75), titled "The Metropolitan Standard," depicted college students engaging in a variety of sports. This campaign complements Murad's college advertising campaigns featured in many student papers that also featured college sports. The following colleges and universities were listed as part of series 51–75:

> Armour Institute of Technology (skiing)
> Berea College (polo scene)
> Baker University (golfers with clubs)
> Colgate University (football game)
> Drake University (duck hunting)
> George Washington University (rowing)
> Georgetown University (track runner)
> Grove City College (pennant and leaves)
> Holy Cross College (pennant and wreath)
> Iowa College (canoeing)
> John Hopkins University (lacrosse)
> Juniata College (fishing)
> Lawrence University (hunting)
> LeHigh University (cricket)
> Mount Union College (sailing)
> Massachusetts Institute of Technology (tennis match)
> Pratt Institute (ice skating)
> Purdue University (golfing)
> Rensselaer Polytechnic Institute (hunting)
> University of Chattanooga (hurdles)
> University of Oklahoma (shooting)
> University of South Carolina (golf)
> Worchester Polytechnic Institute (track)
> Wesleyan University (pennant only)
> Whitman College (ice skating)

The list from this sample series shows that Murad's cigarette card campaign was comprehensive and included a wide range of public and private colleges and universities and institutions with large and small enrollments. The images on the front of the cards portrayed students engaged in a variety of sports including golf, basketball, football, polo, and shooting. Other cards featured pennants and seals from the featured college or university.[2] The series included six sets of cards with 25 colleges in each set for a total of 150 colleges and universities featured. The college series was considered Murad's most successful cigarette card campaign and lasted until 1925.[3]

Although Murad had the largest collegiate card campaign, other tobacco companies also distributed collegiate goods with their products. In addition to cigarette cards, tobacco companies included other college promotions in pipe tobacco pouches or cigarette packs such as decorated leather and silk goods with college seals.[4] For instance, Mogul Egyptian Cigarettes included leather stamped college pennants. The American Tobacco Company's Egyptienne Luxury Cigarettes offered silk pictures or "silkies" featuring pennants as advertising premiums during the early 20th century.[5]

Perhaps drawing its inspiration from the successful college and university card campaigns of the 1920s, Old Gold issued plastic-coated book covers with college and university logos on the front and the Old Gold logo on the back in 1953. The promotional book covers were distributed in most of the country's 1,800 colleges and more than a third of its 25,000 high schools.[6]

Cigarette Advertising at College Football Games and in Game Programs

Football games were a natural fit for cigarette brands. Advertisers could reach large audiences of young people for a reasonable cost. In addition, cigarette brands could foster the association between tobacco and college life, and even college-level athletic performance.

Like the advertisements that ran in college and university newspapers, advertisements in college football game programs contained many of the same themes, and even some of the same campaigns, as other college media. Frequent advertising themes that appeared in the game programs included college romance, school spirit or team spirit, and health claims. Many of the exact same campaigns appeared in the game programs as appeared in the student newspaper such as the "Be Happy—Go Lucky!" and "It's Toasted" campaigns for Lucky Strike and "Johnny" calling for Phillip Morris brand cigarettes. However, one important distinction between the newspaper advertisements and the game program advertising is the number of advertising insertions. It appears that the game programs allowed only one advertising insertion meaning that the same advertisement would have to run for the entire football season.[7] Unlike the football programs, student newspapers typically featured a different advertisement every week. The same advertisements can be found in football programs across the nation from the Rice versus Baylor program to Duke versus the University of Tennessee program. The media placement records show that from the 1930s to the mid–1960s, 250 colleges and universities across the country ran cigarette advertising in their college football programs.[8] Although the football game program advertising campaigns are smaller in scope than the newspaper campaigns, they often supported the newspaper campaigns and made important product associations between smoking, athletics, and college life.

Most universities were eager to collaborate with tobacco companies to help fund college and university athletic programs. This partnership was first created in the 1930s when the economic downturn that created the Great Depression caused cuts in many university budgets.

Before the 1930s, most football programs either didn't contain advertising or only contained advertising for local products and merchants. Very few sports programs contained advertisements for products or services that were available nationally. In the 1920s, football programs contained advertising for local tobacco shops, such as an advertisement for The Smoke House in the University of Tennessee's 1924 program for the Tennessee versus Carson-Newman game.[9] Cigars and pipe tobacco were also advertised locally.

CIGARETTE ADVERTISING IN FOOTBALL PROGRAMS, 1930s

During the early 1930s, national advertising began to appear in game programs. The major national advertisers included Coca-Cola, automotive brands such as Chevy and Oldsmobile, and tobacco brands manufactured by the big tobacco companies such the American Tobacco Company, R.J. Reynolds, Liggett & Myers, and Phillip Morris. Cigarette brands sponsored program covers and the starting roster and schedule pages, and also ran standard full-page advertisements on the back cover and inside of the program. The majority of the advertisements were full color.

During the 1930s Chesterfield, Camel, and Lucky Strike were the major cigarette advertisers in college football game programs. However, media placement records exist only for the American Tobacco Company's Lucky Strike College campaigns. The media records that exist for the American Tobacco Company indicate that Lucky Strike was advertised in game programs at more than 200 major colleges and universities. However, each college and university was contacted separately for the buy and had various rates. For instance, full-page placement for the 1937 season at Princeton University cost $1,120, whereas placement at St. Bonaventure cost $75 for the 1937 season.[10]

Although Lucky Strike was a consistent advertiser, Chesterfield was the most prominent advertiser and ran the largest ads during the 1930s. Chesterfield ran two-page advertisements that featured football rosters for each college game. For instance, Chesterfield sponsored the football roster for the University of Tennessee programs during the 1931 season. During this first season, Chesterfield's two-page spread was black and white. It featured a couple cheering on their team. "*Here they come* Hats off to 'em," the copy read. "In thrilling moments when you're smoking with halfback speed here it's a milder better tasting Chesterfield." In addition to the advertising content, the spread contained the starting lineup for both teams.

In 1932 and 1933, the Chesterfield program advertisement included the team roster and an image of a football stadium. The headline read, "They Satisfy," the same slogan used in the Chesterfield advertisements appearing in the student newspapers. The first full-color Chesterfield advertisement appeared in the game program in 1934. The advertisement again featured a football field and the slogan, "They Satisfy." In 1935, Chesterfield ran an advertisement with the starting team roster. However, unlike the previous four advertisements that focused on the football game, this advertisement features a woman dressed up for the game and appears to be targeting women. The woman in the advertisement is dressed fashionably for the game; she is wearing a dress, high heels, a long coat, gloves, and a hat. The

Advertisement for Camel using a social strategy featured in the University of Tennessee football programs for the 1931 football season, October 10, 1931 (courtesy University of Tennessee Libraries, Knoxville, Special Collections).

advertisement appears to be appealing to an old collegiate tradition of dressing up for football games. The advertisement features the slogan, "They Satisfy" and a cheer that reads:

> Hit the line hard and hit it square
> Play the game and play it fair
> Crash right through—do or die
> You've got to be good to SATISFY![11]

From the reference to the Chesterfield slogan, "They Satisfy!" the cheer seems to be for both the woman's home team and her favorite cigarette. However, the theme of the advertising returned to the football field and the game instead of ladies' attire. For instance, in 1938, Eddie Dooley, an all-America player turned NBC radio announcer, was featured in the Chesterfield spread. In 1939, the last advertisement of the decade featured a woman dressed up for the game and signaling a time out while holding a box of Chesterfields.

Camel advertisements also occupied a prominent spot in the game program. Camel sponsored a full-color back cover in 1931. Camel was the only advertiser to have a full-color ad. The advertisement appears to be targeting women. Two women dressed up for the game are featured smoking with a handsome football player. The headline reads, "A 'SHIFT PLAY' you ought to try." The advertisement positions Camels as a cigarette that brings couples together. The copy also brings football and smoking together. Camel repeats the same advertising approach in 1932. However, in 1933, Camel shifted its strategy and its market. Instead of portraying women dressed up for the game engaging in flirtations with men, the advertisements mirror the "career advisor" approach that appeared in the student newspapers. Even the beginning of the headline, "It takes HEALTHY NERVES..." is the same as the headlines appearing in the campus papers. The advertisement featured on the game program depicts an airmail pilot making a transcontinental flight: It takes healthy nerves to fly the mail at night. From 1934 to 1939, Camel returned to its female target audience. The Camel advertisements showed women dressed for game day while smoking Camel cigarettes, the perfect fashion accessory.

Lucky Strike and Old Gold did not advertise as consistently as Camel and Chesterfield during the 1930s. However, Lucky Strike did sponsor a variety of full-color game day covers in 1935. And, it sponsored the "All American Board of Football" for the 1935 season.

> Ends: Wayne Millner (Notre Dame)
>   James Moscrip (Stanford)
> Tackles: Larry Lutz (California)
>   Edward Widseth (Minnesota)
> Guards: J.C. Wetsel (Southern Methodist)
>   Darrell Lester (Texas Christian)
> Center: Gomer Jones (Ohio State)
> Quarter: Smith Riley (Alabama)
> Halfbacks: Jay Berwanger (Chicago)
>   William Shakespeare (Notre Dame)
> Fullback: Robert Grayson (Stanford)
> Coach: Bernie Bierman (Minnesota)[12]

The pictures of the various men appeared as inserts in the football programs. The inserts included the name of the player, the title "All American Board Selection," the position that they played, their college or university, their hometown, and, of course, their sponsor—Lucky Strike Cigarettes.[13]

Like Camel, Lucky Strike also focused on couples and game-day fashion in the advertisements that it ran on the back covers of the game programs. Old Gold advertised inside the back cover occupied by the full-color Camel advertisement in 1932. However, the Old Gold advertisement seemed like a general national ad for the cigarettes instead of an advertisement that was created especially for the football game audience. The advertisement featured the well-known Old Gold slogan, "Not a Cough in the Carload." Old Gold was not featured in the game programs again until it printed a quarter-page black and white advertisement in 1938. In 1938 and 1939, Phillip Morris sponsored a red and black and white duotone half-page advertisement inside of the front cover featuring "Johnny" the bellhop calling the official football signals. The headline read, "Johnny 'Calls' the signals! For true smoking pleasure call for Phillip Morris." The advertisements are also educational because they instruct the readers about the meaning of various official college football signals.

Although the cigarette industry had just begun its national advertising placements in game programs during the 1930s, the industry executed well-coordinated and sophisticated campaigns that complemented the other promotional efforts on campus. In addition, many brands bought premium placements in the programs. Chesterfield bought double page ads at the center of the program. Camel occupied the back cover. Phillip Morris ads appeared inside the front cover. And, Lucky Strike sponsored some front covers in 1935.

Cigarette Advertising in Football Programs, 1940s

Tobacco promotional efforts shifted focus from colleges and universities to the war front during the 1940s. Like the student newspaper, football programs also lost many of their tobacco accounts due to the shift in marketing focus. No media records were found to trace the frequency and cost of advertising in football programs in the 1940s. However, records show that Liggett & Myers Tobacco Company shifted some of its sports-related promotional activities to high schools in the 1940s. In 1948, Liggett & Myers provided high schools with free football programs with a scorecard in the middle. The scorecard was a two-page advertisement for Chesterfield cigarettes. Apparently, public complaints led to the cancellation of the campaign in spite of the fact that cigarette advertisers had previously supplied programs for football and other high school sporting events.[14] During the 1940s, Chesterfield, Phillip Morris, Camel, and Old Gold advertised in game programs.

At the beginning of the decade, Chesterfield's advertising was as consistent as it was before the war. Chesterfield appeared to be targeting women with its advertising that depicted women dressed up for the game. For instance, Chesterfield ran a two-page full-color roster in 1941 featuring two women in game day fashion. In 1942, the theme of the roster changed so that it featured servicemen in the ads. However, advertising in game programs ended on campus in 1943 due the fact that fewer teams were fielded due to World War II. From 1944 to 1946, Chesterfield resumed its advertising campaign. However, the Chesterfield roster used only red or sepia ink to support the need for green dyes in the war effort. The advertising campaigns were patriotic and featured servicemen with women dressed fashionably for football games.

After the war, cigarette advertising maintained a more consistent game program campaign. In 1947, Chesterfield ran a full-page, full-color roster. The advertisements featured

Advertisement for Camel featuring women dressed for the game published in the University of Tennessee Football Programs for the 1946 football season, September 28, 1946 (courtesy University of Tennessee Libraries, Knoxville, Special Collections).

the "ABC—Always Buy Chesterfield" slogan. The advertisement focused on cigarette smoking as a way to bring couples together. The featured celebrity spokeswoman, singer Jo Stafford, in the advertisement is dressed fashionably for the football game. The celebrity spokesman pictured in the advertisement is singer Perry Como. Both singers were featured in the Chesterfield NBC radio variety program *Chesterfield Supper Club*. In 1948, the slogan "Always Buy Chesterfield" remained but the advertising focused on the football game and featured a televised game. The last advertisement of the decade featured the ABC Chesterfield slogan. However, instead of using the letters for the phrase "Always Buy Chesterfield" the letters were used to spell the names of Chesterfield's big three radio and television stars, "A" for Arthur Godfrey, "B" for Bing Crosby, and "C" for Perry Como.

Old Gold, Camel, and Phillip Morris also advertised occasionally during the 1940s. Old Gold ran quarter page advertisements from in 1942, 1945, and 1946. Although the advertisements were small, they did feature male and female college students socializing with cigarettes. Phillip Morris ran a full-page advertisements featuring "Johnny" calling the signal and calling for Phillip Morris from 1946 to 1949. The advertisements were black and white or duotone with red ink. The ads were usually located inside of the front cover. Camel resumed its advertising after the war ended in 1946. Camel usually ran its full-page, full-color advertisements on the back cover. However, in 1946 the ads were still in black and white due to wartime dye shortages. As before, the advertisements featured women in fur and other high-end fashion enjoying a football game and cigarette. None of the advertisements featured men.

Although advertising for cigarettes in college football game programs was inconsistent during the 1940s, many advertisers still bought premium placements such as Chesterfield's double page center spreads, Camel's back cover placement, and Phillip Morris' placement on the inside cover.

CIGARETTE ADVERTISING IN FOOTBALL PROGRAMS, 1950s

The heaviest push for cigarette promotion at college games occurred during the 1950s. Lucky Strike was absent from football programs during the 1940s. However, in the 1950s, the American Tobacco Company targeted colleges and universities with its largest ever Lucky Strike campaign. Tobacco industry documents in the 1950s show that tobacco companies, such as the American Tobacco Company, were determined to have a strong presence at football games. In a letter dated September 19, 1955, from R.B. Walker, director of sales of the American Tobacco Company, to his district managers, he describes the tactics that the tobacco industry was using. He tells his representatives to contact people at the university who are influential in game planning and to expect "full cooperation" from the colleges and universities that are participating. In addition to the advertisements that appear in the program, the American Tobacco Company also arranged for point-of-sale promotional materials to be present in the stadium during the game. The letter states:

> We have renewed LUCKY STRIKE advertising in college football programs for the 1955 season. Full cooperation can be expected at each stadium where the LUCKY STRIKE ad appears in the official program.... Please call on the colleges when you can conveniently do so and assure yourself that LUCKIES will be offered for sale in the stadium. Make any suggestions that you may have for promoting the brand by placing or arranging for the placement of point-of-sale material.[15]

"Johnny Calls the Signals" advertisement for Phillip Morris published in the University of Tennessee Football Programs for the 1945 football season, October 6, 1945 (courtesy University of Tennessee Libraries, Knoxville, Special Collections).

Lucky Strike advertisement featuring Dorothy Collins published in the University of Tennessee Football Programs for the 1952 football season, October 11, 1952 (courtesy University of Tennessee Libraries, Knoxville, Special Collections).

Camel advertisement featuring a woman dressed for the game published in the University of Tennessee Football Programs for the 1952 football season, November 22, 1952 (courtesy University of Tennessee Libraries, Knoxville, Special Collections).

Likewise, Don Spenser Company Inc., the media company that sold the advertising space in the game programs to the tobacco companies, also contacted the universities to ensure their cooperation and to emphasize the importance of cigarette advertisers, like Lucky Strike. A letter dated August 3, 1953, reads,

> As you know, the makers of Lucky Strike Cigarettes are renewing, <u>for the fourth consecutive year,</u> their advertising in college football programs.
> We consider this a great expression of confidence from the Lucky Strike people, and I know you will too. Confidence in two ways (1) In your football program as a good advertising medium and (2) in the specific merchandising help you have given Lucky Strike in promoting the sale of their product at your games.
> Talk with your concessionaire right away. And tell him that he is to <u>stock</u> and <u>sell</u> Lucky Strike Cigarettes at all of your games. But don't stop there. Re-check each Saturday to make certain the concessionaire has plenty of Luckies on hand and that they are on sale at every stand.
> When the Lucky Strike salesman calls on you before the season, show him where he can set up point-of-sale display material—at the concession stands and in other locations where permissible. Extend him every cooperation.[16]
> [all underlines were present in the original letter]

Implicit in the advertising agreement between colleges and universities, the Don Spenser Company, and the American Tobacco Company was the cooperation of the sporting venue in merchandising the brands advertising in the game programs. Colleges and universities were to allow cigarette companies full access to the football game audiences.

Tobacco companies spent a large portion of their budget on media placement at sporting events. Although media records do not exist for every brand for every year during the 1950s, some complete media plans still exist. For instance, American Tobacco Company records show that placement of advertising in college programs in the 1955 and 1956 cost approximately $111,500 per year.[17] The Don Spenser Company or Spenser Programs, the media placement company for the programs, coordinated the bulk purchase of ads in nearly every major college and university in the United States. In 1955 the number of participating schools was 257[18]; in 1951, 263 schools participated.[19] The estimated circulation was nearly six million.[20] The number of colleges participating in the college football program campaign was fewer than the student newspaper campaign that included 409 colleges and universities, according to a 1958 media plan.[21] The media records indicate that the Lucky Strike ads would appear on the back cover and in full color whenever possible.[22] Back cover placement is considered premium placement for advertising.

During the 1950s, Chesterfield continued to sponsor its double-page, full-color football roster. However, from 1950 to 1952, the Chesterfield advertisements did not depict college students or football games; instead, they showed packs of cigarettes with copy and headlines that stated that the Chesterfield brand was the most popular cigarette on campus. This approach is similar to the ads that were printed in the newspapers. However, in 1953, Chesterfield changed its approach. Chesterfield portrayed a couple walking across a college campus. The headline still promoted the fact that Chesterfield was the top-selling cigarette on campus. This campaign mirrors the "Choice of Young America" newspaper campaign that mentioned individual campuses across the nation where Chesterfield was the top-selling brand.

In 1955, Liggett & Myers began promoting its filtered L&M brand along with Chesterfield in its advertisements. This approach is typical of the 1950s filter wars. Initially, the advertisements focus on the filtered brand instead of the college scene. However, in 1956

Liggett & Myers' center roster spread juxtaposes the rivalry between football teams with the rivalry between the filtered L&M and unfiltered Chesterfield. The headline reads, "Live Modern, Boy...Smoke L&M! My Chesterfields *Satisfy* the Most!" In 1957 and 1958, L&M and its filter that allowed smokers more taste with less tars was advertised in the Liggett & Myers center spread. In 1957 L&M was featured exclusively on the roster or starting line-up page of the game program. The advertisement featured a father and son conversing about their choice of L&M cigarette. The son says, "Hey Dad, light into that Live Modern flavor! The father says, "I'm way ahead of you Son! L&M wins for taste and flavor!" The headline at the top of the ad reads, "Live Modern ... smoke modern L&M." An ad for Liggett & Myers Chesterfield cigarettes occupied the back cover. In 1958, L&M sponsored the roster for the starting squads. The ad addressed health concerns about smoking with the headline, "Puff by Puff, Today's L&M gives you...Less tars & **M**ore taste than ever before!" However, in 1959, the Chesterfield brand was converted to a filtered brand. The new filtered Chesterfield Kings were featured in the 1959 center roster spread. The headline made no references to health. Instead the copy read, "Chesterfield Salutes *King* Football."

In 1951, Lucky Strike ran full-color advertisements inside the programs' front covers that complemented the "Be Happy—Go Lucky" campaign that was running in the student newspapers. However, the campaign focused on cheers for football games. The copy in one advertisement read,

> Eileen Wilson, Lucky Star of TV and Radio says: "At football games I love to cheer, 'Go team' and 'Hip Hooray!' But, for better taste I shout, 'Go Lucky Strike today!'"

In 1952, Lucky Strike continued running full-page ads for the "Be Happy—Go Lucky" campaign in football programs. The celebrity spokeswoman was Dorothy Collins. Collins' voice was also featured in a Lucky Strike college radio campaign. In 1953, Lucky Strike ran the "Be Happy—Go Lucky" campaign without a celebrity spokeswoman. Instead, the advertisements featured cheerleaders and complemented the campus newspaper ads instead of the radio spots.

In 1954, Lucky Strike featured a couple dressed up for the game on the back cover of the football programs. This was the first time a Lucky Strike advertisement was located on the back cover and replaced the Camel ads that routinely appeared on the back of the program. Instead of the "Be Happy—Go Lucky" headline, the advertisement featured a new headline: "IT'S TOASTED to taste better."

The last Lucky Strike ad ran in 1956. The headline read, "Light up a lucky—it's light-up time." In 1956, the Lucky Strike program campaign did not relate to either the newspaper or college radio spot. It seemed that there was some controversy within the organization about advertising Lucky Strike in the program. A memorandum dated February 18, 1958, from Mr. Whelen, assistant treasurer, to Mr. Albert Stevens, advertising manager, highlights some of the issues that the American Tobacco Company was having in with its college football campaign. The letter states,

> We do a considerable amount of advertising in college football programs. Our advertising, however, is confined to one brand, Lucky Strike. We may have had other brands advertised in programs but I do not recall ever seeing them.
> In my opinion, this type of advertising is very close to being institutional in nature and is, therefore, more defensive than offensive. It is my suggestion that we set up an ad under the banner line,

Winston advertisement featuring the Winston filter published in the University of Tennessee Football Programs for the 1958 football season, October 18, 1958 (courtesy University of Tennessee Libraries, Knoxville, Special Collections).

"THE ALL AMERICAN TEAM"

Using cartoon characters the various Company products would serve as the line-up of for a football team. In other words, we might have Half & Half at the center, Lucky Strike and Pall Mall at the guard position, the two Tareytons at tackle, and the two Hit Parade packings at the end.[23]

Although this campaign idea was never used, it shows some of the branding and advertising issues that the American Tobacco Company was experiencing. This memo shows that as the American Tobacco Company was expanding its brand offerings to accommodate the need for filtered cigarettes, the company was losing its campaign focus.

During the 1950s, American Tobacco Company ran image-based advertising that focused on campus spirit. Lucky Strike never mentioned tar or any health issues related to smoking.

For the first time, in 1958, a filtered brand, Winston, occupied the back cover of the football program. The full-color advertisement focused on the filter and did not relate to campus life or sports. Like the newspaper ads, the headline read, "It's What's Up Front That Counts." However, in 1959, R.J. Reynolds altered its generic approach for the Winston brand and ran an image-based campaign featuring a well-dressed college couple smoking at a football game. The headline remained consistent with the other Winston ads by stating, "It's what's up front that counts! Only Winston has FILTER BLEND up front!"

Salem was featured in a game program ad for the first time in 1958. The full-color advertisement featured the usual young couple and emphasized the fresh flavor of the menthol brand. However, the ad seemed more focused on youth and romance than college life. The advertisement appeared to be from Salem's 1958 general campaign. It did not appear to be designed specifically for students.

The American Tobacco Company's Lucky Strike and Liggett & Myers' Chesterfield and L&M brands dominated the college football scene during the 1950s. Phillip Morris, Camel, and Old Gold faded from the college scene in the 1950s. Old Gold did not advertise in football programs in the 1950s. In 1950, Phillip Morris continued to run the "Johnny" calls the signal full-page advertisements. However, the "Johnny" ads disappeared by 1951. Camel ran full-color ads featuring women's college football fashion on the back cover until 1954. New filtered brands such as L&M, Winston, and the new filtered Chesterfield gained prominence at the end of the 1950s.

CIGARETTE ADVERTISING IN FOOTBALL PROGRAMS, 1960s

Cigarette advertising in football game programs slowed during the 1960s. Fewer cigarette brands advertised and the brands that advertised did not always hold the same prominent position in the game programs. Like the advertisements in the student newspapers, cigarette advertising in college football game programs ended in 1963. However, broadcast advertising during college games continued.

In 1960, only Salem advertised in the college game programs. Its ad occupied the back cover of the program. Like most of the Salem cigarette ads that ran in the game programs, the focus was on young love and freshness. The advertisement featured a couple walking along a lush wooded path. The headline reads, "Salem refreshes your taste—'air softens' every puff." No reference was made to college students or football. Therefore, this ad was probably designed for a national audience instead of specifically targeting college students. Studebaker sponsored the center roster instead of Liggett & Myers. Instead of Phillip Morris's "Johnny" calling the signals, Jeep sponsored the official "college signal" page.

A tobacco company sponsored the center game roster spread again in 1961. British American Tobacco's Viceroy brand sponsored the roster. Like Liggett & Myers campaigns for Chesterfield and L&M, Viceroy featured a couple at a football game. The headline read, "Viceroy's got it at both ends...Got the filter! Got the blend!" Salem's full-color advertisement occupied the back cover again in 1961. Like the previous year, Salem's ad featured a couple in a nature scene. No specific reference was made to college life or football.

In 1962 Tiparillo, Viceroy, and Winston advertised in college game programs. In 1962, Viceroy again sponsored the roster spread. The spread featured a group of male and female cheerleaders wearing a "V" for Viceroy. The headline read, "Viceroy's got the taste *that's right*!" Winston ran a full-color advertisement on the back cover featuring a couple camping. The headline consisted of the Winston slogan, "Winston Tastes Good...Like A Cigarette Should!" Like the Salem ads, the Winston ads seemed to relate to a national campaign instead of a campaign that is specifically targeting the college football audience. Tiparillo, a cigarillo brand, launched a national campaign urging men to offer Tiparillos to women. The headlines read, "Should a gentleman offer a Tiparillo..." The advertisement in the game program urged men to offer women Tiparillos at the game and mentioned that the brand was available at the stadium.

Viceroy sponsored the roster in 1963 with a full-color two-page spread that promoted the taste of filtered Viceroy cigarettes. The copy reads, "Viceroy's got the *taste that's right*." Instead of advertising its Winston or Salem brands on the back cover, the back of the program contained a safe driving message from R.J. Reynolds Tobacco Company. The headline states, "Three ways to quarterback the most important drive of the day—your drive home." The copy urged audience members to slow down, turn on their lights, and stay in the line of traffic.

After 1963, cigarette advertising disappeared from the football programs. Coca-Cola sponsored the roster spreads for the next decade. Although the cigarette advertisements ceased to appear in print, other methods of promoting cigarettes during college events remained.

THE TOBACCO BOWL

In addition to advertising in the football game programs, cigarette companies also sponsored The Tobacco Bowl. The Tobacco Bowl or The Tobacco Festival Bowl was held annually from 1935 to 1983. The Tobacco Bowl was not a post-season championship game. Instead, it featured regional teams from Virginia, West Virginia, North Carolina, South Carolina, Maryland, and other southern states. Before the bowl moved to Richmond, Virginia, from 1948 to 1984, it was held in various cities such as South Boston, Virginia; Durham, North Carolina; and Lexington, Kentucky. Starting in 1948, The Tobacco Bowl was played at Richmond City Stadium. After its move to Richmond, game became part of the annual National Tobacco Festival that was held in Richmond and often featured the football rivalry between the Virginia Tech Hokies and the University of Virginia Cavaliers.[24]

Although few programs exist for The Tobacco Bowl or The Tobacco Festival in Rich-

Salem advertisement featuring a young couple published in the University of Tennessee Football Programs for the 1962 football season, November 2, 1962 (courtesy University of Tennessee Libraries, Knoxville, Special Collections).

mond, the two programs that were located did provide insight into how cigarettes and other tobacco products were promoted. According to Governor R. Gregg Cherry of North Carolina, the Tobacco Bowl exists "to pay tribute and to honor those who have worked earnestly in the great Tobacco industry that has made our state famous the world over."[25] The game day schedule of events included a parade, an introduction by Miss Virginia State, Miss North Carolina State, and Miss North Carolina College Alumni. Representatives from the tobacco industry such as Miss Piedmont Tobacco Bowl, Miss Chesterfield, and Miss Lucky Strike, also presented at the game.[26]

The earliest program that was located was for the Piedmont–Tobacco Bowl Classic in Durham, North Carolina. The Virginia State College Trojans competed against the North Carolina College Eagles in the 1945 bowl game at Durham Athletic Park. An interesting facet of this game is that it was a contest between two historically black institutions. This fact is emphasized in a 1945 letter to L. E. Austin published in the game program. The chairman on arrangements for the Tobacco Bowl Classic, R. Gregg Cherry, wrote,

> My attention has been called to the fact that the Alumni Association of the North Carolina College for Negroes and other responsible citizens of our state are planning a Tobacco Bowl Football Classic to be held in Durham on December 8, between two outstanding Negro Elevens of the Country. This homecoming tribute to our returning Negro Veterans of World War II will emphasize the contribution our Negro Citizens have made in the great tobacco industry of our State.[27]

The president of the home university, North Carolina College, also published a message in the program relating to good sportsmanship at the game instead of a promotional message endorsing the legacy of tobacco in state of North Carolina. Dr. James E. Shepard wrote,

> The president extends a cordial welcome to our visiting team and to all who gathered with us today in [the] interest of keen rivalry and clean sportsmanship. May we carry with us something of [the] inspiration from the men "Who play the game." They take the hard knocks without flinching and follow the ball with a strong determination to win.[28]

More than 10 years later, in 1957, the souvenir program of the 9th Annual Tobacco Festival in Richmond showed how the Tobacco Bowl with the addition of the Festival evolved from its beginnings. *The Tobacco Festival Souvenir Program* served as a program for both the festival and The Tobacco Bowl game. The program listed events such as the bowl game, an illuminated parade and pregame show, a variety of dances, the crowning of the tobacco princesses and the tobacco queen, the festival show, and the tobacco markets. Unlike the 1945 program, the 1957 program included a variety of cigarette and tobacco advertising— Lucky Strike, Marlboro, L&M, United States Tobacco Company (manufacturer of Copenhagen, Model Smoking Tobacco, and Bruton Snuff), and Edgeworth pipe tobacco. In addition to cigarette and tobacco advertising, a variety of advertisers publicized their partnership with big tobacco. For instance, DuPont Cellophane advertised how its product keeps cigarettes and cigars fresh. Peter J. Schweitzer, a manufacturer of cigarette paper, also advertised. Five Richmond hotels also advertised their partnership with the tobacco industry and the festival.

Although *The Tobacco Festival Souvenir Program* served as both *The Tobacco Bowl Program* and the festival program, it seemed to be geared toward an industry audience instead of a college audience. Most of the program seemed to work as a public relations tool for the tobacco industry. Only the L&M center roster spread seemed to target the college audience by focusing on the football game between the University of Virginia and Virginia Tech. Liggett & Myers ran the same advertisement for L&M as it ran in its national game program campaign in 1957. It featured a father and son lighting up L&M cigarettes at a college game and the rosters for the two opposing teams.

Broadcast Cigarette Advertising and College Athletics

By the time ABC began broadcasting college football, institutions of higher education had been open to commercial advertising during games for more than one hundred years. The first sponsored athletic event was a crew contest between Harvard and Yale before the Civil War. A railroad sponsored the event.[29] Although college and university administrators have not traditionally approved of corporate sponsorship on college and university campuses, special exceptions are made for extracurricular activities. And, the most lucrative extracurricular activities are typically sports.

The advent of broadcasting brought college athletics to a mass audience via radio and television. The media revolution intensified the commercialization of college and university athletics and amplified the influence of an athletic program on a college or university's reputation. Because a college or university's reputation was linked to the broadcast of athletic events, certain advertisers were taboo, such as laxatives, habit-forming drugs, feminine products, and political advertising. And, at some colleges and universities, advertising alcohol and tobacco was prohibited.[30]

Unlike alcohol, cigarettes and tobacco had established relationships with colleges and universities through the college newspaper and through their educational endowments for research, especially tobacco-related research. Therefore, cigarette companies experienced little difficulty getting access to college and university athletic events. The advertising of tobacco products became especially prevalent at football games, and cigarettes and other tobacco products were soon advertised during the broadcast event. However, the fear that the products might interfere with an athlete's training and performance did raise some concerns and was a drawback for some programs. For instance, Notre Dame and the University of Illinois had policies that pre-dated World War II that prohibited cigarette advertising. However, in the tobacco-growing regions of the South, the policies had been very permissive regarding cigarette and tobacco sponsorships. For instance, an athletic advisory committee for the University of North Carolina decided that potentially harmful substances such as alcohol should not be advertised during sporting events. However, tobacco products did not fall into this category.[31]

After World War II, colleges and universities continued to have divided policies on tobacco and cigarette advertising. However, radio advertising for tobacco products became increasingly common. When Duke University started a broadcasting network for its football program, Chesterfield Cigarettes, manufactured by Liggett & Myers of Durham, North Carolina, became the principal sponsor. Under a policy sanctioned by the National Collegiate Athletic Association (NCAA), a nonprofit association of 1,281 institutions, conferences, and organizations that organize college and university athletic programs, cigarette advertising but not alcohol advertising was permitted. Liggett & Myers also sponsored the Big Ten and Notre

Dame televised regional games. However, the NCAA policy was challenged in the 1960s when research confirmed the harmful effects of smoking and tobacco use.[32]

CIGARETTE ADVERTISING AND NCAA GAME BROADCASTS DURING THE 1930s AND 1940s

Very few scripts exist for broadcast cigarette promotions during college games during the 1930s and 1940s. Tobacco industry documents suggest that during the 1930s and early 1940s, more of the tobacco industry's broadcast youth advertising involved musical programming such as Lucky Strike's *Your Hit Parade,* the American Tobacco Company's *Kay Kyser's Kollege Of Musical Knowledge* and the *Chesterfield Supper Club.* In addition, much of the broadcast marketing efforts during the early 1940s involved the war effort. Although the industry's broadcast efforts targeted young smokers, they did not target the college audience as directly as football game promotions.

During the late 1940s, after the end of World War II, the cigarette brands increased their advertising during college football games. Most of the existing documents suggest that the promotions were made by the radio or sports announcers live or during the broadcast of the game. Sometimes the advertisements were separate from the broadcast of the college game but were read by the sports announcers. Usually the commercials featuring celebrities or experts were pre-recorded. Other times, a script was provided for mentioning the brand at the beginning or end of the game. For instance, announcers were sometimes given a plan from the tobacco company for when the announcer should promote their product. For instance, Lucky Strike provided this schedule for promoting its brand during an early televised Army–Notre Dame football game on November 12, 1947:

PROGRAM

1. STANDARD OPENING... edited for special broadcast
2. PRE GAME COLOR...Stanton comments on film.
3. COMMERCIAL...one-minute spot (Riggs, Burnett) Just before opening
4. FIRST HALF OF GAME...Stanton comments on film opening
5. BALOPTICAN PLATE FIRST HALF SCORE—LUCKY STRIKE SCOREBOARD
6. COMMERCIAL...one minute spot (Currin Testimonial) Just before second half kick-off
7. SECOND HALF OF GAME...Stanton comments on film
8. COMMERCIAL...Stop Motion #1 (Marching Cigarettes) immediately after the end of the game.
9. BALOPTICAN: Still plate giving teaser for Princeton-Yale game. Stanton.
10. STANDARD CLOSING[33]

From the announcer's schedule of the 1947 radio broadcast, it is evident that a variety of media were used during the football game that was broadcast on the radio and to a limited audience on television. The schedule indicates that the announcers promoted Lucky Strike, the game schedule allowed for pre-recorded commercials such as the spot featuring the testimonial of Dan Currin, a tobacco expert, and Riggs and Burnett, tobacco auctioneers. A baloptican projector was also used to project images and film promoting the brand during the live game. And, Lucky Strike sponsored the scoreboard. Lucky Strike also provided a script for the announcers to use to promote the brand during the start of the game, halftime, and the end of the game. For instance, at halftime, announcers said,

Well fans, it the half and it's Notre Dame 15...Army nothing.

And there's just time to say fine tobacco is what counts in a cigarette. And Lucky Strike means fine tobacco ... so round, so firm, so fully packed, so free and easy on the draw.

Now get set for the second half highlights of the thrilling Notre Dame–Army game. And watch for that Army threat in the final quarter.[34]

In the late 1940s, the American Tobacco Company increased its presence during football games. The brand started showing more Lucky Strike films during the game and more commercial spots were featured. Lucky Strike continued to sponsor the scoreboard. For instance, the American Tobacco Company created the following schedule for the first half of the Yale-Connecticut game on September 24, 1949:

ORDER OF COMMERCIALS

Note: If possible, television station to give program BILLBOARD ANNOUNCEMENTS preceding each game

1. Standard Opening (FILM)—(Includes LUCKIES PAY MORE #1: World) Then, to field The Standard Field Sign-on (LIVE).
2. 3–5 Minutes Before Opening Kick-off -(LUCKIES PAY MORE (World plus Survey (FILM) plus Crutchfield Testimonial.)
3. End of First Quarter (FILM)—(STOP MOTION—CB-LA—Edited—Sarra.)
4. Immediately After End of First Half—(STOP MOTION—Spot //27: Square Dance.)
5. Midway Between Halves (LIVE-Studio)—(LUCKY STRIKE SCOREBOARD.)
6. Immediately After Scoreboard (FILM)-(LUCKIES PAY MORE: World.)
7. 3 Minutes Before Second Half Kick-off- (STOP MOTION—Spot #28A: Marching (FILM) Cigarettes.)
8 End of Third Quarter (FILM)—(LUCKIES PAY MORE, Short #1: Auction plus. Stop Motion.)
9. Immediately After End of Game (FILM)—(STOP MOTION—Spot #29: Dancing Packages.)
10. After Recap and Field Sign-off—(LUCKY STRIKE SCOREBOARD.) (LIVE-Studio)
11. Immediately After Lucky Strike -(Includes LUCKIES PAY MORE: World Scoreboard = Closing (FILM) plus Survey and Callis Testimonial.)
12. Oral Mentions (LIVE)
13. Time Out (FILM)[35]

Like before, Lucky Strike gave the game announcers scripts for promoting their product during the game. The Lucky Strike announcer for this particular game was named Jim Stevenson. In addition to providing the script, the American Tobacco Company directed him to light a cigarette and smoke it on the air. The instructions and the script are as follows:

Good afternoon, I'm Jim Stevenson your Lucky Strike announcer for the Yale-Connecticut game here at the Yale Bowl. And, fans, before we get into today's play-by-play, let's light up a Lucky. (LIGHTS UP A LUCKY. DRAWS CONTENTEDLY. EXHALES. LOOKS AT CIGARETTE APPROVINGLY.)

Take it from me! For more ... much more ...real deep-down smoking enjoyment, smoke a Lucky!

(he extends lucky toward camera slightly to feature)
And, remember, in the world there is no finer cigarette than Lucky Strike.[36]

During the late 1940s, the tobacco companies were increasing their efforts to promote cigarette smoking among members of the young college football audience. The evolution of broadcast promotion of cigarettes during the game evolved from various brands being mentioned by announcers to pre-recorded advertisements throughout the game and other multimedia promotions of the brand that integrated with the traditional broadcast efforts.

Cigarette Advertising and NCAA Game Broadcasts During the 1950s

In addition to advertising in football programs, cigarette advertisers also promoted their products during the broadcast of various sporting events including NCAA college football and basketball games. Not only were various cigarette brands promoted in advertisements during breaks in the game broadcasts, but announcers also mentioned their favorite brands during the game. Both live and television audiences could hear these promotions. For instance, Lucky Strike Cigarettes paid $14,834.59 per week during the 1963 NCAA Big Ten Conference basketball season to have celebrity announcer Bill Flemming[37] of ABC's *Today Show* and *Wide World of Sports* promote the brand live during the games. Flemming was the first voice of NCAA Division I Men's Basketball Championship on television. Although many cigarette brands were involved in broadcast college sports promotion, the Legacy Tobacco Documents Library has more documentation for the American Tobacco Company's marketing efforts than any other cigarette manufacturer.

Broadcast advertisements during sporting events were carefully coordinated to match the other promotional efforts. In addition to its sponsorship of the NCAA games, Lucky Strike also sponsored a college newscast during the 1950s that coordinated with its college newspaper advertising campaigns.[38] In 1952, Lucky Strike's advertising agency, Batten, Barton, Durstine, & Osborn, Inc., created television commercials that featured Dorothy Collins to be broadcast during college football games. Collins was also pictured in the Lucky Strike advertisements in the college game programs. The 35-second video described in the broadcast script says that the commercial opens with a medium close-up of Collins in an attractive college-type sweater and skirt against a cigarette screen background. The spot opened with Collins saying, "Now, friends, straight from college campuses all over the country comes more proof that Luckies taste better!" Andre Baruch, the voice of Lucky Strike cigarettes, continued as the voiceover announcer as the images in the commercial shifted from Collins to the entrance of a football stadium where the focus shifts to college couples enjoying a game. There is video of a co-ed dressed for the game; she is wearing a fur coat and chrysanthemum, and the man she is with is smoking a Lucky Strike cigarette and voicing his preference for the brand. At the end of the ad Collins says, "So, friends, take a tip from these college men and women all over America. For a cleaner, fresher, smoother smoke—make your next carton—Lucky Strike!"[39]

In addition to featuring Collins in broadcast commercials and advertisements during the football game, she was also pictured on point-of-sale materials that could be displayed at booths on game day or at local vendors. These point-of-sale materials were designed to complement her television and radio commercials. The point-of-sale promotions for 1952 were announced in a 1951 memo to the entire sales organization. The memo stated:

> Dorothy Collins, the young lady who sings the LUCKY STRIKE BE HAPPY—GO LUCKY comercials on our radio and television shows has become known from coast to coast. Her popularity is particularly great in television areas where one or more of the Lucky Strike shows can be seen. Miss Collins' warm and appealing personality has won many new friends for Luckies. And, she has become "The Sweetheart of LUCKY STRIKE."
>
> To further capitalize on her wide acceptance with the radio and television public, we have designed some LUCKY STRIKE point-of-sale advertising materials with Dorothy Collins the center of attraction.[40]

Due to their popularity on campus, more Dorothy Collins point-of-sale materials were created in 1952.[41]

Ed Thorgersen, a sports radio announcer and commentator, was frequently featured in cigarette advertisements and radio programs sponsored by tobacco companies from the 1930s to the 1950s.[42] Although he was featured in advertising for both Chesterfield and Lucky Strike cigarettes, the majority of his advertising work was done to promote American Tobacco Company's Lucky Strike brand.[43] A contract between Thorgersen and the American Tobacco Company shows that he was paid $650 for filming two spots in 1952.[44] Thorgersen, again under contract with the American Tobacco Company, filmed a television commercial targeting students that linked Lucky Strike with college football. The script reads,

> This is Ed Thorgersen with news about the latest All American! Lucky Strike Cigarette! Nationwide survey based on actual interviews in 80 leading colleges reveals...College students prefer Luckies.[45]

The video that accompanied the spot featured a college football scene. Thorgersen was featured in another television commercial targeting students again in 1953. This spot also promoted the results of Lucky Strike's campus survey. The script reads,

> Hello, I'm Ed Thorgersen, and I have some mighty interesting facts here about college smokers.
> Last year a survey was made in leading colleges throughout the country which showed that smokers in those colleges preferred Luckies to any other cigarette.
> Well sir, this year another nation-wide survey was made—a representative survey of all students in regular colleges from coast to coast. Based on thousands of interviews—this survey shows that as last year, Luckies lead again... lead over all other brands–regular or kingsize—and by a wide margin.[46]

Thorgersen and Lucky Strike made several series of Lucky Strike commercials during the 1950s that connected the popularity of the cigarette brand to football. Many of the commercials used Thorgersen to announce that Lucky Strike had won the popularity contest among college students. Several of the spots began with Thorgersen announcing "Luckies win again" or "Supervised by college professors and based on thirty-one thousand actual student interviews...Luckies lead again."[47]

In 1954, Dorothy Collins again promoted Lucky Strike on the radio. As before, the comparison was made between the popularity of Lucky Strike cigarettes and college victory in sports. Collins' script reads,

> The news is in! And Luckies win... According to the latest and biggest college survey representative of students in colleges throughout the country, Luckies were preferred to any other brand...

and by a really big margin. And listen to this: Once again, the number one reason given by college students was ... better taste.[48]

However, starting in 1955 few industry documents exist that can provide any meaningful information about cigarette companies' broadcast advertising campaigns created for NCAA events. No announcer scripts exist for the late 1950s. The beginning of the filter wars could be one reason for the reduction in the documentation of the industry's advertising efforts at football games. Many of the tobacco companies were shifting their efforts away from promoting their traditional brands to developing a safer cigarette. The American Tobacco Company's absence from the broadcast advertising mirrors its absence in the printed game programs after 1956.

Although no documentation exists stating that the American Tobacco Company was discontinuing advertising in broadcast or print form during games in the late 1950s, the company encouraged its student representatives to take a "personalized and localized"[49] approach. For instance, in the 1955–1956 Campus Representative Guide for the American Tobacco Company, examples are provided for how the student representatives can engage in grassroots efforts to promote smoking Luckies. Two examples are provided:

> NORTH TEXAS STATE COLLEGE Representatives set up this display in the Student Union. Against a background of black corrugated cardboard, were red lips holding LUCKIES. Spun glass wound around thin wire gave the appearance of smoke coming from the cigarettes.
>
> BOSTON UNIVERSITY Representatives tied-in a "personalized-localized" display with the football season. LUCKY STRIKE and PALL MALL cigarettes represented the "home and visiting team." Note that "Terry," the college mascot, appears in both the right and left corners of the display.[50]

In both cases, the students directed the advertising efforts on campus instead of simply using football displays provided by the American Tobacco Company. In addition, the company encouraged its campus representatives to get involved with fundraisers and student welcome week activities. These practices show a shift from a more traditional advertising approach to a social marketing approach that allowed more customization by the students and the individual campus.

In 1959, industry documents suggest that the American Tobacco Company returned to its previous strategy of official sponsorship of broadcasts of NCAA football. However, instead of promoting its lead brand, Lucky Strike, it promoted its new filtered brand Tareyton. The existing documentation indicates that Tareyton cosponsored the Naval Academy games with Gulf Oil Company for the 1959 season to be broadcast in Baltimore, Maryland and Washington, D.C. A 1959 memo from E.F. Mooney, the general sales manager, states,

> On Saturday, September 19, 1959, Dual Filter Tareyton will begin cosponsoring radio broadcasts of the 1959 U.S. Naval Academy Football Games (excluding the Army-Navy game)...Tax-free Dual Filter Tareyton Cigarettes will be awarded to Naval Hospitals located within the broadcast range of the above mentioned radio stations for touchdowns and outstanding plays which occur during the games as follows:

	Cigarettes
Touchdowns	2,000
Outstanding Plays	1,000[51]

Although American Tobacco returned to sponsoring broadcasts, its approach appears to be focused on public relations and the military instead of the general student audience.

Although the sponsorship appears to be a public relations effort, the records do indicate that the announcers' participation in the promotions is part of the contract.[52]

In 1960, the American Tobacco Company sent out a memo to the sales organization stating that it was conducting an aggressive college campaign to promote its new Dual Filter Tareyton brand. A large focus was placed on merchandising, retail, and sports concessions.[53] However, the company continued to sponsor football games. For instance, Dual Filter Tareyton sponsored the radio broadcast of Northwestern football games on WCFL in Chicago for the 1960 season.[54]

Although much of the American Tobacco Company's advertising focused on its new Dual Filtered Tareyton brand, football star Frank Gifford was featured in an advertising campaign targeting college students. Gifford read the following radio script in a 1961 college football advertising campaign for Lucky Strike:

> One of the things I remember about college football is the way we'd look forward to the game. Each day the excitement would build. On Monday morning the kids would quietly wish you luck. But, by Friday night, they'd be so worked up they'd be slapping you on the back. I'll bet it's still the same way today. Now, here is something that I still know is true ... college people really go for Lucky Strike cigarettes. It's a fact that today college students smoke more Luckies than any other regular cigarette.[55]

Although the American Tobacco Company was increasing its promotion of the Dual Filter Tareyton brand at NCAA football games, it started advertising its Lucky Strike brand during NCAA basketball games in the early 1960s. American Tobacco was starting to lose market share to R.J. Reynolds' Camel brand. In fact, since 1959, Lucky Strike had lost 3 percent market share and Camel had gained 4 percent.[56] In response, American Tobacco increased its presence on campus and in collegiate sports. The company made a series of television commercials for Big Ten basketball in December 1960 for the 1960–1961 basketball season that featured "Tommy Trainer" and "Mickey the Manager" as the "Men Who Make the Team."[57] The "Men Who Make the Team" campaign featured various individuals who are instrumental to the success of a basketball team. The "Tommy Trainer" script read,

> Lucky Strike remembers the "Men Who Make the Team." Now we spotlight—Tommy Trainer. Whenever one of his boys get hurt, Tommy takes off like an ambulance driver. And he's a regular medic with the adhesive tape and collodian. In between emergency calls? Well, back in the locker room, here's Tommy enjoying the great taste of a Lucky.[58]

The American Tobacco Company's records show that Lucky Strike cigarettes continued to sponsor NCAA and Big Ten basketball through the 1967 season. The radio broadcasts reached audiences in Michigan, Wisconsin, Ohio, Indiana, Iowa, Illinois, Missouri, Minnesota, South Dakota, and Kentucky. The weekly cost of the NCAA basketball broadcast sponsorship was estimated at $14,834.59.[59]

In 1964, Lucky Strike continued to sponsor spot radio for NCAA basketball. The American Tobacco Company purchased a $40,050 sponsorship of Big Ten basketball and $9,541 in local radio advertising during NCAA basketball games; it can be assumed that this local contract was likely for campus radio stations.[60] Like the Navy football season, American Tobacco shared its University of Kentucky sponsorship with Gulf Oil Company. The cost of the full season on WHAS Louisville was $19,762.50. Instead of pre-recorded spot commercials, the advertising package included radio spots that were read by the announcer at the game. The following spot was read after the scores were announced in the first quarter of the University of Kentucky games:

> When it comes to smoking nothing scores for flavor like fine tobacco. That's why the choice of so many smokers is Lucky Strike. Here's a cigarette that sets a standard in smoking taste. That's because Luckies are blended with fine tobacco from one end to the other. So, with Luckies you get fine tobacco taste at its best. If you're a smoker and you smoke for taste, remember LS/MFT—Lucky Strike means fine tobacco. And that means great taste. Today, taste fine tobacco at its best. Smoke a Lucky Strike. Buy a carton.[61]

After the 1965 basketball season, tobacco sponsorship of NCAA college sports began to decline. The Federal Communications Commission was becoming concerned about cigarette brands advertising during college sports. For instance, Robert B. Meyner, the tobacco industry's attorney who was charged with implementing the self-regulatory Cigarette Advertising Code, stated in a memo to all cigarette manufacturers that he had approved only three sponsorships for bowl games for the 1965–1966 season.[62] In the interest of self-regulation, the tobacco industry was reducing its college sports sponsorships. And, most of the sponsorships that remained involved television advertising during post-season bowl games. Cigarette brand sponsorship of athletic events ended in 1967.[63]

EARLY CONFLICTS ABOUT NCAA AND CIGARETTE COMMERCIALS

The first major clash on advertising tobacco and cigarettes during college athletic events came during the 1960s. Government officials, the NCAA, and the American Cancer Society became concerned about the association between athletics and cigarette smoking and the young audience that the advertisers were targeting during these events. Walter Byers, NCAA executive director, might have been one of the first to express concern about tobacco and college and university athletics. Byers urged the NCAA Television Committee to ban the cigarette advertisements because of the increased awareness of the health dangers associated with tobacco use, particularly smoking. However, his proposal was voted down 8–2. At the same time, the NCAA Television Committee was voting to remove the ban on alcohol advertising to increase revenue.[64]

In 1965, after the removal of the cigarette advertising from game programs, Meyner required that all Cigarette Advertising Code members contact him before advertising during college and university events. The memo, dated September 15, 1965, and sent to all code members, stated,

> Member-companies should not plan to sponsor radio or television coverage of school, college, or university sports events without first clearing such plans with the Code Administrator.
>
> With respect to the 1965–1966 season, the Administrator thus far has approved only three proposals for such sports coverage. These all involve sponsorship of telecasts of post-season college football games.[65]

Meyner sent out another memo addressing concerns that Advertising Code might not allow cigarette advertisers to promote their product during NCAA game-of-the-week broadcasts. Meyner stated that advertising during these broadcasts was still in line with the code. However, cigarette advertising should not be closely identified with a school background nor should any college or university be used as part of cigarette advertising campaigns. Meyner issued a series of guidelines that became effective January 2, 1966, a date chosen because of contracts that cigarette advertisers might have with NCAA football teams for tournament games such as the Rose Bowl. The rules stated that if a member chooses to purchase advertising time during a radio or television broadcast of an NCAA game or any other school athletic event,

1. The broadcast must clearly avoid any inference that any school recommends or approves of cigarette smoking.
2. The cigarette commercial must not suggest a school setting or situation and supers may not be shown over or "voice credits" given with a school background.
3. It must be made clear that the cigarette commercial is not broadcast from the scene of the athletic contest or from any school, campus, or other facility.[66]

Again, in 1966, Meyner set forth more regulations for broadcast advertising during NCAA events. On June 3, 1966, Meyner wrote,

Effective immediately, the following shall apply to cigarette advertising on radio or television broadcasts of athletic events:

1. Radio or television sports announcers who are well-known athletes or former athletes may deliver only lead-ins that have no promotional content, and opening and closing announcements that have no promotional content. Thus and now a word from our sponsor (or the X Tobacco Company) would be allowed. So would "This program is being (has been) brought to you by the X Tobacco Company."
2. Identified sports announcers who are not well-known athletes or former athletes are considered to be "celebrities in the entertainment world" or "persons who would have special appeal to persons under 21 years of age" or both and so they are subject to these restrictions:
    (a) They may deliver no personal testimonials.
    (b) They may deliver no first-person copy, connected to the use of the product, e.g., "I (or we) notice a lot of people switching to Brand X."
    (c) They may not deliver copy, which uses imperative ("Buy a pack today."); horatory ("Let's light up."); or any language of obligation (...should ... ought to ... must ... have to ... owe it to yourself, etc.) in connection with the use of the product. They may not deliver copy which uses rhetorical questions ("Why not try one?") in connection with the use of the product.

Although Meyner tried to work proactively to avoid official government regulation, even with its improvements and stronger regulations, the Cigarette Advertising Code was not enough to prevent concerned citizens and government officials from asking for more regulation of cigarette advertising to youth.

CRITICISM OF THE CODE AND GOVERNMENT REGULATION OF BROADCASTING

In spite of industry efforts toward self-regulation, concerned citizens were beginning to take up the cause against cigarette television advertising and sponsorship. John P. Banzhaf III, who has been called the Ralph Nader of the cigarette and tobacco industry, was responsible for the Federal Communications Commission getting involved in the issue of cigarette advertising. After watching cigarette commercials on television, Banzhaf concluded that the advertisements could be considered legally controversial. Banzhaf wrote to WCBS-TV's headquarters in New York City in December 1966 to request that some other reputable person be given the opportunity to present contrasting views on the issue of whether cigarette smoking is advisable. Banzhaf's letter referenced three advertisements that advocated the view that cigarette smoking is socially acceptable and needed for a rich, full life. CBS ignored the letter. He then sent a second formal letter to WCBS-TV and the FCC in Washington, D.C.[67]

Like Banzhaf, the FCC's commissioner, Paul Dixon, was also concerned about the effectiveness of the current self-regulatory cigarette advertising code. On March 29, 1967, Dixon wrote to Meyner with questions about the current cigarette advertising code that had been put into effect in 1964. In response, Meyner defended the current code and mentioned the many changes in youth advertising that the code mandated. Meyner mentioned the removal of cigarette advertising from comic books and other sorts of media that are appealing to children. In addition, Meyner mentioned the removal of cigarette promotions from college and university campuses. He mentioned that all sanctioned distribution of sample cigarettes on campus had ceased. Meyner mentioned that four instances of sampling had occurred since the new code and that he had rebuked and warned the violators of the code about their lack of adherence. Meyner also mentioned the removal of cigarette advertising from all college publications and the current restrictions on broadcasting during college sporting events that the code had enacted.[68]

In the spring of 1967, Meyner wrote to the members of the Cigarette Advertising Code cautioning them against advertising in pre-season professional football games played in college and university stadiums to ensure compliance with Article IV, Section 1 (c) of the current code.[69]

In addition to writing to Meyner, the Federal Communications Commission also contacted the broadcasters. In a letter to the television station dated June 2, 1967, the FCC wrote that the programs that CBS broadcast relating to smoking and health were insufficient to counteract the advertising supporting cigarette smoking that ran from 5 to 10 minutes each day. The FCC held that the fairness doctrine applied to Banzhaf's claims. However, the FCC rejected the idea that the issue required equal time.[70] Instead it was determined that one anti-smoking PSA was needed for every four cigarette commericals.[71]

In response to Banzhaf's complaint, the FCC required that stations provide free time each week for public service announcements launched by the government under the cigarette labeling law. The FCC decided that it was not in the public interest for the airwaves to be used to advertise cigarettes without some warning of the health dangers associated with cigarette smoking.[72] Therefore, the broadcast stations were obligated to provide free airtime in opposition to cigarette commercials.[73]

The FCC was inundated with requests to reconsider its action. The FCC's ruling that cigarette advertising was covered under the fairness doctrine was attacked by a variety of television stations, including WTMJ-AM-FM-TV, Milwaukee. The television and radio stations called it a "classic example" of one government agency operating against another agency. And, in the end, both entities use tax dollars to support their conflicting interests.[74]

The broadcasters' argument centered on the fact that while the United States government was attempting to counteract cigarette advertising domestically, it was spending money promoting the product abroad. The various stations claimed that the government spent nearly $30 million during the 1966 fiscal year to regain and expand foreign cigarette markets. The broadcasters also noted that cautionary statements required on cigarette packs were not mandatory on cigarettes packaged for export. The editorials also mentioned that the U.S. Department of Agriculture was spending $240,000 in Japan, Austria, and Thailand to promote products of domestically grown tobacco. The broadcasters also cited the Department of Agriculture's $106,000 outlay toward producing a documentary film promoting U.S. tobacco. Therefore, the broadcasters concluded that the Department of Agriculture and the Federal Communications Commission's activities represented "another Washington conflict on the subject of tobacco and your health. How could a film extolling the pleasures of tobacco be shown here when American radio and television stations are forced to carry anti-cigarette messages?"[75]

Despite the controversy, the FCC stood firm on its decision. As a result of the FCC's ruling, many of the voluntary health agencies and the Public Health Service created public service announcements and other kinds of broadcast content to be utilized during the airtime provided by the television and radio stations.[76] From the time the ruling took effect in 1967 to 1970, counteradvertising from the voluntary health organizations appeared in a volume of approximately one-quarter of the cigarette commercials. While the counterads were broadcast, there was a decline in cigarette consumption. The counterads were eliminated on January 2, 1971, when cigarette advertising was formally banned from the airwaves.[77]

Senator Robert Kennedy also adopted the cause of restricting cigarette advertising that targets youth in the mid–1960s. Senator Kennedy challenged many of the tobacco industry's advertising interests to deter youth from smoking. In the fall of 1967, Senator Kennedy met with the administrators of the current cigarette advertising code to express his concerns about the effectiveness of the voluntary cigarette advertising code. He wrote to Robert Walker, the chairman of American Tobacco Company, expressing his concerns. In response, in a letter written on September 14, 1967, Walker attempted to satisfy Kennedy's concerns and defend the industry's and his company's current course of action. Walker wrote,

> With respect to advertising, it is and has been our Company's position that smoking is a form of pleasure for adults. In June 1963, for example, I announced our Company's decision to discontinue advertising in college periodicals and promotion of cigarettes on college campuses. In 1964, our Company discontinued the use of sports personalities in advertising. These steps were taken so that our position with respect to youth smoking would not be misunderstood by the general public. As to television advertising, in which you show a particular interest, we have taken and intend to continue to take steps to see that our advertising does not appear in programs which have a disproportionately high percentage of young people among their viewing audience.[78]

On November 27, 1967, *Broadcasting* reported that Senator Kennedy sent off another group of telegrams on November 17, 1967, to the three major television networks, the Tobacco Institute, the Cigarette Advertising Code administrators, the coaches and owners of professional football teams, and the NCAA, in his continuing battle against cigarette television commercials that reached young people.[79] The telegram stated,

> I continue to be concerned at the spectacle of seeing cigarette advertising on televised football games. I noted this past weekend that it appears not only on telecasts of professional games but on telecasts of college games as well. Although young people do not constitute 45 percent of the viewing audience for these events there are unquestionably millions of young people among the viewers. I think your responsibility in this matter is very great. I urge you to cease advertising on telecasts of football games.[80]

Senator Kennedy received only a few replies to his telegram. Walker responded to the telegram and quoted his letter to Senator Kennedy that he sent on September 14, 1967. He added the following to his previous statement: "First, in view of your particular mention of college football games, I should like you to know that we are not advertising on telecasts of college sports and have no plans to do so."[81]

In response to Kennedy's telegram, the NCAA said that its television committee would discuss the topic of cigarette commercials at its next meeting. Walter Byers, the NCAA president from the University of Michigan, sent the reply to the telegram. He noted that the NCAA's current advertising contract with ABC allowed cigarette commercials.[82]

In addition to confronting the tobacco industry about its product and advertising practices, Senator Kennedy also addressed the broadcasting industry and its role in the cigarette advertising and youth problem. In December 1967, Senator Kennedy and Julian Goodman, executive director of NBC, had sharp disagreements about cigarette advertising on television. The dispute between NBC and Kennedy came to a head when Kennedy suggested that cigarette advertising should not be broadcast during football games.[83]

The NCAA's president, Marcus Plant, agreed with Kennedy's views on cigarette advertising during NCAA broadcasts. He promised Kennedy to "use every influence possible to reduce and ultimately eliminate" cigarette advertising from NCAA broadcast programming. In 1967, the NCAA's contracts with tobacco companies ran through the 1969 college football season. Pressing for greater self-regulation, Kennedy said, "We all have a responsibility to act on our own regarding this serious health hazard." According to Kennedy, a failure of the government to act did not diminish the responsibilities of other Americans for voluntary action in the public interest.[84]

In addition to criticizing NBC's Goodman for resisting self-regulation, Kennedy also wrote to ABC and CBS regarding the issue. However, executives from each of the big three networks, ABC, CBS, and NBC, felt that the broadcast media was being singled out for self-regulation. In response, Kennedy said that he did not recognize any such distinction among the media insofar as the desired influence of advertising was concerned. According to Kennedy, regardless of the medium, the purpose of advertising is to convince people to smoke. Kennedy felt that television was particularly influential for the young. He said,

> It is true that television is particularly formative of youth attitudes. And a recent poll showed that of all television advertisements, the one most appealing to teenagers was a cigarette ad which was part of a campaign for a new brand. The broadcast media are unique, too, in that they already refrain from advertising liquor and firearms, a step which newspapers and magazines have not taken. And there are irrational distinctions regarding the government's regulatory power.... The airwaves belong to the public and the FCC (Federal Communications Commission) was established for the purpose of regulating their use in the public interest.[85]

Although all three of the networks disagreed with Kennedy, NBC's Goodman was the most vocal in his disagreement. He wired Kennedy with the following message:

> Since young people are included in the audiences for magazines, newspapers, billboards, and most radio and television programs, the sense of your suggestion is tantamount to a proposal that all cigarette advertising be barred, a suggestion urged by the Congress and rejected by it.[86]

In his response to the criticism by the broadcast media, Kennedy suggested that it was "not at all inconceivable" that cigarette advertising might be forbidden in print media such as magazines and newspapers.[87]

The issue created so much controversy that *Television Magazine* featured the debate on cigarette advertising and youth in its regular feature "Encounter" on December 8, 1967. The title of the bylined articles by Senator Robert Kennedy and President of the Tobacco Institute, Earl C. Clements, was "Should Cigarette Advertising on Television Be Subjected to Stringent Regulations?" Senator Kennedy made many of the same arguments that he made to the television executives the week before to the head of the Tobacco Institute. One of the major subjects of the debate was audience composition. During the 1960s, cigarette advertisers were not to advertise on programs that had more than 45 percent youth audience. Although the NCAA broadcast events had a smaller youth audience by percent, they had such a large audience that the number of youth reached outnumbered many of the programs already off-limits to the cigarette and tobacco industry. Senator Kennedy wrote,

> For example, cigarette advertising is not carried on programs with an audience more than 45 percent of which is under 21 years of age. But there are many programs with audiences in the tens of millions—notably sports events—that are watched by millions of young people even though the youthful portion of the audiencemay not reach 45 percent. A lower percentage figure and an absolute limit on the number of young people in the audience would be notable steps forward in self-regulation.[88]

In addition to his concerns about the cigarette marketers' young target audience, Senator Kennedy was also concerned about the tobacco industry's large media budget of $300 million and its role in influencing 1.5 million American children to start smoking each year. In response to the criticism, Clements wrote,

> The tobacco industry's position is that smoking is for adults, not children, is properly limited to those people who are mature enough to make their own decisions.
>
> The industry has amply demonstrated this belief through the rules of its voluntary Cigarette Advertising Code. The youth provisions of the Code are adhered to by all members of the industry.
>
> In spite of attacks on it, the Code has been quite successful in limiting the exposure and appeal of cigarette advertising to young people. Code Administrator Robert B. Meyner recently listed a number of substantial accomplishments of the code in this area. Among them are:
>
> Today, college and university campuses are barren of cigarette advertising. All school premises are barred to cigarette promotions. "The ban is absolute and it is observed scrupulously," the governor [Meyner] says.[89]

In a column published in *Broadcasting* on December 11, 1967, the NCAA's president, Marcus Plant, supported Senator Kennedy's position. He stated that "it is not desirable" to have cigarette advertising on NCAA broadcasts. However, Plant also stated that he did not have control over this phase of the NCAA's affairs and that he would use his influence in every way possible to phase out and eventually eliminate cigarette advertising.[90]

On February 2, 1968, Senator Kennedy won a major battle with the big tobacco companies. Manuel Yellen, the chairman of the board for P.J. Lorillard Co., announced in his response to Senator Kennedy's telegram sent in November that he had allowed the football advertising "option date to pass without renewal." In his statement to Kennedy, Yellen stressed a policy of "cooperation with government in arriving at a resolution of these problems."[91]

On February 5, 1968, on the eve of the American Advertising Federation's annual conference on government relations, Senate Commerce Committee chairman Warren Magnuson, who was scheduled to be a keynote speaker at the annual conference, told the Senate that his committee was "deeply disturbed about the role of advertising, especially television advertising, for cigarettes." Senator Magnuson said that the particular focus on youth appeals by the tobacco industry and pending measures that would require stronger warnings on cigarette packs would require warnings in other cigarette advertising, including broadcast. The FCC would also be given the power to regulate broadcast cigarette commercials.[92]

In addition to the Federal Communications Commission and Senate's continued concern about cigarette advertising and youth, Banzhaf, now the executive director of Action on Health and Smoking, accused the Tobacco Institute of "unfair and deceptive trade practices" and "planting" pro-cigarette articles in two national publications in March 1968. Banzhaf filed complaints with the Federal Trade Commission's Bureau of Deceptive Practices, the Post Office's fraud section, and the New York state attorney general's Bureau of Consumer Frauds.

The complaints charged that the Tobacco Institute, its public relations firm, Hill & Knowlton, and Tiderock Corporation "conspired together to plant in a number of national publications apparently factual and unbiased reports discounting the evidence against smoking." However, Banzhaf charged that the articles were actually "prepared and written by persons in the employ of the Tobacco Institute's public relations firm in an attempt to mislead the public ... by leading them to believe that the articles were actually the results of careful research by unbiased journalists."[93]

In anticipation of upcoming hearings on cigarette advertising, on May 15, 1968, Code Administrator Meyner wrote to Federal Communications Commission chairman Dixon to provide information for the commission's use as the commission prepared a report for Congress relating to the terms of the Cigarette Labeling and Advertising Act. The six-page letter covered a variety of subjects on the topic. However, advertising to youth was of particular concern. Meyner wrote,

> They [Senators Kennedy and Magnuson and the Senate Commerce Committee] seemed to be interested exclusively in the area of youth appeal, the restrictions on health claims were not urged. We discussed a possible revision of television-youth audience guideline—perhaps a cutoff percentage based on the 12-to-17 age range rather than the whole up-to-21 grouping. The staff people felt strongly too, that cigarette advertising should be prohibited on college and professional football telecasts. The guideline change remains under consideration and the Administrator hopes that the conversations with the staff will be continued.
>
> The Administrator remains unconvinced that the percentage of young viewers of football on television is excessive. I have studied the audience composition figures and restudied them. In only one case were the findings close to breaching 45 percent and I am at a loss to explain the exception. It is somewhat academic because this one telecast carried no cigarette advertising but I was interested to know why a relatively unpopular, post-season college all-star game (North-South), aired at a time when the season is tired, should attract more than 40 percent of its watchers in persons under 21. "Freak" and "fault in the sample" are the best explanations given.[94]

Meyner concluded the letter by stating that he felt that it was "vain" to hope for an "absolute expungement of all associative ties between smoking and sports." Meyner cited the instances of coaches and players smoking after games and on the sidelines. Meyner also asked Dixon for fairer play and to provide Congress with all of the facts.[95]

On November 21, 1968, the Federal Communications Commission's decision to regulate the tobacco industry under the fairness doctrine was upheld by the U.S. Court of Appeals. The court said, "The danger that cigarettes may pose to health is, among others, a danger to life itself." As the commission had emphasized, normal use of cigarettes is inherently dangerous, not just cigarette addiction. Cigarette smoking is affecting a large population of the country, not just an insignificant fringe group. The danger of cigarette smoking is documented by compelling statistical evidence.[96] The cigarette manufacturers then asked the Supreme Court to review their case. The high court turned down their request, leaving the appeals court standing.

After the completion of the 1968–1969 NCAA season, a contract allowing the continuance of cigarette advertising during NCAA events on ABC had already been signed. Senators Robert Kennedy and Warren Magnuson and the American Cancer Society requested that the NCAA ban cigarette advertising from college football. Kennedy argued that removing the advertising from college football would set a good example for young Americans. The American Cancer Society said that the NCAA would "fight this scourge" by removing the cigarette advertising. Marcus Plant joined Byers in an attempt to have the cigarette advertisements removed. Plant, a law professor, spoke so strongly on the issue that R.J. Reynolds voluntarily discontinued its sponsorship of NCAA football. However, this move angered the ABC executives who responded by campaigning to reauthorize beer advertising to make up for the lost revenue.[97]

The debate on whether cigarette advertising should be permitted during college athletic events helped to spark an even larger discussion. Congress was now deciding whether cigarette advertising should be allowed on broadcast media at all. In the course of their lobbying for tobacco interests, the broadcasters had put forth the argument that they were already monitoring and regulating cigarette advertising through the National Association of Advertisers Review Board. By using the code, the industry was maintaining a continuing review of cigarette advertising on the radio and television. However, in mid–June, Representative Brock Adams (Democrat, Washington), revealed evidence to the contrary. Warren Barren, the former manager of the Code Authority's New York office, told the House Committee investigating the matter that, as early as 1966, evidence existed that the guidelines were being violated. A confidential study by the Code Authority found that a large portion of broadcast advertising portrayed smoking as attractive and socially acceptable to young people, in violation of its own guidelines. However, the board ignored the study. Following an April 1968 meeting of National Association of Broadcasters (NAB), a review of cigarette commercials was virtually abandoned. Stockton Helffrich, the Code Authority director, denied accusations that the NAB was negligent in enforcing its cigarette advertising guidelines.[98]

A delegation of broadcasters visited Senator Magnuson in the summer of 1968 proposing a phase-out of advertising for cigarette brands with high nicotine content. After Senator Robert Kennedy's death on June 6, 1968, Senator Magnuson took Kennedy's place leading the fight against cigarette commercials targeting youth. A network of policy-makers in the Washington offices of NBC created the proposal with the idea that commercials for low-tar-and-nicotine cigarettes would be less controversial. Broadcast revenues also stood a chance with this proposal.[99]

The tobacco industry was rather surprised by the phase-out plan from the broadcasters. Although Senator Magnuson rejected the broadcaster's idea, the proposal opened the door for further concessions in secret talks that exploited the uneasy broadcast-tobacco alliance. On July 8, 1968, the National Association of Broadcasters announced a plan to start to phase out broadcast cigarette advertising over a period of three and a half years, starting January

1, 1970. In response, the angered tobacco industry promised to remove all broadcast advertising by September 1970, if the broadcasters would release them from their contracts.[100]

The broadcasters were aggrieved by this suggestion, having just lobbied for the House bill in favor of the tobacco industry. The industry stood to lose $200 million in advertising revenue to other media. The broadcasters decided not to release the tobacco industry from its contracts. Dr. Frank Stanton, the president of CBS, stated,

> If the public interest should require legislation in this area, should not the legislation deal with the problem as a whole and not direct its restraints only against the television and radio media? To put it another way, if the product is considered sufficiently dangerous to ban it from one form of advertising, should it not be outlawed entirely?[101]

The United States government came to a consensus in advocating the removal of cigarette advertising. On December 5, 1968, the Senate Commerce Committee voted out a bill removing cigarette commercials from the air starting midnight January 1, 1971. The bill was signed by President Richard M. Nixon on April 1, 1970. The case of cigarette brands advertising to youth during the NCAA events was instrumental in this decision. In 1970, Congress banned television advertising of cigarettes effective January 2, 1971. This was the chosen date because of the cigarette advertisers' sponsorship of college bowl games on New Year's Day. Congress did not want to intensify the tobacco industry's anger by prohibiting their participation in the college bowl games. The NCAA television committee voted 6–4 to allow cigarette advertising in the fall of 1970. The committee also voted to lift restrictions on beer advertising during broadcasts of college games to recoup the lost revenue from the cigarette accounts.[102]

The End of Cigarette Advertising and Youth?

Although the tobacco industry suffered a major defeat when cigarette advertising was removed from NCAA broadcast and print venues and banned from the airwaves, the cigarette manufacturers had other promotional methods at their disposal. Cigarette brands could still advertise in a variety of print and outdoor media to reach the younger mass market. And, cigarette brands still retained some event and venue sponsorships. For instance, the Tobacco Bowl was played until 1983. Cigarette companies, such as R.J. Reynolds, sponsored scoreboards during bowl games, such as the Hula Bowl, until the late 1970s. Even after stadium signage was banned during college sports, many venues simply left the signs unlit during college games. Tobacco industry documents indicate that the signs were designed specifically to be readable even when they were not lit.[103]

Although removing cigarette commercials from the airwaves and from the game programs did not eliminate all youth exposure to cigarette advertising, it did reduce the cigarette brands' college presence and association with athletics. And, collegiate athletics and the NCAA had an important role to play in the final elimination of cigarettes from the most prominent media at college games as well as radio and television.

PART III

CONCLUSION

11

Cigarette Advertising Themes
and Regulations
Spanning Five Decades

One of the primary contributions research on cigarette advertising is providing is information regarding how the tobacco industry targeted young adults in the absence of effective government regulation. Without regulations, cigarette smoking became an important element of collegiate culture from the 1920s to the 1960s. By promoting smoking in venues such as student newspapers, football programs, and campus broadcast stations, the tobacco industry helped persuade college students across the United States that smoking was a socially desirable habit and that smoking would help them adapt to collegiate life and to adult life after graduation.

The purpose of this last section is to discuss some of the most frequent advertising themes that appeared in campus newspapers and to demonstrate how governmental intervention through the FTC influenced the various advertising approaches that the tobacco industry used to attract new smokers. The themes discussed in this chapter were identified by examining the cigarette advertisements published in a variety of college and university newspapers from 1920 to 1963.

Popular Cigarette Advertising Themes on Campus

From the early 1920s when advertising campaigns began appearing in student newspapers and other student media to the early 1960s when the campaigns ended, certain themes were popular in advertising campaigns. These advertising themes were inductively grouped into several categories that emerged from the study of cigarette advertising in college newspapers. These categories include "Matchmakers," marketing cigarettes as a way to make a connection with the opposite sex, "Career Advisors," selling cigarettes by associating smoking with career success, "Study Buddies," suggesting that smoking enhances scholastic performance, "Smoking and Health," promoting the health benefits or physiological consequences of smoking a specific brand, "Advertorials and Cartoons," creating a cigarette advertisement that entertained students by mimicking editorial content, or "Promotional Advertising," encouraging students to tune into tobacco-sponsored broadcast programming.

CAREER ADVISORS

From the beginning of cigarette marketing, the tobacco industry positioned cigarettes as a way to achieve success in life. At the start of the industrialization of cigarette manufacturing, Buck Duke realized that upward mobility was an important part of the American psyche. He capitalized upon this facet of American culture by associating cigarettes with sophistication and success.[1]

Both Chesterfield and Camel often featured professional-looking men smoking their brands during the early 1930s.[2] However, Chesterfield was the first brand to directly associate smoking with career success in its advertisements. A headline published in 1933 reads, "I'm working and Smoking overtime—hence a *Milder Cigarette*." From the leather-bound books in the background and his professional attire, the man in the image appears to be a young lawyer. The man provides his endorsement for Chesterfield by stating, "When I work hard, I usually smoke more; and when I smoke more I usually work harder—and that's why I want a cigarette that is milder." Therefore, the man suggests that smoking Chesterfield is going to help him in his work by keeping him alert.

During the 1934–1935 academic year, Camel ran advertisements that made the most direct connection between career success and smoking. The advertisements featured men and women from a variety of career and social backgrounds providing their endorsement for Camel. In addition to featuring men in various careers, the campaign also features women in a variety of nontraditional career paths such as being a "Horsewoman" or a "Girl Explorer." Careers mentioned in the campaign include engineer, transport pilot, reporter, trans–Pacific flyer, explorer, cameraman, and rancher. Although the individuals are involved in a variety of different vocations, they all attest to the fact that they "get a Lift with a Camel."

Because of World War II, the use of the career advisor approach continued to be popular. During the war, Chesterfield's campaigns gave a tribute to "The Workers of America" and their contributions. For instance, the text in one such advertisement reads,

> ALL OVER THE WORLD—America's 900,000 aviation workers combine their skill and experience to satisfy today's demand for war necessities. Thanks to our airplane makers, ground crews and pilots like Capt. Haakon Gulbranson (shown here), of Pan American airways, needed supplies are flown to our fighting men all over the world.[3]

On the other hand, if joining the military is considered a vocation, cigarette marketers have advice to give their audience relating to getting ahead in the armed forces. For instance, the advertisements give slang terms used in the various branches of the military and testimonials from servicemen.

During the early 1950s, the popularity of the career advisor approach waned in favor of other creative appeals. However, from the mid- and late 1950s to the early 1960s the Career Advisor approach returned. The reason for the return of this approach is likely the fierce competition of filter wars. The brands that used this approach were the older non-filter brands, Camel and Chesterfield. In addition to using business tycoons, Camel also connected its brand to stardom. In its 1953–1954 campaign, Camel provided stories of "How the Stars Got Started." In this series of advertisements, Hollywood stars would provide endorsements for the brand as well of their story of breaking into the movie business. This approach encourages the reader to connect the brand with becoming famous. In the 1956–1960 Camel campaign, the headline read, "HAVE A REAL CIGARETTE...have a Camel!"[4] In a

Advertisement for Camel using a career advisor theme featured in the University of Tennessee football programs for the 1933 football season, September 30, 1933 (courtesy University of Tennessee Libraries, Knoxville, Special Collections).

1956 advertisement, Murray Golub, a civil engineer on the Connecticut Turnpike, says, "I want a real cigarette—one I can taste. That's why I'm a Camel smoker and have been ever since college."[5] Chesterfield had a similar campaign; however, instead of featuring a testimonial, the advertisement gave the forecast for particular lucrative careers. For example, an advertisement featuring a uranium geologist includes text that mimics a job posting. The advertisement's headline reads, "New Careers for Men of America: Uranium Geologist." The body copy describes the career path more specifically:

Exciting opportunities are opening up in the hunt for more uranium. Known for reserves of ore, 75 million tons will be used up in 10 years. Wanted: more geologists.[6]

It seems that the Career Advisor theme was a powerful persuasive approach for cigarette marketers wanting to target a college audience. Most students attending college are interested in learning skills that can be applied to a future career. This approach seemed to be targeting college-aged men as it featured men almost exclusively. In addition, during the late 1950s and 1960s the advertisements were for non-filtered brands that positioned them as the more masculine cigarettes. The Career Advisor theme seems to combine a social strategy with referent tactics. The advertisements present cigarette smoking as a way to break into the career world that students are aspiring to join. The advertisements also present individuals that students hope to emulate when they graduate.

MATCHMAKERS

The theme of dating and relationships with the opposite sex is one of the most popular in cigarette advertisements appearing in student media. Because there was some question about the social acceptability of women smoking before 1930, most of the advertisements that used a dating context focused on women approving of their husband's or boyfriend's smoking habit. However, once smoking became acceptable for both sexes, advertisements promoted cigarette smoking as a way to connect with the opposite sex.

Advertisements began featuring cigarette smoking as a way to break the ice with a member of the opposite sex in the early 1930s. Although it might have been suggested that men and women might smoke together in the 1920s, advertisements first began to feature couples smoking during the 1930–1931 academic year. In a Chesterfield advertisement that ran in 1932, the headline reads, "They Click with Me, too—." The image shows a couple sharing a pack of cigarettes. The text follows,

THE young man is saying the reason he smokes Chesterfields is because they satisfy. The young lady agrees with him. She says, "They click with me, too. I'm not what you would call a heavy smoker. But even I can tell that they are milder."[7]

The advertisement seems to reflect the sentiment of the time. It was socially acceptable for women to smoke. But, women were not to be heavy smokers. During 1935, Lucky Strike ran a similar campaign. The headline reads, "'Remember how I brought you two together.' I'm your best friend. I am your Lucky Strike."[8] The image features a couple sharing a pack of Luckies.

The Matchmaker approach virtually disappeared from campus papers during the 1940s when advertising focused on the war effort. However, the theme reappeared in 1954 during the filter wars. It seems that the filter wars were an impetus for cigarette brands to either develop new strategies or return to previous strategies that had been successful in the past.

Winston, a filtered cigarette, was the first brand to resume this strategy. In an advertisement that ran in 1955, the headline reads, "YOU'LL BOTH GO FOR THIS CIGARETTE! Get together on Winston." The image features a young man and woman smoking together. Like Winston, Tareyton also used a matchmaking approach and featured a young man and woman smoking together.

As the filtered cigarettes entered the college football scene, they soon integrated the cigarette filter into the college dating scene at games during the late 1950s. The 1959 Winston campaigns used the classic slogan, "It's what's up front that counts" while featuring a college couple enjoying a smoke at a football game. The image featured a woman dressed for a game, wearing a fur and chrysanthemum. The man is wearing a felt jacket. The couple is seated on a blanket and appears to be enjoying a fall afternoon while watching a game. Like Winston, Salem also featured young couples in romantic settings smoking filtered fresh menthol cigarettes in football programs. However, unlike the Winston advertisements, Salem used a more generic natural setting instead of a college campus for its football advertising campaigns.

The matchmaking approach was also popular among the non-filtered brands. For instance, Camel also advertised using a dating theme. The text reads, "When classes are through, And your girl's next to you, Here's a good thing to do—have a CAMEL!" In 1955, Chesterfield also ran advertisements that used a dating theme.

Using the Matchmaker approach to advertising demonstrated how smoking could serve a social need. Many young people are interested in dating and meeting people of the opposite sex. Cigarette manufacturers demonstrated how their product could help facilitate conversation with new people. The Matchmaker theme employed a social strategy and positions cigarettes as a way to relieve the anxiety associated with communicating with members of the opposite sex. In addition, the advertisements used a referent tactic by showing couples that students either relate to or to emulate.

CAMPUS CIGARETTE

Many cigarette brands worked to position themselves as the most popular brand among college students. These advertisements targeted college students directly by mentioning their particular school or other colleges and universities by name.

In the 1920s, Old Gold was the first cigarette brand to directly target college students. The campaign headline reads, "AT LEADING COLLEGES...*This is an Old Gold year.*" Tobacconists that served local college students provided their observations. The local tobacconist that served Princeton students, Skirm's Smoke Shop, 68 Nassau Street, Princeton, New Jersey, was quoted in an ad printed in *The Princetonian*. Perhaps not coincidentally, he was quoted exactly the same as the tobacconist at Gray Piper Drug Co. in Knoxville, Tennessee:

> The growth of OLD GOLD Cigarettes' popularity here has been amazing to me, but what interests me most is the way students stick to the brand after they start smoking it. OLD GOLD smokers don't switch.[9]

However, use of the collegiate theme lost popularity after 1928 and did not reappear in most student papers until the 1950s when it was one of the most popular advertising approaches. Lucky Strike used the collegiate approach consistently from 1950 to 1962. Lucky Strike regularly mentioned specific colleges and universities by name and claimed to be the most popular cigarette among students. Lucky Strike based its brands' claims on surveys that sampled 30,000 college students. Chesterfield also claimed to be the most popular cigarette at a variety of college campuses that included Rice,[10] Northwestern,[11] Princeton,[12] Cornell,[13] University of Virginia,[14] and M.I.T.[15] Like the Old Gold ads, the advertisement asked local tobacconists to certify that Chesterfield was the most popular brand. In 1953, Chesterfield claimed to be the "Choice of Young America for the *Fifth* Straight Year." The copy continued by stating that Chesterfield was the best selling cigarette at America's colleges and universities.[16] Chesterfield used this same approach combined with the "Choice of Young America" slogan in its football centerfold roster in the early 1950s.

In addition to making claims about being the most popular cigarette on campus, various cigarette brands sponsored contests to recruit college smokers. Lucky Strike sponsored campus contests that included jingles, word puzzles called "Sticklers," and picture puzzles called "Droodles." In addition to winning a $25 prize, both students and their universities would be mentioned in Lucky Strike advertisements. L&M, Oasis, and Chesterfield, the Liggett & Myers cigarette brands, sponsored a contest between popular college football rivals such as Tennessee and Kentucky,[17] Iowa and Notre Dame,[18] and Minnesota and Wisconsin[19] to see which school could collect more cigarette packs. Viceroy also sponsored a contest that centered on school spirit and college football. In the fall of 1961, Viceroy sponsored a contest where students were challenged to select the winning teams and scores for select football games. The winner would win a cash prize and would have his or her picture featured in a Viceroy advertisement. Therefore, the contests published in the campus paper often were integrated with football game promotions.

Associating particular cigarette brands with school spirit on campus was a popular advertising theme during the 1950s and early 1960s. Sponsoring a contest or mentioning specific colleges and universities by name was a way to get students interested in smoking. In addition, promoting brands based on their popularity on certain college and university campuses reinforced the idea that cigarette smoking is a desirable habit among students. Like the Career Advisor theme, these campaigns combined a social strategy with a referent appeal. However, these advertisements focused more intently on the present. Instead of considering the careers students wanted to pursue in the future and the social circles that they hope to join, the advertisements focused on fitting in with their peers and being a socially desirable member of the campus community.

STUDY BUDDIES

Because college campuses are academic institutions, the primary target audience for cigarette advertisers was the student population. Students, by their very nature, were concerned about their academic performance on exams and written assignments. A good way to appeal to the student population is to make the claim that cigarette smoking enhances academic performance. The primary way that cigarette advertisements claimed to enhance academic performance was by heightening mental acuity and alertness. R.J. Reynolds' Camel brand used this particular tactic regularly from the 1934–1935 to the 1937–1938 academic year. The advertisements featured male students' testimonials. The headline for the campaign reads, "GET A LIFT WITH A CAMEL!" The campaign featured a variety of students such as Lawrence Alfred Brewer studying history,[20] Alfred Archer specializing in agriculture,[21] and

James Casey majoring in business.[22] Each student provided his endorsement. One student testimonial by Charles Stephes, a pre-med student, states,

> I've followed the recent scientific investigations that confirm Camel's "energizing effect." But I already knew from my own personal experience that Camels lift up my energy and enable me to tackle my next assignment with renewed vigor. It has definitely been established that Camels are a milder cigarette.[23]

In addition to offering their endorsements as fellow students, the men continued by providing scientific information that relates to the benefits of smoking.

Students continued to offer their testimonials during 1937. However, as time passed the students provided more ambiguous endorsements that offered less information about them as individuals. For instance students endorsed smoking "For Digestion's Sake" and "To Avoid Mental Strain."[24] Arthur H. Waldo Jr.'s testimonial reads,

> "I GET MORE ENJOYMENT FROM CAMELS" says *Arthur H. Waldo Jr.* College Class of '38. "I've found that Camels help offset the strain of long hours of study. Working out a tough assignment often can make me feel tense inside. So at mealtime, you'll see me enjoying my Camels." Yes, Camels speed up digestive fluids—increase alkalinity.[25]

The Study Buddy approach to advertising cigarettes was particularly popular with Camel cigarettes during the 1930s. However, this creative theme disappeared after the 1930s—probably to avoid FTC sanctions. The Study Buddy theme used a rational strategy by persuading students that smoking tobacco would enhance academic performance. This rational strategy was combined with referent tactics. The campaigns showed successful students attributing their academic achievements to smoking cigarettes.

SMOKING AND HEALTH

Although the smoking and health controversy did not become a public concern until the 1950s, many cigarette advertisements mentioned health-related topics in their advertisements before the dangers of smoking became well known. Before the 1950s, cigarette advertisements claimed that certain brands did not cause throat irritation or coughing, aided digestion, calmed smokers' nerves, and did not influence athletic performance. Once health and smoking issues began to cause concerns about smoking, health claims centered on filters and the quality of particular brands of cigarettes.

During the 1920s, Old Gold was the only cigarette advertiser making health-related claims. In its campaigns that ran from 1926 to 1929, Old Gold used its famous slogan "not a cough in the carload." In addition, many of its advertisements mentioned coughing and throat irritation and prescribed Old Gold as a solution to these undesirable consequences of smoking. In many of the advertisements, someone has consistent problems with coughing and their cough disrupts a particular situation, such as a photo shoot. A friend or relative suggests Old Golds as a coughing remedy.

During the 1931–1932 academic year, Lucky Strike began to make health-related claims regarding cigarette smoking. The first health-related campaign that Lucky Strike ran asked the question, "DO YOU INHALE?" The text reassured the reader by stating, "More than 20,000 physicians, after Luckies had been furnished them for tests, basing their opinion on their smoking experience, stated that Luckies are less irritating to the throat than other cigarettes."

Toward the end of the decade, Lucky Strike used celebrities to attest to the healthfulness of their cigarette. In a 1937 advertisement, actor Cary Grant says, "A light smoke rates aces high with my throat." The advertisement continues by stating, "A Light Smoke 'It's Toasted'— Your Throat Protection AGAINST IRRITATION—AGAINST COUGH."[26]

Like Lucky Strike, Camel also created advertisements that mentioned the physiological effects of smoking. However, instead of mentioning the side effects that smoking Camels does not cause, the brand focused on the positive effects of smoking. For example, Camel used athletes, such as professional golfers Densmore Shute, Tommy Armour, and Gene Sarazen, as well as students to attest that smoking soothed their nerves. Likewise, Camel used the testimonials from athletes such as New York Giants pitcher Carl Hubbell and tennis champion George M. Lott Jr. to attest that smoking does not impede athletic performance because "THEY DON'T GET YOUR WIND." In addition to not impeding athletic performance, Camel used the testimonials of students and professionals to claim that smoking was beneficial to digestion.

During the 1940s, most advertisements connected cigarette smoking with patriotism. However, Camel continued to mention the physiological benefits of smoking Camel. In addition to mentioning the health benefits of the brand, Camel also advertised the fact that it contained 28 percent less nicotine than other leading brands. However, the advertisements failed to mention why lower nicotine content is beneficial for smokers. To further Camel's health claims, it used athletes such as Ralph Flanagan to promote the brand. Camel also claimed that smoking Camel did not affect the "T-Zone." The "T-Zone" was comprised of the smoker's nose, mouth, and throat. Camel encouraged smokers to give its brand a 30-day test to prove the brand's mildness. Toward the end of the decade, Old Gold also made some claims that related to the healthfulness of smoking. This simple advertisement emphasizes the fact that the makers of Old Gold are tobacco men and that the only thing that they attest about their product is that it is made for enjoyment. This advertisement also seems to be an effort on the part of Lorillard Tobacco Company to dismiss health concerns about smoking. Although this advertisement does not directly address health issues, it suggests that health-related concerns are not important. Instead, the tobacco's quality and enjoyment should be the smoker's concern.

During the early to mid–1950s, health claims regarding cigarette smoking increased in collegiate campaigns. This increase was due to published reports that linked smoking to health problems and the introduction of filtered brands to help eliminate public fears about smoking. However, FTC regulations limited any health-related claims and the mention of a particular filter effectiveness, tar content or nicotine content after the mid–1950s. Therefore, health related claims disappeared from student papers after 1958.

Both filtered and non-filtered brands made health claims during the 1950s. Non-filtered brands such as Camel and Chesterfield promoted the healthfulness of their cigarette based on the quality of their tobacco. Other unfiltered brands such as Lucky Strike, Old Gold, and Pall Mall avoided health related advertising during the 1950s. Filtered brands such as Tareyton, L&M, Viceroy, and Winston made claims about the effectiveness of their filters. As in the 1940s, Camel continued to advertise that its cigarettes had no effect on the smoker's "T-Zone" and that smokers should give Camel a 30-day test for "mildness." Like Camel, Chesterfield claimed that the nose, throat and sinuses are not affected by smoking their brand. In addition, Chesterfield claimed that its high-quality cigarettes had low nicotine content. On the other hand, filtered brands such as Viceroy and L&M centered on the quality and effectiveness of the filter. For instance, L&M referred to its filter as a miracle tip and Viceroy stated that its filter was made from the same pure and natural materials found in fruit.

Whether promoting the physiological benefits of smoking or reassuring smokers about the healthfulness of smoking, the relationship between smoking and health was a frequent topic in cigarette advertising on campus. Referring to the physiological or health related aspects of cigarette is a rational approach to advertising. This rational strategy uses product information as a means of persuading students that smoking is healthful or has desirable physiological results.

ADVERTORIALS AND CARTOONS

In order to entice their audience to read their advertisements, cigarettes brands mimicked editorial formats. Cigarette advertisements used comic strips, advice columns, and celebrity columnists to attract readers. This advertorial approach was almost always combined with humor. However, on a few occasions it was combined with novel or surprising information. These advertorials usually appeared in serials that ran for more than one academic year. The Max Shulman column, sponsored by Phillip Morris and Marlboro, was the longest running advertorial in most major campus newspapers including *The Orange and White*,[27] *The Minnesota Daily*,[28] *The Daily Iowan*,[29] *The Ram*,[30] *The Spectrum*,[31] *The Tech*,[32] *The Aztec*,[33] and *The Princetonian*.[34] Phillip Morris sponsored the column from 1953 to 1963. After 1963, when cigarette advertising was removed, Burma Shave and other non-tobacco sponsors continued the column.

The comic strip was the first advertorial format used by tobacco advertisers. The first comic strip printed in *The Orange and White* was printed on October 1, 1927. The sponsor was Old Gold. The comic strip was, "Somebody Is Always Taking The Joy Out of Life," by Briggs. The comic strip ran during the 1927–1928 and 1928–1929 academic years. However, the title and format of the cartoon frequently changed. During the 1929–1930 academic year, Old Gold used John Held, Jr. to create a comic in linoleum cuts that mimicked his famous "Gay Nineties" feature that poked gentle fun at the previous generation. Old Gold's use of Held's creative abilities helped the brand resonate with the college student audience during the 1920s. Old Gold discontinued the comic approach until the 1934–1935 academic year when it began the "AT TRYING TIMES...TRY A *Smooth* OLD GOLD" comic campaign. This serial cartoon positioned smoking Old Golds as a "smooth" way to get out of awkward situations such as being "Pawed by a Pudgy Wudgy"[35] or "Dished by a Dilemma."[36] In addition to providing a social use for smoking, the cartoons were intended to be humorous.

Camel began to use a comic strip during the 1932–1933 academic year in its "It's Fun to be Fooled..." series. In this series Camel revealed the secrets behind popular magic tricks. The point of the cartoon was to point out that it's fun to be fooled during a magic show but not when choosing a cigarette. Although it was popular during the 1930s, the comic approach did not return to most student papers until the 1950s, when Camel introduced the "Campus Interviews on Cigarettes Tests." This campaign featured a series of cartoons that personified animals describing their individual smoking habits. For instance, in cartoon number 27, "The Lynx" asks, "What's par for the course?" The text reads,

This sporty student really teed off on a long tirade when he found himself stymied on the "single puff" and "one sniff" cigarette tests. "They're strictly for the birdies said he."[37]

The Lynx, and other characters in the series, continue by endorsing the "30-day Camel mildness test." The serial comic ran in all major campus papers during the 1950–1951 and 1951–1952 academic years. The following academic year Camel advertised with the "...But only Time will Tell" comic. The point of the cartoon was to try to persuade students that, like everything else, you can tell if you like smoking only after you have given the habit a chance. For instance the text of one advertisement reads,

ONLY TIME WILL TELL about a football team! And only time will tell about a cigarette! Take your time ... make the sensible 30-day Camel mildness test. See how Camels suit you as your steady smoke![38]

Camel resumed the serial comic approach during the 1958–1959 academic year. This serial cartoon used the slogan "Have a *real* cigarette—have a CAMEL." This series of cartoons focused on the importance of having a real cigarette. And, Camel is, of course, a real cigarette. The text adjacent a cartoon reads,

More buxom blondes with shipwrecked sailors insist on Camels than any other cigarette today. It stands to reason. The best tobacco makes the best smoke. The Camel blend of costly tobaccos has never been equaled for rich flavor and easygoing mildness. No wonder Camel is the No. 1 cigarette of all.[39]

Although Camel used the cartoon approach more than any other brand, Winston, Pall Mall, and Lucky Strike also used comics to advertise their brands. During the 1958–1959 academic year, Winston used cartoons to create a comic satire of popular literary works such as Arthurian legends and *Moby-Dick*. In each comic, Winston cigarettes allow the hero to save the day. Each cartoon ends with the familiar slogan, "Winston tastes good! Like a Cigarette Should!" Pall Mall also ran a cartoon series called "The Girl Watchers Guide." This comic was a satirical guide for young men looking for a mate. The cartoon series ran during the 1961–1962 and 1962–1963 academic years. Lucky Strike's "Lucky Puffers" comic ran during the 1961–1962 academic year. This humorous column personified cigarettes and satirized campus life.

Although cartoons and comics are a popular way to mimic editorial content, student newspapers also published other forms of advertorials. For example, the popular Max Shulman wrote, "On Campus," a column where the humorist provided humorous stories and observations relating to college and university life. Although the column often was illustrated with a cartoon, the image was a subordinate feature of the advertorial. In addition, Kool's advertising campaign during the 1959–1960 academic year used a crossword puzzle format.[40] The "Kool Krosswords" used a popular word game to mimic editorial content. In addition to columns and crosswords, various cigarette brands used quizzes to engage with the college market. For instance, Viceroy created a quiz that tested whether college smokers think for themselves. The tagline for the ad stated, "The man who thinks for himself knows only Viceroy has a thinking man's filter and a smoking man's taste."[41]

From the 1920s to the 1960s, advertorials were popular in a variety of forms. Using the same format as editorial content was a popular way for cigarette advertisers to get students interested in their advertising and entice them to try their product. Advertorials can include a variety of promotional tactics. Most of the cartoons and advertorials use humor to sell their brand. Other cartoons present product information or other novel kinds of facts to advertise the product.

PROMOTIONAL ADVERTISING

In addition to purchasing advertising space, cigarette manufacturers also sponsored radio and television programming and sports broadcasts. Many cigarette advertisers used their advertising space in print media, especially newspapers, to promote their product and their programs. Often, sponsoring programs also involved promoting the stars of these broadcasts.

The first advertisements that promoted cigarette-sponsored radio programming appeared in *The Orange and White* in 1929. The *Paul Whiteman Radio Hour* was promoted in a February 28, 1929, advertisement for Old Gold. The text reads,

> On your radio...OLD GOLD PAUL WHITEMAN HOUR...Paul Whiteman, King of Jazz, and his complete orchestra, broadcasts the Old Gold Hour every Tuesday ... from 9 to 10 p.m. Eastern Standard Time, over entire network of Columbia Broadcasting System.

Although the advertisement promotes the broadcast, it is subordinate to the image, the headlines, and main body text. The promotions were printed in Old Gold's advertisements from February to October of 1929. Like Old Gold, Lucky Strike included a promotion for *The Lucky Strike Dance Orchestra* in its 1931–1932 advertising campaign. Again, the promotional text was subordinate to the other text and images in the advertisements. Chesterfield gave one of its first promotional plugs for its radio shows in a February 19, 1932 advertisement. The promotional text reads,

> CHESTERFIELD'S RADIO PROGRAM—Nat Shilkret's Orchestra and Alex Gray, well-known soloist, will entertain you over the Columbia Coast-to-Coast Network, every night, except Sunday, at 10:30 E.S.T.

Like the promotional spots in the other advertisements, the text relating to the radio programming is the smallest in the advertisement and has nothing to do with the rest of the cigarette advertisement.

However, by the end of 1932, Chesterfield was frequently using its entire advertising space in campus papers to promote its radio programs, such as an advertisement featuring the Boswell Sisters. In fact, this advertisement was more focused on the sponsored broadcasting than Chesterfield cigarettes. Chesterfield continued to run advertisements that focused almost exclusively on its programming for the remainder of the 1931–1932 academic year. However, the following academic year, Chesterfield ran only one promotional advertisement for Arthur Tracy in campus papers. The rest of the advertisements only mentioned Chesterfield's programming in subtext. On May 7, 1937, Chesterfield printed a promotional advertisement that invited readers to dance and sing with featured artists Hal Kemp and Kay Thompson on their program at 6:30 on Fridays on CBS. Chesterfield's final promotional advertisement before the outbreak of the Second World War featured Glenn Miller. The advertisement was printed January 10, 1940.

Starting in April 1933, Camel ran the first promotional advertisements for its *All-Star Camel Caravan*. The full-page advertisement focused more on the programming schedule and the stars, such as singers Annette Hanshaw and Walter O'Keefe, than Camel cigarettes.

However, Camel did not run another promotional advertisement for the *Camel Caravan* until October 1935. Again the advertisement focused more on the programming schedule and the performers, such as Walter O'Keefe, Deane Janis, Ted Husing and Glen Gray, than the Camel brand itself. In 1937, Camel introduced *Jack Oakie's College*. The Camel-sponsored radio program aired every Tuesday night. The comic variety show presented college life as Jack Oakie thought it should be. Jack Oakie was an actor and comedian who was dubbed "The World's Oldest Freshman" because he was rather old for the collegiate roles he was frequently asked to play, including roles in *College Humor* (1933), *College Rhythm* (1934) and *Collegiate* (1935). In the movie *Rise and Shine* (1941), the 38-year-old was asked to play an 18-year-old senior.[42] *Jack Oakie's College* also featured performances from Benny Goodman's Swing Band and George Stoll's Orchestra. Promoting Camel cigarettes among college students was an integral part of the program. The following is a vignette from the May 11, 1937, broadcast of *Jack Oakie's College*:

> GOODWIN:
> Now back to the present, ladies and gentlemen...
> Here's a scene at the Victor Hugo Restaurant, Beverly Hills. One of the most famous restaurants in the world. A charming young couple has just sat down at a table in the Palm Garden.
> (FADE IN MUSIC)
> MAN:
> Well, Janet, we've certainly seen a lot today—Malibu Beach this morning—lunch at the Brown Derby, watching a picture being shot in the afternoon—and ...
> GIRL:
> And now—dinner at one of the finest restaurants in the world!
> MAN:
> Yes. Well, to be practical, here's the menu! What appeals to you?
> GIRL:
> U-m-m, let's see. Oh—this sounds good. Jumbo squab with broccoli and candied sweet potatoes.
> MAN:
> That's quite an order after, an exciting day!
> GIRL:
> Don't worry, I'll enjoy every bit of it! Oh! Have we plenty of CAMELS?
> MAN:
> Of course. For "digestion's sake!"
> GIRL:
> You're right! It's grand to enjoy CAMELS. They give you such a delightful sense of well-being!
> GOODWIN:
> And, it's not surprising that CAMELS—the cigarette that's made from costlier tobaccos—appear on so many tables in the Victor Hugo. Here's what Hugo himself says: QUOTE. Our patrons know fine tobacco as well as fine food. CAMEL Cigarettes are the overwhelming favorite here. END QUOTE. "For digestion's sake—smoke CAMELS" is a good idea to remember during and after every meal.[43]

In addition to featuring a number of vignettes and sketches, this particular program featured actress and singer Judy Garland and musician Benny Goodman.

Camel also promoted Benny Goodman's Great Swing Band's performance on the *Camel Caravan* in April 1938. Camel began promotional advertising for Goodman's Tuesday night program in January 1939. The program gained popularity when it capitalized on young people's cravings for swing music. The swing music craze spanned from the mid–1930s to 1950. In addition to Goodman's Tuesday night performances, the advertisement introduced Eddie Cantor's Monday evening comedy act. However, in 1940 all promotional advertisements in student media stopped because of the war. However, the radio program was broadcast on NBC radio for more than 20 years, spanning from 1933 to 1954.

In 1947, cigarette-sponsored promotional advertising resumed in college newspapers. Phillip Morris along with its famous bellhop promoted *Phillip Morris Night with Horace Height*. The NBC radio program was promoted as "The Newest Most Thrilling Hunt in America Including Top Stars from the Colleges." Several advertisements for *Phillip Morris Night with Horace Height* were printed during the 1947–1948 academic year. Chesterfield began promoting the *Chesterfield Supper Club* in November 1948. The NBC radio program featured musicians Perry Como, Jo Stafford, and Peggy Lee.

In 1950, the promotional advertising for cigarette-sponsored radio programming came to an end. However, in 1952, Phillip Morris began running promotional advertisements for its new television program, *I Love Lucy*. This series of advertisements comprised the last promotions for cigarette-sponsored programming in campus newspapers.

Although cigarette advertisements promoting broadcast programming were far from the most frequent advertisements in campus newspapers, it is important to mention them because they demonstrate how various cigarette brands used an integrated marketing strategy to promote cigarette smoking among college and university students. Many of these programs use a social strategy by demonstrating the popularity of the brand among students. Some combine a social strategy with celebrity tactics by associating their product with celebrities. These advertisements demonstrate how broadcast and print media worked together to target students. The strategies and tactics that are used in the print advertisements seem to be consistent across media.

The Use of Endorsements

A common theme found across campus media is the use of endorsement. To sell cigarette smoking to the collegiate audience, advertisements used a variety of testimonials. Cigarette brands used the "Career Advisor" theme by including the testimonials of celebrities and successful businessmen to try to persuade students that smoking would help them reach their career goals. Advertisements also used student endorsements in the study buddy approach to convince their audience that smoking was a popular habit on campus. Celebrities, athletes, and peers provided endorsements to help persuade students about the healthfulness of smoking. The promotional programming also implicitly or directly provided the endorsement of the musicians and actors who participated in the broadcasts. In addition to the use of spokespeople, cartoons or comic characters also provided product testimonials.

The use of endorsement was a powerful persuasive tool for cigarette advertisers because it works to help persuade the young audience that smoking is popular among their peer group and the social groups that they aspire to join. The advertisements communicate that cigarette smoking is both a socially acceptable and desirable habit. Cigarette smoking is also positioned as a way to create and manage social relationships. For instance, offering a stranger a cigarette is shown as a way to start social or dating relationships. It is also depicted as a way to manage uncomfortable or stressful social situations. Cigarette smoking is marketed as a tool for young people learning how to navigate the social system of the adult world that they are about to join. In this way, cigarettes, an unnecessary product, are given a useful and desirable role in American collegiate culture.

The Influence of Legislation on Advertising Appeals

Cigarette advertising was effective at persuading young adults and teenagers that cigarette smoking was an essential rite of passage for joining adult society. The Federal Trade Commission (FTC) recognized that the tobacco industry was engaging in some unethical practices to entice the college audience. Therefore, the FTC worked to limit the tools that the advertising industry could use before persuading the industry to completely remove the advertisements from student-oriented publications. One of the most intriguing aspects of studying cigarette advertising in student newspapers is that the advertisements were virtually unregulated until the early 1950s. And, the regulations of the 1950s were minimal.

In January 1930, the FTC passed some of its first cigarette advertising regulations. These related to testimonials that Lucky Strike published that were from celebrities that did not smoke. The FTC ruled that the American Tobacco Company had to stop creating advertising that included the testimonies of endorsers that never used their product. Further, the American Tobacco Company needed to identify paid testimonials.[44]

The first celebrity testimonials used in Lucky Strikes included a disclaimer that stated that the endorsement was made without monetary compensation. For instance, an advertisement featuring Jean Harlow that ran in *The Orange and White* on October 29, 1931, included the following statement.

> **Is Miss Harlow's Statement Paid For?** You may be interested in knowing that not one cent was paid to Miss Harlow to make the above statement. Miss Harlow has been a smoker of LUCKY STRIKE cigarettes for 2 years. We hope that the publicity herewith given will be as beneficial to her and to Fox and Columbia, her producers, as her endorsement of LUCKIES is to you and to us.

In addition to including Jean Harlow's endorsement, the advertisement also mentions her current films. This same advertising approach was also used in advertisements that featured actress Lorette Young,[45] aviatrix Sally Eliers,[46] actress Dorothy Mackaill,[47] actor Robert Montgomery,[48] actor Douglas Fairbanks,[49] actress Sue Carol,[50] and actress Mary Ceston.[51] Although the advertisements mentioned that the celebrity spokespeople were not compensated, both the actors and their films received publicity in the advertisements. In fact, it seemed that Lucky Strike was able to capitalize on the FTC's restriction. Actors seemed more credible when the audience was informed that they were not being paid for the testimonial. In spite of Lucky Strike's skillful management of the situation, celebrity endorsements lost popularity by the mid–1930s. However, in 1937, Lucky Strike again began advertising using celebrity testimonials. However, the testimonials were printed without any mention of whether the celebrities were compensated.

In proceedings culminating in 1950 with cease and desist orders against every major tobacco company, the FTC found virtually all cigarette advertisements had been false, misleading, and deceptive.[52] For instance, in the proceedings against R.J. Reynolds, like the previous case against Lucky Strike and American Tobacco Company, the FTC found that many of the celebrity endorsements for the Camel brand were deceptive because either the celebrities did not smoke or they did not smoke Camels exclusively.[53] The Chesterfield "Nose, Throat, and Accessory Organs Not Adversely Affected by Smoking Chesterfields" campaign was also the subject of an FTC investigation that resulted in a cease and desist order entered against Liggett & Myers Tobacco Company.[54]

In 1951, the FTC ordered the American Tobacco Company's Lucky Strike brand to abandon any claims regarding the acid levels of its cigarettes, throat irritation, and nicotine levels. Likewise, R.J. Reynolds' Camel cigarettes received a mandate that it had to stop advertising that smoking Camel brand aids digestion, calms the nerves, increases energy levels, doesn't impede athletes' "wind," and that it contains less nicotine than other brands.[55] Likewise, the FTC prohibited Phillip Morris from stating that its brand was less irritating than other brands of cigarettes.[56]

These regulations initiated a major shift in creative strategy. Before the 1950s, many of Camel's advertisements focused on the physiological effects of smoking. For instance, the brand gave you energy and calmed your nerves but it did not impede your ability to perform in athletic events or affect the "T-Zone." Therefore, many Camel advertisements in campus newspapers encouraged students to consider the effects that smoking might have on their bodies. However, after 1950, Camel changed tactics and began advertising using either stories of how celebrities and tycoons became successful or light-hearted cartoons to promote its brand. Likewise, during the late 1940s and early 1950s Chesterfield ran numerous advertisements to counteract health concerns. After the FTC regulations, Chesterfield changed its approach and advertised to students by suggesting that it was the most popular cigarette on college campuses, that it was a popular cigarette among members of the opposite sex, and that people who were successful in their careers smoked the brand. Health concerns were completely ignored in advertising for non-filtered cigarette brands.

Another set of FTC guidelines were created in 1954. The purpose of these 1954 "cigarette advertising guides" was to close the gaps in its brand-specific decrees. The guides specifically prohibited all references to "throat, larynx, lungs, nose or other parts of the body," or to "digestion, nerves or doctors." A later press release stated, "No advertising should be used which refers to either the presence or absence of any physical effect of smoking."[57] In addition, the guides banned all tar and nicotine claims unless definite scientific evidence existed to prove the claims. However, the guides permitted the advertising of pleasure and taste.[58]

Again, these guidelines changed the advertising approaches that were used in the campus paper. From the middle of the 1950s to the early 1960s, advertising for filtered brands was increasing while the advertising for the non-filtered cigarettes was gradually declining. Instead of advertising referring to the effectiveness of or benefits of various filters, the advertising began to refer more exclusively to what the filters did not do. For instance, the filters did not impede the flavor or pleasure of smoking. This change in approach probably made smoking even more appealing to the college student audience. Young people typically are not interested in the long-term health consequences that result from smoking. Instead, they are more interested how their peers will react to the habit. From the late 1950s to the early 1960s the tobacco industry created advertisements that focused almost exclusively on the pleasure and social benefits that cigarette smoking provided. During the last five years that cigarettes were advertised in campus newspapers, more cigarette advertising was printed than ever before. And, the cigarette advertising was more image-based than ever before. Thus, in some ways, the FTC increased the appeal of the filtered brands by preventing them from discussing any health-related issues.

Although the FTC regulations might have prevented an older generation from feeling a false sense of security about the healthfulness of cigarette smoking, the regulations did little to help young adults and teenagers who were the industry's primary target audience. The FTC regulations prevented the cigarette manufacturers from addressing much factual product information and forced the industry into highly successful image-based advertising campaigns that were much more appealing to young people. Not surprisingly, most students found comic strips and other humorous appeals and collegiate appeals to be much more enticing than detailed explanations of the various types of cigarette filters. The only FTC regulation that protected the college market was the 1964 Cigarette Advertising Code that prevented cigarette companies from advertising in student newspapers.

The 1964 Cigarette Advertising Code formally brought tobacco promotion in student newspapers to an end. On June 19, 1963, the Tobacco Institute decided to pull its advertising from student media. American Tobacco, R.J. Reynolds, Lorillard, and Liggett & Myers all agreed to discontinue their cigarette advertising immediately. During the meeting of the Tobacco Institute, Paul Smith of Phillip Morris said that his company had not made a decision on the question of college advertising.[59] Phillip Morris was the last cigarette advertiser to remove its cigarette promotions from campus newspapers. The code did not formally go into effect until January 1964. For instance, the final Marlboro-sponsored Max Shulman column was printed in *The Orange and White* on November 26, 1963. It was the last cigarette advertisement to be printed in the student newspaper at the University of Tennessee.

Conclusion

This book provides the reader with a glimpse into a relatively unknown world. Very little research in advertising or history makes any reference to the presence of tobacco on college and university campuses from the 1920s to the 1960s. This research provided insights into the strong presence of cigarette advertising in student publications on college and university campuses. It is hoped that this research will help reveal how and why generations of America's young adults and youth became attracted to cigarette smoking and, eventually, addicted to nicotine.

12

Promotions Targeting Young
Adults and Youth After Cigarette
Advertising Was Discontinued
at Colleges and Universities

After cigarette advertisements were removed from student publications and NCAA sporting events, the tobacco companies had to regroup. The tobacco industry was being systematically eliminated from college campuses and separated from one of its most profitable audiences. This shift would produce large changes in cigarette marketing because so much of the tobacco industry's efforts to recruit young smokers had been focused on college and university students. Instead of partnering with tobacco and its tobacco research goals, many institutions of higher education were researching how to prevent smoking among teens and young adults. In addition to discontinuing marketing research collaboration, a number of actions were being taken on campus to dissuade college students from smoking.

1. In 1962, a number of campuses prohibited the dispensing of sample cigarettes and cigarette contests on campus.
2. In 1963, some colleges and universities began to remove cigarette vending machines on campus.
3. By 1966, a variety of campuses had started health education programs related to the dangers of cigarette smoking. Colleges and universities also started engaging in more tobacco-related research activities.[1]

As a result of the advertising restrictions and the campus initiatives, most college students were well aware of the actual health risks associated with cigarette smoking by the early 1960s. And, due to these efforts, between 1962 and 1965 the number of college freshmen that smoked was steadily decreasing at a statistically significant level.[2] The tobacco industry needed to change its approach to continue to recruit new smokers.

The national attitude toward smoking was rapidly changing and causing the number of new smokers to drop and existing smokers to quit. The industry's concern was stated in the introduction of a 1969 report providing survey data on cigarette smoking trends during the 1960s. The report states,

> Current trends in consumer purchases of cigarettes make it apparent that substantial changes are occurring in the underlying cigarette smoking habits and attitudes. An understanding of these changes is essential for an evaluation of the future patterns of cigarette sales.[3]

The report continued by revealing that the cigarette market had experienced steady growth in the total domestic cigarette consumption from 1955 to 1963. However, after 1963, when the surgeon general's report was released linking cigarette smoking to adverse health consequences, the trend of growth started to reverse. With more regulations on advertising in the later 1960s, cigarette consumption overall continued to decline. [4] However, there was a increase in the number of female smokers. The sharpest increase was in the 16 to 24 age group.[5] Women were also trying their first cigarettes at an earlier age than men.[6] This was a trend that the cigarette manufacturers could use to their benefit in their future marketing efforts. However, one obstacle that faced the female market is that men often disapprove of women smoking. This trend was especially strong among men who did not smoke.[7]

A 1971 poll of college students reflected these general findings. The college poll revealed that in 1968, 52 percent of college students smoked. However, in 1971 the number dropped to 44 percent. Although the number of female smokers was on the rise, the number of college-educated female smokers was dropping. Many college men disapproved of women smoking. In 1971, 96 percent of college students felt that cigarette smoking was dangerous to one's health. Young adults and teenagers were still starting to smoke in large numbers. However, the numbers were certainly declining. In 1971, 36 percent of adults were smokers. In 1966, 42 percent of adults smoked. This reduction equaled 29 million ex-smokers.[8]

Although cigarette smoking was decreasing in popularity on campus because of the increased awareness of the health hazards associated with smoking and the reduction or elimination of cigarette advertising, students and faculty were not always supportive of smoking bans. On several occasions, both students and faculty protested cigarette bans on campus. Many schools and boards of education were pressured to permit student smoking, even in high schools.[9]

During the late 1960s and early 1970s, the tobacco industry began to turn to other markets outside of the college campus. The two major markets where the tobacco industry was working to improve its presence were the female market and the Black market. Both of these markets had room for growth. For instance, in 1965, the prevalence of smoking among women was 18 percent less than men.[10] The tobacco industry also saw opportunities to market to Blacks using the mentholated brands. Industry research showed that in the 1960s and 1970s, approximately 60 percent of Black smokers smoked menthol.[11] In addition, during the 1960s and 1970s, the Black population was growing faster than the White population and smoking at a higher rate than the White population. And, according to industry documents, the Black population was 44 percent functionally illiterate.[12] Therefore, market researchers felt that the Black population could be easily persuaded to smoke with simple out-of-home messages (billboards, subway signs, etc.) about the product.[13] To replace the college smoker market, the industry quickly turned to more vulnerable populations. This chapter will focus on the tobacco industry's advertising and marketing strategy after cigarette and tobacco marketing became increasingly restricted on campus during the late 1960s and 1970s.

THE FEMALE MARKET AND THE FEMINIST
AND FEMININE CIGARETTES

Women had been an important market for cigarette advertisers since Lucky Strike's "Reach for a Lucky Instead of a Sweet" campaign in the early 1920s. However, despite many attempts to create a women's cigarette, no cigarette designed for women had ever found success. Although the proportion of female smokers was growing, before the 1960s, the vast majority of cigarette advertising targeted men. Phillip Morris wanted to develop the first successful women's cigarette that would help grow the women's market. Virginia Slims was the first cigarette brand to find success in the female market. After Phillip Morris' success with Virginia Slims, many other manufactures began to introduce brands to the market in the late 1960s and early 1970s.

Tobacco industry research documents show that the industry was expecting growth in the women's market. From 1958 to 1973, women proved to be one of the most dynamic forces in the cigarette market. And, industry leaders expected this trend to continue into the future. The percentage of women smoking rose from 27 percent to 32 percent from 1955 to 1966. During the same period of time, the percentage of men smoking declined from 54 percent to 49 percent. From 1966 to 1969, the only increase in the men's market was among young smokers aged 16 to 24 and those over 65. However, in contrast to men, women showed growth in every age group, with the greatest growth in young smokers aged 16 to 24. Young female smokers increased by more than 20 percent.[14]

The introduction of the first women's cigarette brands in the late 1960s and early 1970s created large growth in the cigarette market. From 1958 to 1973, the percentage of women smoking rose from slightly more than one-third to nearly 40 percent of cigarette sales volume. The primary reason for this growth was the 100mm market, which was growing at a rate of three to four times of the standard 85mm category. Female smokers strongly preferred the longer and thinner 100mm cigarettes. Although the failure rate among the new women's brands was fairly high, 77 percent of the growth brands in the early 1970s were female-oriented.[15]

THE BIRTH OF VIRGINIA SLIMS

In 1968 Phillip Morris hired the Leo Burnett Agency to work a marketing strategy for a women's cigarette. The agency drew its inspiration from the idea that women saw a style feature to a slim, long cigarette. Phillip Morris drew its inspiration for the name Virginia Slims from American Tobacco Company's Silva Thins and a current brand name that they owned, Virginia Rounds. Silva Thins were the first thin cigarette on the market and Virginia Slims added the name of the state of Virginia, which has a strong association with tobacco and was the name of a tobacco executive's wife.[16] The brand launched in San Francisco in July 1968. The brand was so successful that the test market was cut short after seven weeks. The brand had achieved 3 percent market penetration in unprecedented time.[17]

One of the unique features of the Virginia Slims brand is that it was the first cigarette to be marketed with a particular consumer segment in mind. And, the body copy and concept of the brand communicated directly to this audience in a meaningful way. A 1969 memo to Milton R. Rusk, director of marketing for Phillip Morris, from Edward Grey, director of marketing research at Phillip Morris, explains that Silva Thins and Virginia Slims were developed with a particular consumer segment in mind. The memo states,

> [T]he concept for a consumer segment did precede the development of the reduced diameter cigarette ... research and creativity worked together for both Silva Thins and Virginia Slims. In both instances the usual process was reversed. Historically, the products were developed by the manufacturing people and then tested or then turned over to market to sell. In the case of the thin cigarettes, the concept of a market segment came first and then the development of the product.[18]

The Leo Burnett Agency developed the "You've come a long way baby" campaign for Virginia Slims in 1968. The campaign focused on comparing the differences between men and women in a fun way and also featured vignettes related to the women's rights movement at the turn of the 20th century. Both Leo Burnett and Phillip Morris attributed Virginia Slims' success to its brand personality resonating with young women. Virginia Slims was feminine but nonthreatening. The women featured in the advertisements were women who could make choices but still retained their femininity. Therefore, the brand was both "aspirational" and "user-friendly."[19]

Virginia Slims' early success is primarily attributed to the success of its advertising creativity. The slogan, "You've come a long way baby," resonated with the values of women during the late 1960s and 1970s and was used for many advertising campaigns over a span of nearly 20 years.[20] The advertising team from the Leo Burnett Agency that developed the slogan described its creative genius like this:

> "You've come a long way, Baby." The story was simple, and went like so: "It used to be that women had no rights. Now they have the rights. Now they have everything. You've come a long way, Baby. And now you even have a cigarette brand for your very own." It was fun, it was simple, and it was fresh. And like all good ideas, it was easy to write.[21]

According to the creative team at Leo Burnett, there were three ingredients that were needed to create a successful cigarette brand. First, there needed to be enough of a product difference to make the brand interesting. Second, the brand needs to appeal to a particular market. And, third, the appeal needs to fit that market. The personality needs to be a strong fit and in the right mood for the target audience.[22] The creative team presented the following copy for the first Virginia Slims campaign,

> "It used to be, lady, you had no rights. But now you've got a new thin cigarette all your own." And it's signed with a Queens pack and "You've come a long way, Baby." And there's the suffragette carrying her sign "No Vote, No Tax." And a *Chicago Tribune* headline: "Woman's victory needs one more step," And the copy says, "No right to vote, no right to property. No right to the wage you earned. That was back when you were laced in, hemmed in, and left to while away your time among the what-nots. That was back when you had to sneak up to the attic if you wanted a cigarette. Smoke in front of a man? Heaven forbid: You've come a long way. Now you can vote and own and earn, and, well—you've come a long way. Now you can smoke downstairs, or even out of the house if you please. And now you have a cigarette all your own. You have a right to your own cigarette."[23]

To add to the sophistication of the brand, Walter Landor, a renowned product and packaging designer, was hired to design the first Virginia Slims package. Landor's firm, Landor and Associates, consulted on the design of all of the Virginia Slims packages until 1998 when Phillip Morris decided that they wanted an updated design for the brand.[24]

Over the next 20 years, Virginia Slims showed a steady increase in market share. A review of the female cigarette market by R.J. Reynolds, a competitor, noted that Virginia Slims' success had increased the size of women's share of the cigarette market. Female smokers grew from 45 percent to 48 percent of the total population of smokers between 1970 and 1979. It was also observed that brand awareness and recall was particularly strong among young female smokers aged 18 to 34. In addition to cigarettes, sports sponsorships, such as tennis matches, and branded non-tobacco items reinforced the brand image.[25]

Advertising placement also grew significantly. Virginia Slims had one of the most extensive introductory campaigns in industry history. For instance, in 1968 it was estimated that if the measured media used in the San Francisco launch were national, it would have cost in excess of $30 million. The media included prime time television and radio spots and placement in 15 women's magazines.[26] After unprecedented success in its introductory campaign, measured media expenditures continued at a high level of $6 million in television alone in 1969 and more than $7 million in 1970.[27]

EVE: A FEMININE CIGARETTE

Because of Virginia Slims' unprecedented success, other companies began to develop women's cigarette brands. Liggett & Myers introduced Eve on May 18, 1970, in Tulsa, Oklahoma; Denver, Colorado; Columbus, Ohio; and Phoenix, Arizona.[28] The basic premise of the introduction of Eve was that cigarette smoking was unfeminine and that feminine smokers needed a more feminine cigarette.[29] The Young and Rubicon research report states,

> Since a woman is feminine to begin with, Eve cannot add to her femininity.
>
> The only thing Eve can do is prevent her from looking less feminine when she smokes a cigarette.
>
> If this further implies that a woman who smokes Eve will look less masculine (or more feminine) than a woman who smokes Lucky Strike, we shouldn't blame the advertising.
>
> This implication grows out of the product itself. And the features that make it tangibly different from other cigarettes.
>
> The tip, the shape and the package make this an obviously more feminine cigarette than a Lucky, a Pall Mall, or a Winston.[30]

Unlike Virginia Slims that aligned itself with women's liberation and feminism, Eve was designed to make smoking appear beautiful. It was a cigarette for the feminine woman. Eve spent less money on television advertising than Virginia Slims. Eve only spent $400,000 on advertising in 1970. After the television ban in January 1971, Eve mounted an extensive print campaign with the following themes that related to beauty, flowers, and femininity, "Farewell to the ugly cigarette—smoke pretty Eve,"[31] "Flowers on the outside flavor on the inside," and "Eves of the world you are beautiful."[32] Because of the brand's success, in 1972, Liggett & Myers spent two million dollars on magazine advertising for Eve.[33]

To make the act of smoking appear beautiful to its audience, Eve and its advertising agency, Young and Rubicon, planned to work with artists and the fashion industry to create a desirable and sophisticated product image. Eve was introduced with an apple shaped lighter and a matching ashtray designed to keep the used cigarettes out of sight as premiums that could be ordered. In addition, Liggett & Myers was offering prints by artists such as Van Dyck and Michelangelo who had painted famous paintings of Eve. Liggett & Myers was also working with high-end department stores such as Saks and Neiman Marcus to create Eve make-up, hairstyles, and fashion to help promote the brand. Liggett & Myers would also sponsor in store sampling of the Eve brand at department stores and art museums such as the Modern Art Museum or the Museum of Contemporary Crafts. To promote the brand among stylish women, Liggett & Myers planned to advertise in high fashion magazines such as *Vogue* and *Harper's*.[34]

In addition to making the act of smoking beautiful, Liggett & Myers wanted to design the most beautiful cigarette possible for the Eve brand. Like Virginia Slims, Eve was a long, slender 100mm cigarette; however, the packaging was less modern and more feminine. Both the cigarettes and the cigarette packaging for Eve featured an intricate floral design. John Alcorn, an up-and-coming artist, designed the cigarettes and packaging to reflect the art nouveau movement and textile designs.[35] The floral pattern on the cigarette was positioned to mask any lipstick left on the cigarette while smoking. The art nouveau floral design was reminiscent of traditional product designs from the turn of the 20th century, but it also reflected the growing popularity of the psychedelic movement of the late 1960s and early 1970s that were inspired by art nouveau design.

Eve also ran a series of broadcast advertising to enhance its feminine brand appeal. The first Eve television commercials featured a woman, Eve, in a garden smoking a cigarette. After the shot of Eve in the garden, a series of "classic beauties" are shown ruining their appearance with traditional masculine cigarettes. The copy reads,

> Women have always been beautiful in a garden. But, cigarettes have never helped them look that way. Announcing the end of the ugly cigarette. And, the beginning of a beautiful new one. Eve. A slender cigarette with a feminine filter tip. Women have been beautiful since Eve. Now cigarettes are beautiful. Since Eve.[36]

Although Eve succeeded in its niche market of ladylike smokers, it never enjoyed the same success as Phillip Morris' Virginia Slims brand. Eve lacked the strong personality, voice, and consistent branding of Virginia Slims. Eve changed its packaging, branding, and slogan numerous times, preventing it from being the leader in the women's cigarette market.

OTHER WOMEN'S BRANDS

In addition to Phillip Morris and Liggett & Myers, R.J. Reynolds and Brown & Williamson also worked to create women's brands of cigarettes. However, none of their brands attained the level of success of Virginia Slims or Eve. R.J. Reynolds introduced Dawn, Flair, Embra, More, and Winnie. Most brands failed shortly after introduction.

In 1969, Brown & Williamson and R.J. Reynolds both worked to develop a cigarette to compete with Virginia Slims. In January 1970, Brown & Williamson introduced a new cigarette named Flair. Flair's tagline was, "It does something for a woman." It was a longer 100 mm cigarette. The brand never competed well against Virginia Slims or Eve. In fact, Flair's share of the market never exceeded .5 percent in its test markets.[37] R.J. Reynolds introduced Embra to compete with Flair and Virginia Slims as another women's market newcomer. However, Embra was even less popular among female smokers. In consumer tests, most participants preferred Flair's packaging, name, and style to Embra.[38] Like Eve, Embra was marketed as a feminine cigarette. However, R.J. Reynolds attributed the failure of the brand to the fact that it illustrated women as being too sexual and submissive. The ads positioned Embra as the cigarette that men wanted women to smoke and placed women in a somewhat submissive or subservient role.[39] The tagline was, "Embra. For My Woman."[40] This advertising approach did not appeal to the market. The industry found that women typically do not smoke cigarettes to please men.

In 1974, R.J. Reynolds introduced its first successful women's brand, More, to take advantage of trends in king-size cigarettes. The brand added extra length to the king-size cigarette. More was fundamentally different than other kinds of cigarettes. According to the More positioning statement, consumers "of the brand are viewed as possessing a strong measure of independence and strength of character, characteristics of people who would smoke so unique a product." One of More's unique features is that the cigarette came in colors other than white, often tan or brown, making the cigarette look like a cigarillo. This product feature distinguished it from other women's cigarettes. Consequently, when compared with smokers of the Virginia Slims brand, More smokers were more individualistic, mature, sophisticated, and self-assured.[41] The brand name, More, was not only representative of the fact that there is "more" length to the cigarette, but it also provides psychological associations for consumers as well, as is evidenced by the tagline, "More: Never settle for less."[42]

Although R.J. Reynolds had finally reached a degree of success with the introduction of More, it still had not reached the mainstream female cigarette market. Many women felt that the dark color of the cigarette was too distinctive for them. To address these concerns, R.J. Reynolds was developing female version of Winston that they called Winnie. Winnie began product development 1973 to be a mainstream women's cigarette; it would be white, slender, and long like the Virginia Slims. Winnie was to be both a brand name for the first Winston cigarette marketed for women and the female spokeswoman in a series of advertisements promoting the new brand. The Winnie brand was designed to be more casual, sporty, and carefree than Eve and Virginia Slims. In the first campaign, Winnie was to be pictured on a swing, riding a horse, and driving a sports car. The headline would read, "Meet Winnie: The new 120mm Winston with a personality all its own."[43] The copy described the cigarette's personality:

> Winnie is today's woman. Spirited, full flavored—and totally unique. There's never been a WINSTON like Winnie before. 120mm's of real taste—the kind of taste that's never been available in a cigarette with your kind of style—slender, elegant, and womanly. No other woman's cigarette has ever been able to offer so much. Yet costs no more than ordinary 100's. Maybe Winnie is for you.[44]

Dancer-Fitzgerald-Sample, Inc., Winnie's advertising agency, tested the campaign with female focus groups. The participants perceived Winnie (the spokeswoman) in a favorable but somewhat superficial manner. The focus groups found her to be an attractive, well-groomed, and fashionably attired young woman. She was not housebound nor overly serious. Winnie was fun loving, spirited, and playful.[45] However, the women perceived Winnie to be very similar to the women featured in the Virginia Slims ads. One focus group member said, "She (Winnie) is like that chick they had on Virginia Slims. The same type, a girl that's with the swinging set, the jet set."[46] However, some minor differences existed between Winnie and the women in the Virginia Slims advertisements. Winnie was perceived to be more casual, less urban, less sophisticated, and more into the outdoors. Therefore, for many of the participants, they believed themselves to be more similar to Winnie than the women in the Virginia Slims advertisements. Overall, the focus groups' perceptions of the advertisements were not entirely positive. Many of the participants thought that she looked like a "spoiled brat," "pampered" or like an "athletic snob."[47] No evidence was found that showed that Winnie 120mm was ever introduced to the market.

In another attempt to reach Virginia Slims smokers, R.J. Reynolds introduced Dawn in May 1975, the first 120mm filtered cigarette for women, even longer than Virginia Slims.[48] The tagline was "Slender. Spirited, Deeply Satisfying. The first 120mm for women."[49] Two months after the introduction of Dawn 120mm, the outcome was decidedly mixed. Foot Cone & Belding, Dawn's advertising agency, found that new brand's sales were very slow. Retailers stated, "They're dogs" and "they're the worst of the 120's."[50] The women interviewed said that they were offended by the inclusion of "for women" in the advertising and thought the brand was just an imitation of Virginia Slims and Eve. In addition to the marketing, the women who had tried Dawn did not like the taste.[51] After three attempts, R.J. Reynolds still had not created a successful mainstream women's cigarette.

Although the women's market for cigarettes was growing, only three brands found success during the 1970s: Virginia Slims, More, and Eve. The key to success for these brands was associating a cigarette with a particular lifestyle. Virginia Slims was associated with feminism and career women. Eve was the cigarette for the feminine smoker. The other mainstream brands that were introduced failed to find a market to match the image that they were selling. Although the brand was not considered mainstream, More found a smaller market of female smokers who valued self-expression and an unconventional image. Through its consistent marketing efforts, the tobacco industry was able to reach a large market of young female smokers.

THE BLACK[52] MARKET AND THE GROWING POPULARITY OF KOOL AND OTHER MENTHOL BRANDS

As the tobacco industry was losing its young adult target market on campus, it was gaining the urban youth market. During the 1960s and 1970s, few product categories exemplified the differences between White and Black consumers as much as cigarette brand preferences. While Marlboro was the fastest-growing brand among young White smokers, Brown & Williamson's mentholated Kool was the fastest growing cigarette brand among young Black smokers. Although Kool represented only 10 percent of the total cigarette market, it represented at least 35 percent of the Black cigarette market.[53] To better understand this market, cigarette manufacturers conducted periodic Black smoking studies. For instance, Brown & Williamson conducted a Black smoking study each year starting in 1968.[54] These studies used focus groups, census data, surveys, interviews and other methods. Most of the studies were conducted in metropolitan areas because the majority of Black smokers were urban. Unlike the women's brands, most cigarette companies had existing and successful menthol brands that they were positioning for the Black market. Therefore, less emphasis was placed on new product development. These Black smokers studies provided the majority of the information to be discussed in this section. Although Lorillard, R.J. Reynolds and Brown & Williamson produced menthol cigarettes targeting Black smokers, nearly all of the documents on menthols that were found were located in the R.J. Reynolds collection.

The distinct patterns of cigarette consumption were first established by the broadcast cigarette advertising that was popular before its removal from the airwaves in 1971. The Marlboro Country campaign that aired on television was a successful image builder for the brand and appealed to the young white males in the youth market. Marlboro represented 15 percent of the total cigarette market share. But, it only represented 4 percent of the market share among

Black smokers. To the peer-oriented Black market of the 1960s and 1970s, the idealized lone cowboy of Marlboro Country was a foreign concept.[55] At one point in time a Marlboro ad featuring a Black cowboy was run, but the image did not resonate with the audience.[56]

The market research conducted by R.J. Reynolds and Brown & Williamson in the 1960s and 1970s showed that the Black youth market desired a more social brand that appealed to their product preferences without being exclusive to the Black market. The Kool brand combined the Black market's preference for mentholated taste with a brand name that resonated with young Black men. "Keeping cool" was not only an important part of the Black idiom during the 1960s and 1970s, but cool is also a state that Blacks, more than Whites, wish to maintain. Black smokers often feel less in control over external forces and often must struggle to maintain inner composure.[57]

During the 1960s and early 1970s, most of the Black market felt that the majority of advertisers had chosen not to market to them directly and in a meaningful way. Brown & Williamson's Kool was one of the first mainstream brands to communicate effectively with the Black market without using tokenism or other trivial methods.[58] However, Lorillard's Newport brand, first introduced in 1957, also was successful in the menthol market and targeted the young Black market heavily. The Newport brand started to gain significant popularity in the mid–1970s and was reported to be the fourth fastest growing cigarette brand in the mid–1970s.[59] Even though its popularity was growing among young smokers in high school and college, Newport possessed only about 4 percent of the total menthol market share.[60] Newport positioned itself between R.J. Reynolds' lighter Salem brand and Brown & Williamsons' stronger Kool brand.[61] Although the Newport advertising campaigns were not recognized as being as successful among Black smokers, Newport used aggressive direct marketing methods during the 1960s to attract a young urban audience. These efforts involved distributing free cigarettes to Black urban-dwellers. Children living in housing projects during the 1960s reported consistently receiving sample packs of Newport cigarettes.[62]

Although Kool was praised by the advertising industry as being one of the first successful national brands to target an ethnic market, it is also important to note that Brown & Williamson was also exploiting Black inner city youth by taking advantage of the market's illiteracy. A 1979 letter from Daniel Murphy, a marketing research executive, to J.B. Stewart mentions the fact that the Black market suffers from a high rate of illiteracy. For instance, in 1979, 44 percent of Black people were functionally illiterate. In addition, the fact that many Black youth lived in densely populated urban environments during the 1960s made them easy to reach with outdoor media. The letter mentions that more than 50 percent of the Black population lived in the top 25 metropolitan areas in the U.S. To promote the Kool brand, Brown and Williamson utilized billboards and other out-of-home media to reach Black and urban youth.[63]

The tobacco industry worked to create brand messages reflecting this urban lifestyle of the 1970s. An industry document titled, "Menthol and the Black Smoker," states,

> [Blacks] state that smoking Kools is almost dictated by the ghetto lifestyle. It's a "hard," "tough" place and Kools is a "hard," "tough" cigarette.[64]

In addition to reflecting the harsh life that many Blacks experienced in the inner city, the brand also worked to boost the smokers' self-esteem in this "hard," "tough" place. The document continues by stating,

To the majority of Blacks, Kools gives them an ego, a feeling of identity with the "dudes" who have made it. It gives them a sense of having coped with their environment and, in their own way, coming out on top of it.[65]

Therefore, the key themes that emerged from the documents indicate that the Black market felt that Kool cigarettes gave them more of a high, almost like a joint. And this high helped them cope with their difficult lives.

A 1975 survey of Black smokers titled "The Black Smoker as Part of the Cigarette Industry" highlighted Kool's distinct "in," macho image among young men in Black urban communities. This image contrasted sharply with R.J. Reynolds' feminine and establishment-oriented Salem brand that was somewhat popular among Black women. Young Black male smokers thought that Kool was a cigarette that is "cool" or for people that style themselves as "cool." These men had a positive brand image of Kool. They defined Kool as being

1. With it; Up to Date
2. Self-confident, Assured, Independent, Self-reliant, Aggressive, Ambitious, Brave, Tough
3. Sociable, Enjoys Parties
4. A Leader
5. Casual, Easy Going
6. Concerned About Appearance
7. Likes to be Noticed
8. Manly
9. Daring, Adventurous
10. Sexy, Sensual[66]

Although other menthol brands existed at this time, none had advertising campaigns that resonated as well with the Black audience as the Kool brand. Some Black women preferred R.J. Reynolds' Salem cigarette that was traditionally associated with white smokers. Most Black smokers believed that smoking Salem demonstrated a person's desire to break away from the Black "ghetto" life and obtain a higher social status. Industry research indicated that for some Blacks, smoking Salem cigarettes meant that they were trying to identify more with White culture.[67] For most Black smokers, Salem was viewed as a cigarette for middle-aged suburban housewives or a cigarette for "clean-cut, blue-eyed, blonde haired people" living in an "antiseptic" world.[68]

Tobacco industry executives believed that reaching the Black market was essential. Murphy, an executive at R.J. Reynolds, stated that reaching future Black smokers was "critical to the company's future."[69] Tobacco industry research demonstrated that the Black population was growing and was becoming increasingly educated. Increasing numbers of Black people were attaining middle class status and working in white collar jobs. In addition, members of the Black population were 10 percent to 15 percent more likely to smoke than the average White. Black smokers were also found to feel both less guilty and more tolerant of smoking.[70] The Black market was ideal for the tobacco industry. Although various cigarette brands were experiencing success in the Black market, this consumer group was expected to diminish with time.[71] The research states,

While the Black population will continue to be significantly younger on the average than the White population over the next five years (to 1985), the "young adult" (25 to 44 age) segment of

the Black population will expand, as the "bulge" in Black population represented by the generation of young KOOL smokers of the 1966 to 1976 heyday of the brand among Blacks move into
the more mature and stabilizing phases of their lives. According to Census Bureau data, the 25 to
49 age segment will represent half of the adult Black population by 1985.[72]

Murphy's letter concluded by emphasizing the importance of creating integrated advertising
for the Black market that doesn't focus too much on Black or White smokers.[73] In other
words, it was important that it not be too obvious that a cigarette brand was advertising to
the young urban Black market.

    In addition to a highly effective brand and advertising, Kool was also popular by virtue
of the fact that Black smokers had a strong preference for menthols. A research document
from 1974 shows that R.J. Reynolds was aware of this "mystique" regarding menthols.

> There appears to be a mystique about menthol among Blacks. Not only do they see it as sooth-
> ing, refreshing, good tasting flavor but at the same time it appears to give them heightened sen-
> sation above what other tobacco will do.[74]

The report continues by saying that the menthol flavor helps the Black smoker feel that he
can cope with his environment by giving him a pleasurable sensation.[75]

    In addition to their preference for the sensation that menthol cigarettes provided, mar-
keting research showed that many Black smokers were under the impression that menthol
cigarettes did not pose the same health risks as traditional cigarettes. Black menthol smokers
stated that they were a "better" smoke because they were "cooler and milder" as opposed to
the harsh standard cigarettes. Therefore, many Black smokers believed that menthol cigarettes were a "more healthy" option.[76] Unfortunately, menthol actually inhibits nicotine
metabolism, resulting in a greater health risk.[77]

    The Ted Bates agency in New York found that one of the key challenges in advertising
menthol cigarettes to urban youth was communicating the freshness of the menthol through
images of natural scenes such as water or snow while integrating a Black model into the ad.
During the 1970s, most Black youth related exclusively to an urban environment. Featuring
a Black model in a natural setting seemed unnatural to the test audiences. They perceived
this type of advertising to be White-oriented.[78]

    Ted Bates advised Kool to run separate ads with the natural scenes communicating the
taste of Kool and other ads featuring Black models in social scenes. Overall, the Black respon-
dents preferred the social advertising to the nature scenes.[79] One respondent stated, "The
people are the product users while the scenery is just there."[80] When asked to respond to
advertisements that featured Black models in natural settings, the focus group members
stated,

> It's a setting that you seldom see Black people in.
> Most Black people are not used to that type of scenery. They can't relate to that. It's not the
> everyday life. That's not even seen on vacation.
> That picture relates to the suburbs. You are not in the city proper where the Black people live.[81]

If the advertisement did not feature models, the audience members interpreted the scenes
as a metaphor for the taste and menthol level in the brand. The researchers felt that the
Black smokers were conditioned to associate the amount of water and green with the strength
of the menthol flavor in the cigarette.[82]

    By 1980, approximately 89 percent of Black smokers between the ages of 18 and 24 smoked mentholated cigarettes. However, a preference for menthol appears to decline with age. In 1980, only 40 percent of Black smokers between 45 and 55 smoked menthols.[83] A large percentage of the Black population smoked in 1980. Overall, approximately 60 percent of Black men between the ages of 21 and 34 smoked and 45 percent of Black women between the ages of 12 and 34 smoked. The incidence of smoking among Blacks became much higher than the population in general. By 1980, 48 percent of Black people smoked as opposed to 36 percent of the total population.[84]

Although much of what is discussed about advertising cigarettes to the Black market seems to be characteristic of what one would expect before the success of the civil rights movement, documents from the 1990s show that the tobacco industry maintained this same approach for decades. However, in the 1990s, it was Lorillard's Newport brand that was targeting the young Black market. The focus remained on the urban market and using outdoor advertising and other out-of-home venues.[85]

SUCCESS AND CONSEQUENCES OF ADVERTISING TO MINORITIES AND WOMEN

Although cigarette manufacturers during the 1960s and 1970s took different approaches when trying to reach the female and Black markets, the advertising contained some of the same themes. The most successful brands, Kool and Virginia Slims, both addressed the market's ego and status needs. Kool made Black smokers feel higher social status by smoking a cool brand of cigarettes. Virginia Slims helped women feel empowered at home and in the workplace. Therefore, both brands fed the audience's ego and social needs and maintained the smokers' brand loyalty and faith in their smoking habit. In addition, the success of these campaigns helped the tobacco manufacturers to replace the college students with other markets of young smokers.

Brand personalities became increasingly important to cigarette advertising in the 1960s and 1970s. Instead of marketing to a general audience of college smokers by evoking a sense of school spirit and coming of age, the tobacco industry took on a more niche approach to reaching individuals and their particular needs. The industry also adapted to the loss of broadcast advertising by using print and out-of-home media more extensively. According to Pollay, during the 1960s and 1970s the cigarette industry saw advertising and brand positioning as being essential to how consumers perceived the product, themselves, and ultimately how well brands succeeded. Lorillard listed the psychological role of product marketing as being as important as the cigarette's ability to deliver the physiological stimulation of nicotine.[86]

Advertising also played a key role in reassuring smokers about the social acceptability and desirability of smoking. The advertising often contrasted sharply with the health risks that many smokers, especially women, were already aware of. For instance, Brown & Williamson's consumer research recognized smokers' addiction psychology, and their inner guilt, anxiety, conflict, and need for reassurance.

> Most smokers see themselves as addicts. The typical smoker feels guilty and anxious about smoking but impotent to control it. Psychologically, most smokers feel trapped. They are concerned about health and addiction. Smokers care about what commercials say about them. Advertising may help to reduce anxiety and guilt. [Smokers] may be receptive to advertising, which helps them escape from their inner conflicts about smoking.[87]

Although cigarette advertising in the 1970s provided consumers with information about how various brands related to their particular market segment, little or no meaningful information about the product itself is contained in the advertising. Leaving out important product information fueled ignorance among smokers, especially those in poor Black communities who were ignorant about much of the research about tobacco and health. Many Black smokers believed that the mentholated brands were not as harmful as the regular brands. A large number of female smokers also held inaccurate beliefs about the harms of smoking. Female smokers believed that smoking lighter brands, such as the women's brands, might reduce the health hazards of smoking. Advertising did not address any of these misconceptions that were motivating smokers and their choice of cigarette brands.

Black and female smokers were also essential to the cigarette industry because they are especially loyal and experience difficulty quitting the habit. Women and Black smokers are much less likely to successfully quit smoking than White men.[88] So, once the female and Black smokers were recruited, they were better customers than White men.[89]

Cigarette smoking became particularly burdensome for the Black community and caused high mortality and cancer rates even though Black smokers tended to start later than White smokers and smoked fewer cigarettes per day on average. Smoking among the Black community started to exceed the rates of smoking in the general population because of the difficulties that many Blacks experienced when trying to quit. In addition, many of the menthol brands that the Black smokers preferred had the highest tar and nicotine content so they presented a greater health hazard than the other brands.[90]

Cigarette advertising during the 1970s contributed to a dramatic increase in women suffering from tobacco addiction. Historically, men smoked with greater frequency than women. But, this trend reversed in the 1970s.[91] In 1971, the *U.S. Tobacco Journal* reported that a five-year study sponsored by the U.S. Public Health Service found that a far greater percentage of women than men had no desire to quit smoking and that a much greater percentage of women than men return to cigarettes after trying to quit. One of the researchers suggested that women tended to rely on cigarettes as a means of controlling their frustration and anger. Men did not appear to use cigarettes in the same way.[92] This idea of using smoking to deal with frustration is reflected in the 1960s and 1970s Virginia Slims advertisements that position smoking as a way to rebel against patriarchy.

ADVERTISING BAN, NEW MARKETING TECHNIQUES AND THE SMOKING PREVALENCE AMONG COLLEGE STUDENTS

The U.S. government's interventions to stop cigarette marketing on campus were relatively effective. By the early 1970s, nine out of ten teenagers believed that smoking was harmful to one's health. Consequently, most teenagers expressed the opinion that they would not become smokers in the next five years.[93] A longitudinal study conducted in 1979 by the Department of Health, Education and Welfare indicated that only 14.5 percent of male college students aged 17–23 smoked. The findings indicated that the incidence of smoking among college students dropped to half the rates reported in 1970[94] and was greatly reduced from 45 percent in 1965.[95] The incidence of smoking on campus in 1979 was also reduced to about half of the smoking rate of the general population aged 17 to 24.[96] Therefore, the reduction of the smoking rates correlated with the television advertising ban and other efforts to reduce the tobacco industry's ability to target college students.

Although the advertising restriction was effective at reducing smoking among male college students, the tobacco industry's retargeting efforts in the 1970s maintained the population of female smokers. In 1979, 20 percent of female college students smoked and 37 percent of women aged 22 to 23, most of whom were just out of school, smoked. The rates among men who were out-of-school were also high at 35 percent. The highest rate of smoking was among women who were out-of-school at age 20 to 21. The rate was 45.5 percent. Therefore, the industry's efforts to target women and young men who were out of school were effective during the 1970s.[97] No data was found that specifically reported the frequency of smoking among minority and Black college students during the 1970s.

By 1980, Marlboro was the leading brand among college students. However, Virginia Slims was the top brand among female college students and the fourth most popular brand on campus. By the spring of 1980, college smokers were predominantly female (61 percent). More college-aged women smoked than women in the general population. In 1979, 49 percent of women in the general population aged 17 to 23 smoked. Phillip Morris had the largest market share (49.6 percent) among college students in 1980 with its Marlboro, Merit, and Virginia Slims brands becoming the most popular cigarettes on campus.

The tobacco industry's marketing campaigns targeting women, especially the Virginia Slims ads, were effective in persuading female college students that smoking was either feminine or a feminist social statement. A survey of college students found that female students did not believe that smoking made them less feminine. However, two out of three men preferred to date women that did not smoke. Therefore, the campaigns had not worked to persuade men that smoking was feminine or attractive.[98]

Although cigarette brands could no longer reach college students using student media, the industry used traditional print media popular among college students and young adults to reach their market. For instance, in the 1970s, *Time* (30 percent), *Playboy* (26 percent) and *Newsweek* (24 percent) were the most popular magazines among college smokers. Among men, the top three magazines were *Playboy* (46 percent), *Time* (36 percent) and *Penthouse* (34 percent). Female college students read *Cosmopolitan* (36 percent), *Glamour* (33 percent) and *Time* (26 percent).[99] Therefore, the industry could still reach its audience using alternative forms of media popular among college students and young people. The data seem to indicate that instead of reducing advertising, the regulations simply encouraged the industry to change the media that it used to reach its market.

ANTI-SMOKING EFFORTS IN THE 1970S

Although the advertising restrictions were somewhat effective during the 1970s, many educators and researchers concerned about young people and smoking were unhappy with the reduction in anti-smoking campaigns during the 1970s. A number of schools enacted smoking bans on campus, which helped reduce smoking among students. Many of these bans were publicized and were enforced more consistently during the 1970s. In addition, many students on campus formed groups such as GASP, Global Advisors on Smokefree Policy, to help reduce smoking on campus.[100]

Although the grassroots efforts were somewhat effective, researchers in the 1960s felt that advertising required an adequate share of voice to be effective. During the Fairness Doctrine tobacco broadcast enforcement period from 1966 to 1970, Lewit and his fellow researchers estimated that one anti-smoking ad for every four smoking ads was needed for the anti-smoking PSAs to be effective. During this time period, the undergraduate smoking rate was reduced by 3 percent.[101] After 1970 antismoking groups had to purchase their own airtime for anti-smoking PSAs, and the frequency of the PSAs was greatly reduced.

To reach college students after the broadcast PSA space was eliminated by the enactment of the 1970 broadcast ban, the American Cancer Society developed a campus antismoking poster campaign. Posters were an attractive option because poster space is often free or inexpensive on high school, college, and university campuses. The Creative Advertising Workshop at the University of Michigan developed a campaign for the American Cancer Society targeting the college and teenage market. The net result was a campaign that used sexual innuendo and was somewhat controversial. Pictured in an accepted poster design for the university was a naked woman offering a pack of cigarettes to a naked man. The caption read, "No thanks Eve, I'd rather have an apple."[102] In addition to using grassroots creative generated by college students, Peter Max, a regarded graphic artist, also designed posters, book covers, and a television commercial campaign for the American Cancer Society with the tagline, "Happy People Don't Smoke" and "Beautiful Things Happen When You Don't Smoke Cigarettes" that were used in the late 1960s and early 1970s.[103]

FUTURE OF CIGARETTE MARKETING

During the 1970s, the tobacco industry in the United States began to face marketing restrictions that continue today. In the 1980s and 1990s, the tobacco industry faced increasing advertising regulations, more detailed warnings on advertisements and cigarette packs, and high taxes. These efforts have continued to reduce smoking prevalence in the United States. However, some populations in the United States remain vulnerable. The tobacco industry continues to target youth that live in poverty or immigrant populations. For many young people, cigarette smoking still serves as an escape from depression and stress. In addition to serving as an escape, people suffering from depression and anxiety also have a more difficult time quitting smoking if they do try to quit. People suffering from mental illnesses are also much more likely to relapse.[104]

In addition to targeting the disadvantaged in the United States, the tobacco industry is still reaching a global market. The United States remains one of the largest tobacco producing nations in the world. It is second only to the People's Republic of China. Although restrictions and regulations have reduced cigarette smoking in the United States and Western Europe, American cigarette brands have become status symbols in Eastern Europe and Asia. In 2010, the international tobacco industry generated sales of almost $721 billion. The U.S. tobacco industry had sales of approximately $96 billion in 2010. In total, 1.3 billion people smoke; this number is expected to increase 4 percent annually. Approximately 35 percent of men in developed countries smoke cigarettes, compared with 50 percent of men in developing countries. About 22 percent of women smoke cigarettes in developed countries, compared with less than 10 percent in developing countries.[105]

The Chinese cigarette market is the largest in the world. For instance, more than 300 million people smoke in China and advertising campaigns encourage more to start. By 2025, smoking-related diseases are expected to kill two million Chinese people a year.[106] American cigarettes have become increasingly popular in China.[107] In a survey of Chinese college students in 1995, two of the top eight cigarette brands most familiar to the participants were American: Marlboro and Kent. More participants reported seeing advertisements for American brands than domestic brands; those for Marlboro were reported most often (29.7 percent). Kent (18.1 percent) was also popular. Among smokers, Marlboro was the most preferred foreign brand, by 44.2 percent. The research showed that preference for Marlboro was also correlated with smokers being exposed to Marlboro advertisements.[108]

Although other markets are not as lucrative as the Chinese market, cigarette smoking in Eastern Europe, Asia, and parts of the Middle East is increasing in popularity. For instance, more than 60 percent of men smoke in the Russian Federation, Serbia, Romania, Albania, Turkey, Yemen, Tunisia, and Kenya. Smoking rates among men remain above 50 percent in most of Eastern Europe, Asia, and the Middle East.[109] Researchers believe that smoking rates are high in these nations because taxes are low and there are fewer restrictions on marketing and advertising. However, poverty does reduce smoking rates in a number of developing nations.[110]

Although the United States has reduced smoking significantly by limiting the tobacco industry's access to the youth market, cigarette smoking remains popular among young people all over the world. New markets continue to open up to the tobacco industry. Because of the cigarette industry's marketing campaigns and promotions, millions of young people still start smoking each year. According to the World Health Organization, tobacco use kills six million people each year. This rate is expected to increase to eight million people each year by 2030.[111]

Chapter Notes

Preface and Introduction

1. Stanley C. Whitehead, and David A. Goodman, "A Saga of Cigarette Ads: Free Cigarettes and Tobacco Advertising are Fading From the College Scene," *America*, October 5, 1963.

2. "Master Settlement Agreement," *Office of the Attorney General: State of California Department of Justice*, p. 23 (retrieved December 6, 2006).

3. "Master Settlement Agreement," *Office of the Attorney General: State of California Department of Justice*, p.23 (retrieved December 6, 2006).

4. "Master Settlement Agreement," *Office of the Attorney General: State of California Department of Justice*, p. 23 (retrieved August 12, 2012).

5. Tobacco Documents Online, TobaccoDocuments.org (retrieved December 6, 2006).

6. The Legacy Tobacco Documents Library Online (retrieved December 6, 2006).

7. The Legacy Tobacco Documents Library Online (retrieved December 6, 2006).

8. Stanley C. Whitehead, and David A. Goodman, "A Saga of Cigarette Ads: Free Cigarettes and Tobacco Advertising are Fading From the College Scene," *America*, October 5, 1963.

9. R.J. Reynolds, "A Guide for Selecting Which Student Representatives Should Be Employed," 1947. Legacy Tobacco Documents Online, University of California, San Francisco, Legacy.library.ucsf.edu, Bates number: 502397291/7293 (retrieved August 13, 2012).

10. The American Tobacco Company, "The American Tobacco Company Campus Campaign: Student Marketing Institute Recommendations for 1955–1956," 1956. American Legacy Tobacco Collection, Bates number: 990992760/2775 (retrieved July 30, 2012).

11. The American Tobacco Company, "The American Tobacco Company Campus Campaign: Student Marketing Institute Recommendations for 1955–1956," 1956. American Legacy Tobacco Collection, Bates number: 990992760/2775 (retrieved July 30, 2012).

12. C. M. Sprinkle, "Annual Research Report. Agricultural Research 1955 (550000)." *Agricultural Research,* January 26, 1956, Legacy Tobacco Documents Archive, University of California, San Francisco, Legacy.library.ucsf.edu, Bates number: 504166682–504166686 (retrieved July 30, 2012).

13. Charles L. Click, *A History of the University of Tennessee Experiment Station* (Knoxville: University of Tennessee, 1990), pp. 43–73.

14. Charles L. Click, *A History of the University of Tennessee Experiment Station* (Knoxville: University of Tennessee, 1990), pp. 43–73.

15. Charles L. Click, *A History of the University of Tennessee Experiment Station* (Knoxville: University of Tennessee, 1990), pp. 43–73.

16. Charles L. Click, *A History of the University of Tennessee Experiment Station* (Knoxville: University of Tennessee, 1990), pp. 43–73.

17. Charles L. Click, *A History of the University of Tennessee Experiment Station* (Knoxville: University of Tennessee, 1990), pp. 74–76.

18. Charles L. Click, *A History of the University of Tennessee Experiment Station* (Knoxville: University of Tennessee, 1990), pp. 74–76.

19. Stanley C. Whitehead and David A. Goodman. "A Saga of Cigarette Ads: Free Cigarettes and Tobacco Advertising are Fading From the College Scene," *America*, October 5, 1963; Mary Ellen Wolfe "Colleges Do Little to Discourage Smoking, Health Survey Indicates." *Dayton Journal Herald*, October 4, 1961.

20. The American Tobacco Company, "The American Tobacco Company Campus Campaign: Student Marketing Institute Recommendations for 1955–1956," 1956. American Legacy Tobacco Collection, Bates number: 990992760/2775 (retrieved July 30, 2012).

21. Peter Bart, "Madison Avenue Tobacco Troubles," *Saturday Review*, August 10, 1963.

Chapter 1

1. Paul J. Chung, Craig F. Garfield, Paul J. Rathouz, Diane S. Lauderdale, Dana Best and John Lantos, "Youth Targeting by Tobacco Manufacturers Since the Master Settlement Agreement," *Health Affairs* 21 (March 2002): pp. 254–263.

2. James C. Crimmins, *Successful Publishing on the Campus* (New York: Newsweek, 1968), p. 71.

3. Susan Wagner, *Cigarette Country: Tobacco in American History and Politics* (New York: Praeger, 1971), p. 77.

4. Susan Wagner, *Cigarette Country: Tobacco in American History and Politics* (New York: Praeger, 1971), p. 77.

5. Steve Craig and Terry Moellinger, "'So Rich, Mild, and Fresh': A Critical Look at TV Cigarette Commercials, 1948–1971,"

Journal of Communication Inquiry 25 (January 2001): 55.

6. Susan Wagner, *Cigarette Country: Tobacco in American History and Politics* (New York: Praeger, 1971), p. 4.

7. Pamela Walker Laird, "Consuming Smoke: Cigarettes in American Culture," *Reviews in American History* 28 (2000): pp. 96–104.

8. Steve Craig and Terry Moellinger, "'So Rich, Mild, and Fresh': A Critical Look at TV Cigarette Commercials, 1948–1971," *Journal of Communication Inquiry* 25 (January 2001): pp. 55–71.

9. Susan Wagner, *Cigarette Country: Tobacco in American History and Politics* (New York: Praeger, 1971), p. 77.

10. Tara Parker-Pope, *Cigarettes: Anatomy of an Industry from Seed to Smoke* (New York: The New Press, 2001), p. 9.

11. Robert Sobel, *They Satisfy: The Cigarette in American Life* (Garden City, NJ: Anchor Press, 1978), 13.

12. Tara Parker-Pope, *Cigarettes: Anatomy of an Industry from Seed to Smoke* (New York: The New Press, 2001), p. 11.

13. Michael Schudson, *Advertising: The Uneasy Persuasion* (New York: Basic Books, 1984), p. 185.

14. Robert Sobel, *They Satisfy: The Cigarette in American Life* (Garden City, NJ: Anchor Press, 1978), p. 33.

15. John A. Meyer, "Cigarette Country," *American Heritage* 43, 1992, p. 72.

16. Michael Schudson, *Advertising: The Uneasy Persuasion* (New York: Basic Books, 1984), p. 185.

17. Robert Sobel, *They Satisfy: The Cigarette in American Life* (Garden City, NJ: Anchor Press, 1978), p. 35.

18. Robert Sobel, *They Satisfy: The Cigarette in American Life* (Garden City, NJ: Anchor Press, 1978), p. 45.

19. Michael Schudson, *Advertising: The Uneasy Persuasion* (New York: Basic Books, 1984), p. 185.

20. John A. Meyer, "Cigarette Country" *American Heritage* 43, 1992, p. 72.

21. Susan Wagner, *Cigarette Country: Tobacco in American History and Politics* (New York: Praeger, 1971), pp. 54–55.

22. Stephen Fox, *The Mirror Makers: A History of American Advertisers & Its Creators* (Chicago: University of Illinois Press, 1997), p. 114.

23. Edward L. Bernays, *Biography of an Idea: Memoirs of Public Relations Counsel Edward L. Bernays* (New York: Simon and Schuster, 1965), p. 387.

24. Juliann Sivulka, *Soap, Sex, and Cigarettes: A Cultural History of American Advertising* (Belmont, CA: Wadsworth, 1998), pp. 166–167.

25. Susan Wagner, *Cigarette Country: Tobacco in American History and Politics* (New York: Praeger, 1971), p. 60.

26. Stephen Fox, *The Mirror Makers: A History of American Advertisers & Its Creators* (Chicago: University of Illinois Press, 1997), p. 114.

27. Stephen Fox, *The Mirror Makers: A History of American Advertisers & Its Creators* (Chicago: University of Illinois Press, 1997), p. 114.

28. Juliann Sivulka, *Soap, Sex, and Cigarettes: A Cultural History of American Advertising* (Belmont, CA: Wadsworth, 1998), pp. 166–167.

29. Juliann Sivulka, *Soap, Sex, and Cigarettes: A Cultural History of American Advertising* (Belmont, CA: Wadsworth, 1998), pp. 166–167.

30. Stephen Fox, *The Mirror Makers: A History of American Advertisers & Its Creators* (Chicago: University of Illinois Press, 1997), p. 114.

31. Robert H. Miles *Coffin Nails and Corporate Strategies* (Englewood Cliffs, NJ: Prentice Hall, 1982), p. 32.

32. Debra J. Ringold and John E. Calfee, "The Informational Content of Cigarette Advertising, 1926–1986," *Journal of Public Policy & Marketing* 8 (1989): pp. 1–23.

33. John E. Calfee and Debra J. Ringold, "What Can We Learn From the Informational Content of Cigarette Advertising? A Reply and Further Analysis," *Journal of Public Policy & Marketing* 9 (1990): pp. 30–42.

34. Richard W. Pollay, "Filters, Flavors...Flim-Flam, Too! On 'Health Information' and Policy Implications in Cigarette Advertising," *Journal of Public Policy & Marketing* 8 (1989): pp. 30–39.

35. John E. Calfee and Debra J. Ringold, "What Can We Learn From the Informational Content of Cigarette Advertising? A Reply and Further Analysis," *Journal of Public Policy & Marketing* 9 (1990): pp. 30–42.

36. John A. Meyer, "Cigarette Country," *American Heritage* 43, 1992, p. 72.

37. Karen S. Miller, "Smoking Up A Storm: Public Relations and Advertising in the Construction of the Cigarette Problem 1953–1954," *Journalism Monographs* 36 (December 1992): p. 6.

38. John A. Meyer, "Cigarette Country," *American Heritage* 43, 1992, p. 72.

39. Thomas Whiteside, *Selling Death: Cigarette Advertising and Public Health* (New York: Liveright, 1970), pp. 28–29.

40. John L. Solo, "Exorcising the Ghost of Cigarette Advertising Past: Collusion, Regulation, and Fear Advertising," *Journal of Macromarketing* 21 (2001): pp. 135–145.

41. Debra J. Ringold and John E. Calfee, "The Informational Content of Cigarette Advertising 1926–1986," *Journal of Public Policy & Marketing* 8 (1989): pp. 1–23.

42. Richard W. Pollay, "Filters, Flavors...Flim-Flam, Too! On 'Health Information' and Policy Implications in Cigarette Advertising," *Journal of Public Policy & Marketing* 8 (1989): pp. 30–39.

43. Debra J. Ringold and John E. Calfee, "The Informational Content of Cigarette Advertising 1926–1986," *Journal of Public Policy & Marketing* 8 (1989): pp. 1–23.

44. Steve Craig and Terry Moellinger, "'So Rich, Mild, and Fresh': A Critical Look at TV Cigarette Commercials, 1948–1971," *Journal of Communication Inquiry* 25 (January 2001): p. 55.

45. Michael F. Jacobson and Laurie A. Mazur, *Marketing Madness: A Survival Guide for a Consumer Society* (Boulder, CO: Westview Press, 1995), p. 150.

46. Michael F. Jacobson and Laurie A. Mazur, *Marketing Madness: A Survival Guide for a Consumer Society* (Boulder, CO: Westview Press, 1995), p. 150.

47. Steve Craig and Terry Moellinger, "'So Rich, Mild, and Fresh': A Critical Look at TV Cigarette Commercials, 1948–1971," *Journal of Communication Inquiry* 25 (January 2001): p. 55.

48. Thomas Whiteside, *Selling Death: Cigarette Advertising and Public Health* (New York: Liveright, 1970), pp. 3–5.

49. John E. Calfee and Debra J. Ringold, "What Can We Learn from the Informational Content of Cigarette Advertising? A Reply and Further Analysis." *Journal of Public Policy & Marketing* 9 (1990): pp. 30–42.

50. Steve Craig and Terry Moellinger, "'So Rich, Mild, and Fresh': A Critical Look at TV Cigarette Commercials, 1948–1971," *Journal of Communication Inquiry* 25 (January 2001): p. 61.

51. Steve Craig and Terry Moellinger, "'So Rich, Mild, and Fresh': A Critical Look at TV Cigarette Commercials, 1948–1971," *Journal of Communication Inquiry* 25 (January 2001): p. 62.

52. Juliann Sivulka, *Soap, Sex, and Cigarettes: A Cultural History of American Advertising* (Belmont, CA: Wadsworth, 1998), pp. 254–255.

53. Juliann Sivulka, *Soap, Sex, and Cigarettes: A Cultural History of American Advertising* (Belmont, CA: Wadsworth, 1998), pp. 254–255.

54. Susan Wagner, *Cigarette Country: Tobacco in American History and Politics* (New York: Praeger, 1971), p. 26.

55. Jane L. McGrew, "History of Tobacco Regulation" based on a paper prepared for the National Commission on Marihuana and Drug Abuse. DrugLibrary.org (retrieved July 19, 2005).

56. Jane L. McGrew, "History of Tobacco Regulation" based on a paper prepared for the National Commission on Marihuana and Drug Abuse. DrugLibrary.org (retrieved July 19, 2005).

57. Susan Wagner, *Cigarette Country: Tobacco in American History and Politics.* (New York: Praeger, 1971), p. 26.

58. Susan Wagner, *Cigarette Country: Tobacco in American History and Politics* (New York: Praeger, 1971), p. 26.

59. Karen S. Miller, "Smoking Up A Storm: Public Relations and Advertising in the Construction of the Cigarette Problem, 1953–1954," *Journalism Monographs* 36 (December 1992): p. 4.

60. Pamela Walker Laird, "Consuming Smoke: Cigarettes in Amer-ican Culture," *Reviews in American History* 28 (2000): pp. 96–104.

61. Robert Sobel, *They Satisfy: The Cigarette in American Life* (Garden City, NJ: Anchor Press, 1978), p. 53.

62. Robert Sobel, *They Satisfy: The Cigarette in American Life* (Garden City, NJ: Anchor Press, 1978), p. 54.

63. Susan Wagner, *Cigarette Country: Tobacco in American History and Politics* (New York: Praeger, 1971), p. 26.

64. John A. Meyer, "Cigarette Country," *American Heritage* 43, 1992, p. 72.

65. Karen S. Miller, "Smoking Up A Storm: Public Relations and Advertising in the Construction of the Cigarette Problem, 1953–1954," *Journalism Monographs* 36 (December 1992): p. 5.

66. Robert Sobel, *They Satisfy: The Cigarette in American Life* (Garden City, NJ: Anchor Press, 1978), p. 63.

67. Michael Schudson, *Advertising: The Uneasy Persuasion* (New York: Basic Books, 1984), p. 196.

68. Michael Schudson, *Advertising: The Uneasy Persuasion* (New York: Basic Books, 1984), p. 196.

69. Michael Schudson, *Advertising: The Uneasy Persuasion* (New York: Basic Books, 1984), p. 196.

70. John A. Meyer, "Cigarette Country," *American Heritage* 43, 1992, p. 72.

71. John A. Meyer, "Cigarette Country," *American Heritage* 43, 1992, p. 72.

72. Karen S. Miller, "Smoking Up A Storm: Public Relations and Advertising in the Construction of the Cigarette Problem, 1953–1954," *Journalism Monographs* 36 (December 1992): p. 5.

73. Stephen Fox, *The Mirror Makers: A History of American Advertisers & Its Creators* (Chicago: University of Illinois Press, 1997), p. 116.

74. Maurine Neuberger, *Smoke Screen: Tobacco and the Public Welfare* (Englewood Cliffs, NJ: Prentice Hall, 1963), p. 23.

75. Karen S. Miller, "Smoking Up A Storm: Public Relations and Advertising in the Construction of the Cigarette Problem, 1953–1954," *Journalism Monographs* 36 (December 1992): p. 7.

76. Karen S. Miller, "Smoking Up A Storm: Public Relations and Advertising in the Construction of the Cigarette Problem, 1953–1954," *Journalism Monographs* 36 (December 1992): p. 7.

77. Robert H. Miles, *Coffin Nails and Corporate Strategies* (Englewood Cliffs, NJ: Prentice Hall, 1982), p. 39.

78. Karen S. Miller, "Smoking Up A Storm: Public Relations and Advertising in the Construction of the Cigarette Problem, 1953–1954," *Journalism Monographs* 36 (December 1992): p. 7.

79. Karen S. Miller, "Smoking Up A Storm: Public Relations and Advertising in the Construction of the Cigarette Problem, 1953–1954," *Journalism Monographs* 36, December 1992, p. 7.

80. Robert H. Miles, *Coffin Nails and Corporate Strategies* (Englewood Cliffs, NJ: Prentice Hall, 1982), p. 39.

81. David T. Courtwright, "'Carry on Smoking': Public Relations and Advertising Strategies of American and British Tobacco Companies since 1950," *Business History* 47, July 2005, p. 423.

82. David T. Courtwright, "'Carry on Smoking': Public Relations and Advertising Strategies of American and British Tobacco Companies since 1950" *Business History* 47, July 2005, p. 423.

83. David T. Courtwright, "'Carry on Smoking': Public Relations and Advertising Strategies of American and British Tobacco Companies since 1950" *Business History* 47, July 2005, p. 426.

Chapter 2

1. Mary Ellen Wolfe, "Colleges do Little to Discourage Smoking, Health Survey Indicates," *Dayton Journal Herald*, October 4, 1961.

2. Mary Ellen Wolfe, "Colleges do Little to Discourage Smoking, Health Survey Indicates," *Dayton Journal Herald*, October 4, 1961.

3. Kerry Segrave, *Women and Smoking in America, 1880–1950* (Jefferson, NC: McFarland, 2005), p. 156.

4. "Vassar History 1915–1922," *History of Vassar, 1999* (retrieved from Vassar Website January 16, 2007).

5. Kerry Segrave, *Women and Smoking in America, 1880–1950*

(Jefferson, NC: McFarland, 2005), p. 98.

6. Kerry Segrave, *Women and Smoking in America, 1880–1950* (Jefferson, NC: McFarland, 2005), p. 99.

7. *New York Times*, March 2, 1925, on Radcliffe; *New York Times*, November 20, 1925, on Smith.

8. Michael Schudson, *Advertising: The Uneasy Persuasion* (New York: Basic Books, 1984), p. 189.

9. *New York Times*, November 24, 1925, p. 1; November 25, 1925, p. 20

10. Michael Schudson, *Advertising: The Uneasy Persuasion* (New York: Basic Books, 1984), p. 189.

11. Kerry Segrave, *Women and Smoking in America, 1880–1950* (Jefferson, NC: McFarland, 2005), p. 157.

12. "Letter to R.J Reynolds on November 15, 1933," November 15, 1933, Tobacco Documents Online, TobaccoDocuments.org, Bates number: 50180–8113 (retrieved on June 30, 2006).

13. Michael Schudson, *Advertising: The Uneasy Persuasion* (New York: Basic Books, 1984), p. 191.

14. Kerry Segrave, *Women and Smoking in America, 1880–1950* (Jefferson, NC: McFarland, 2005), p. 159.

15. Maureen Neuberger, *Smoke Screen: Tobacco and the Public Welfare* (Englewood Cliffs, NJ: Prentice Hall, 1963), p. 46.

16. Maureen Neuberger, *Smoke Screen: Tobacco and the Public Welfare* (Englewood Cliffs, NJ: Prentice Hall, 1963), p. 46.

17. Maureen Neuberger, *Smoke Screen: Tobacco and the Public Welfare* (Englewood Cliffs, NJ: Prentice Hall, 1963), p. 46.

18. Maureen Neuberger, *Smoke Screen: Tobacco and the Public Welfare* (Englewood Cliffs, NJ: Prentice Hall, 1963), p. 47.

19. Maureen Neuberger, *Smoke Screen: Tobacco and the Public Welfare* (Englewood Cliffs, NJ: Prentice Hall, 1963), p. 47.

20. Maureen Neuberger, *Smoke Screen: Tobacco and the Public Welfare* (Englewood Cliffs, NJ: Prentice Hall, 1963), p. 48.

21. Maureen Neuberger, *Smoke Screen: Tobacco and the Public Welfare* (Englewood Cliffs, NJ: Prentice Hall, 1963), p. 48.

22. "About The Dartmouth: Past and Present," *The Dartmouth*

Online (retrieved November 11, 2006).

23. Julius Duscha and Thomas Fischer, *The Campus Press: Freedom and Responsibility* (Washington, DC: American Association of State Colleges and Universities, 1973), p. 9.

24. "About the Yale Daily News," YaleDailyNewswwwe (retrieved November 11, 2006).

25. "About the Harvard Crimson," *The Harvard Crimson: Online Edition* (retrieved November 11, 2006).

26. Bob Peterson, "Spartan Daily Debated at Friday Night Forum," *Spartan Daily* (San Jose State College), May 4, 1964.

27. Edwin E. Slosson, "The Possibility of a University Newspaper," *Independent* 72, February 15, 1912.

28. Norman Struder, "The New College Journalism," *Nation* 122, May 26, 1926.

29. Robert H. McNeil, "Training on College Newspapers," *School and Society* 34, March 30, 1929, pp. 419–420.

30. Robert H. McNeil, "Training on College Newspapers," *School and Society* 49, December 1961.

31. "Daily News: Intercollegiate Paper First to Unite Schools," *Newsweek*, October 21, 1933, p. 26.

32. "Daily News: Intercollegiate Paper First to Unite Schools," *Newsweek*, October 21, 1933, p. 26.

33. "Doiley," *Time*, March 11, 1940.

34. Julius Duscha and Thomas Fischer, *The Campus Press: Freedom and Responsibility* (Washington, DC: American Association of State Colleges and Universities, 1973), p. 9.

35. Julius Duscha and Thomas Fischer, *The Campus Press: Freedom and Responsibility* (Washington, DC: American Association of State Colleges and Universities, 1973), p. 10.

36. Julius Duscha and Thomas Fischer, *The Campus Press: Freedom and Responsibility* (Washington, DC: American Association of State Colleges and Universities, 1973), p. 10.

37. Julius Duscha and Thomas Fischer, *The Campus Press: Freedom and Responsibility* (Washington, DC: American Association of State Colleges and Universities, 1973), p. 11.

38. Julius Duscha and Thomas Fischer, *The Campus Press: Freedom*

and Responsibility (Washington, DC: American Association of State Colleges and Universities, 1973), p. 21.

39. Kenneth Stowe Devol, *Major Areas of Conflict in the Control of College and University Student Daily Newspapers in the United States* (Los Angeles: University of Southern California: 1965), p. 47.

40. Julius Duscha and Thomas Fischer, *The Campus Press: Freedom and Responsibility*. (Washington, DC: American Association of State Colleges and Universities, 1973), p. 21.

41. Kenneth Stowe Devol, *Major Areas of Conflict in the Control of College and University Student Daily Newspapers in the United States* (Los Angeles: University of Southern California: Graduate School University Press, 1965), p. 47.

42. Julius Duscha and Thomas Fischer, *The Campus Press: Freedom and Responsibility* (Washington, DC: American Association of State Colleges and Universities, 1973), p. 22.

43. Julius Duscha and Thomas Fischer, *The Campus Press: Freedom and Responsibility* (Washington, DC: American Association of State Colleges and Universities, 1973), p. 22.

44. Julius Duscha and Thomas Fischer, *The Campus Press: Freedom and Responsibility* (Washington, DC: American Association of State Colleges and Universities, 1973), p. 22.

45. Robert Andrew Schoonover, *Working Relations of Faculty Advisers to Student Staffs on Collegiate Newspapers* (Washington, DC: American University, 1962), p. 11.

46. Herman A. Estrin, "What is a College Newspaper?" in *Freedom and Censorship of the College Press*, Herman A. Estrin and Arthur M. Sanderson, eds. (Dubuque, IA: Brown, 1966), p. 14.

47. Herman A. Estrin "What is a College Newspaper?" in *Freedom and Censorship of the College Press* Herman A. Estrin and Arthur M. Sanderson eds. (Dubuque, IA: Brown, 1966), p. 15.

48. Julius Duscha and Thomas Fischer, *The Campus Press: Freedom and Responsibility* (Washington, DC: American Association of State Colleges and Universities, 1973), p. 11.

49. Julius Duscha and Thomas Fischer, *The Campus Press: Freedom and Responsibility* (Washington, DC: American Association of State Colleges and Universities, 1973), p. 11.

50. Julius Duscha and Thomas Fischer, *The Campus Press: Freedom and Responsibility* (Washington, DC: American Association of State Colleges and Universities, 1973), p. 12.

51. Julius Duscha and Thomas Fischer, *The Campus Press: Freedom and Responsibility* (Washington, DC: American Association of State Colleges and Universities, 1973), p. 12.

52. Julius Duscha and Thomas Fischer, *The Campus Press: Freedom and Responsibility* (Washington, DC: American Association of State Colleges and Universities, 1973), p. 13.

53. Robert Andrew Schoonover, *Working Relations of Faculty Advisers to Student Staffs on Collegiate Newspapers* (Washington, DC: American University, 1962), p. 11.

54. Burges Johnson, "Cigarette Advertising and Censorship," *School and Society* 32, December 31, 1932, pp. 856–856.

55. Ruth Strang, *Group Activities in College and Secondary School* (New York: Harper & Brothers, 1941), p. 185.

56. Burges Johnson, "Cigarette Advertising and Censorship," *School and Society* 32, December 31, 1932, pp. 856–856.

57. Burges Johnson, "Cigarette Advertising and Censorship," *School and Society* 32, December 31, 1932, pp. 856–856.

58. Burges Johnson, "Cigarette Advertising and Censorship," *School and Society* 32, December 31, 1932, pp. 856–856.

59. Burges Johnson, "Cigarette Advertising and Censorship," *School and Society* 32, December 31, 1932, pp. 856–856.

60. "Letter to R.J Reynolds on November 15, 1933," November 15, 1933, Tobacco Documents Online, TobaccoDocuments.org, Bates number: 50180–8113 (retrieved on June 30, 2006).

61. Burges Johnson, "Cigarette Advertising and Censorship," *School and Society* 32, December 31, 1932, pp. 856–856.

62. Burges Johnson, "Cigarette Advertising and Censorship," *School and Society* 32, December 31, 1932, pp. 856–856.

63. "Letter to R.J Reynolds on November 15, 1933," November 15, 1933, Tobacco Documents Online, Bates number: 50180–8113, Retrieved: on June 30, 2006.

64. "It's No Go Chesterfield," *The Bardian*, March 7, 1941, p. 3.

65. "It's No Go Chesterfield," *The Bardian*, March 7, 1941, p. 3.

66. "It's No Go Chesterfield," *The Bardian*, March 7, 1941, p. 3.

67. James C. Crimmins, *Successful Publishing on the Campus* (New York: Newsweek, 1968), p. 71.

68. Louis Ingelhart, *Freedom for the College Student Press: Court Cases and Related Decisions Defining the Campus Fourth Estate Boundaries* (Westport, CT: Greenwood Press, 1985), p. 173.

69. Louis Ingelhart, *Freedom for the College Student Press: Court Cases and Related Decisions Defining the Campus Fourth Estate Boundaries* (Westport, CT: Greenwood Press, 1985), p. 169.

70. *New York Times Company v. Sullivan*, 376 U.S. 254 (1964).

71. James C. Crimmins, *Successful Publishing on the Campus* (New York: Newsweek, 1968), 71.

72. Louis Ingelhart, *Freedom for the College Student Press: Court Cases and Related Decisions Defining the Campus Fourth Estate Boundaries* (Westport, CT: Greenwood Press, 1985), p. 175.

73. James C. Crimmins, *Successful Publishing on the Campus* (New York: Newsweek, 1968), 71.

74. *CASS Student Advertising v. National Educational Advertising Services Inc.*, 374 F. Supp. 754 (United States District Court, N.D. Illinois E.D., 1976) reversed and remanded and rehearing denied (United States Court of Appeals, Seventh Circuit, 1975) cert. denied 96 S. Ct. 394 (United States Supreme Court, 1975) affirmed 407 F. Supp. 520 (United States District Court, N.D. Illinois E.D., 1976).

75. Louis Ingelhart, *Freedom for the College Student Press: Court Cases and Related Decisions Defining the Campus Fourth Estate Boundaries* (Westport, CT: Greenwood Press, 1985), p. 175.

76. James C. Crimmins, *Successful Publishing on the Campus* (New York: Newsweek, 1968), p. 71.

77. James C. Crimmins, *Successful Publishing on the Campus* (New York: Newsweek, 1968), p. 72.

78. Robert Andrew Schoonover,

Working Relations of Faculty Advisers to Student Staffs on Collegiate Newspapers (Washington, DC: American University, 1962), p. 164.

79. Robert Andrew Schoonover, *Working Relations of Faculty Advisers to Student Staffs on Collegiate Newspapers* (Washington, DC: American University, 1962), p. 164.

80. Ivan Livingston Jones, *An Analysis of the Educational Problems Peculiar to School-Newspaper Advertising* (Seattle: University of Washington, 1961), p. 8.

81. Ivan Livingston Jones, *An Analysis of the Educational Problems Peculiar to School-Newspaper Advertising* (Seattle: University of Washington, 1961), p. 8.

82. Ivan Livingston Jones, *An Analysis of the Educational Problems Peculiar to School-Newspaper Advertising* (Seattle: University of Washington, 1961), p. 8.

Chapter 3

1. "Smoke Still Swirls Around Cigarettes: Top Tobacco Companies Agree to Discontinue Advertising and Promotion in College Publications," *Business Week,* June 29, 1963.

2. Stanley G. Whitehead and David A. Goodman, "A Saga of Cigarette Ads: Free Cigarettes and Tobacco Advertising are Fading from the College Scene," *America,* October 5, 1963, p. 387.

3. Stanley G. Whitehead and David A. Goodman, "A Saga of Cigarette Ads: Free Cigarettes and Tobacco Advertising are Fading from the College Scene," *America,* October 5, 1963, p. 387.

4. Stanley G. Whitehead and David A. Goodman, "A Saga of Cigarette Ads: Free Cigarettes and Tobacco Advertising are Fading from the College Scene," *America,* October 5, 1963, p. 388.

5. Stanley G. Whitehead and David A. Goodman, "A Saga of Cigarette Ads: Free Cigarettes and Tobacco Advertising are Fading from the College Scene," *America,* October 5, 1963, p. 388.

6. Stanley G. Whitehead and David A. Goodman, "A Saga of Cigarette Ads: Free Cigarettes and Tobacco Advertising are Fading from the College Scene," *America,* October 5, 1963, p. 388.

7. Stanley G. Whitehead and

David A. Goodman, "A Saga of Cigarette Ads: Free Cigarettes and Tobacco Advertising are Fading from the College Scene," *America,* October 5, 1963, p. 388.

8. Stanley G. Whitehead and David A. Goodman, "A Saga of Cigarette Ads: Free Cigarettes and Tobacco Advertising are Fading from the College Scene," *America,* October 5, 1963, p. 389.

9. Stanley G. Whitehead and David A. Goodman, "A Saga of Cigarette Ads: Free Cigarettes and Tobacco Advertising are Fading from the College Scene," *America,* October 5, 1963, p. 389.

10. The Tobacco Institute, "The Tobacco Institute—Roots in the Tobacco Industry Research Committee," no date, Tobacco Documents Online, TobaccoDocuments. org (retrieved August 21, 2012).

11. The Tobacco Institute, "The Tobacco Institute—Roots in the Tobacco Industry Research Committee," no date, Tobacco Documents Online, TobaccoDocuments. org (retrieved August 21, 2012).

12. T. Abrams, P. Crist, S. Kaczynski, and W. Marple, "Confidential Report Containing Legal Advice and Attorney Opinion Work Product Regarding Numerous Smoking and Health Issues Relevant to Litigation, Prepared by Outside Counsel for RJR, with Whom B&W Maintains A Common Legal Interest, and Forwarded to B&W in–House Counsel," no date, p. 9, Tobacco Documents Online, TobaccoDocumnets.org, Bates number: 681879254–681879715 (retrieved August 21, 2012).

13. T. Abrams, P. Crist, S. Kaczynski, and W. Marple, "Confidential Report Containing Legal Advice and Attorney Opinion Work Product Regarding Numerous Smoking and Health Issues Relevant to Litigation, Prepared by Outside Counsel for RJR, with Whom B&W Maintains A Common Legal Interest, and Forwarded to B&W in–House Counsel," no date, p.18, Tobacco Documents Online, TobaccoDocuments.org, Bates number: 681879254–681879715 (retrieved August 21, 2012).

14. T. Abrams, P. Crist, S. Kaczynski, and W. Marple, "Confidential Report Containing Legal Advice and Attorney Opinion Work Product Regarding Numerous Smoking and Health Issues Rel-

evant to Litigation, Prepared by Outside Counsel for RJR, with Whom B&W Maintains A Common Legal Interest, and Forwarded to B&W in–House Counsel," no date, p.18, Tobacco Documents Online, TobaccoDocuments.org, Bates number: 681879254–681879715 (retrieved August 21, 2012).

15. Shook, Hardy, and Bacon LLP, "Overview," April 11, 1988, Tobacco Documents Online, TobaccoDocuments.org, Bates number: 2024972574–2024972598 (retrieved August 21, 2012).

16. "The Tobacco Institute— Roots in the Tobacco Industry Research Committee," no date, Tobacco Documents Online, Tobacco Documents.org (retrieved August 26, 2006).

17. T. Abrams, P. Crist, S. Kaczynski, and W. Marple, "Confidential Report Containing Legal Advice and Attorney Opinion Work Product Regarding Numerous Smoking and Health Issues Relevant to Litigation, Prepared by Outside Counsel for RJR, with Whom B&W Maintains A Common Legal Interest, and Forwarded to B&W in–House Counsel," no date, p. 265, Tobacco Documents Online, TobaccoDocuments.org, Bates number: 681879254– 681879715 (retrieved July 26, 2006).

18. T. Abrams, P. Crist, S. Kaczynski, and W. Marple, "Confidential Report Containing Legal Advice and Attorney Opinion Work Product Regarding Numerous Smoking and Health Issues Relevant to Litigation, Prepared by Outside Counsel for RJR, with Whom B&W Maintains A Common Legal Interest, and Forwarded to B&W in–House Counsel," no date, p.265, Tobacco Documents Online, TobaccoDocuments.org, Bates number: 681879254– 681879715 (retrieved July 26, 2006).

19. Mark Parascandola, "Public Health Then and Now: Cigarettes and the U.S. Public Health Service in the 1950s," *American Journal of Public Health* 91, 2001, pp. 196– 205.

20. Mortin L. Levin, Hyman Goldstein, and Paul R. Gerhardt, "Cancer and Tobacco Smoking: A Preliminary Report" *Journal of the American Medical Associatio,* 143, 1950, pp. 336–338.

21. Gene Borio, "Tobacco Timeline," *Tobacco.org,* last modified 2007.

22. John E. Calfee, "The Ghost of Cigarette Advertising Regulation Past," *Regulation* 20, 1986, pp. 35– 45.

23. "What Cigarette Smokers Should Know," *U.S. News & World Report,* April 14, 1950, p. 20.

24. "What Cigarette Smokers Should Know," *U.S. News & World Report* April 14, 1950, pp. 20–21.

25. T. Abrams, P. Crist, S. Kaczynski, and W. Marple, "Confidential Report Containing Legal Advice and Attorney Opinion Work Product Regarding Numerous Smoking and Health Issues Relevant to Litigation, Prepared by Outside Counsel for RJR, with Whom B&W Maintains A Common Legal Interest, and Forwarded to B&W in–House Counsel," no date, p. 271, Tobacco Documents Online, TobaccoDocuments.org, Bates number: 681879254– 681879715 (retrieved August 21, 2012).

26. R.J. Reynolds Tobacco Co., 46 FTC 706 (1950). modified, 192 F. 2d 535 (7th Cir. 1951), order modified, 48 FTC 682 (1952) (retrieved August 21, 2012).

27. 55 FTC 354 (1958) (Bruff Depo. Exh. 7).

28. "FTC Office of Information, Orders 4795 and 4922," April 5, 1950, p. 1, Legacy Tobacco Documents Online, University of California, San Francisco, Legacy.library.ucsf.edu, Bates number: 980300567/0572 (retrieved August 7, 2006).

29. "FTC Office of Information, Orders 4795 and 4922," April 5, 1950, p. 3, Legacy Tobacco Documents Online, University of California, San Francisco, Legacy.library.ucsf.edu, Bates number: 980300567/0572 (retrieved August 7, 2006).

30. T. Abrams, P. Crist, S. Kaczynski, and W. Marple, "Confidential Report Containing Legal Advice and Attorney Opinion Work Product Regarding Numerous Smoking and Health Issues Relevant to Litigation, Prepared by Outside Counsel for RJR, with Whom B&W Maintains A Common Legal Interest, and Forwarded to B&W in–House Counsel," no date, p. 274, Tobacco Documents Online, TobaccoDocuments.org,

Bates number: 681879254–68187 9715 (accessed July 26, 2006).

31. James M. Mead and FTC, "Order To Cease And Desist," June 20, 1951, Legacy Tobacco Documents Online, University of California, San Francisco, Legacy.library.ucsf.edu, Bates number: 980297792/7793 (retrieved August 21, 2012).

32. FTC, "Modified Order to Cease and Desist," January 17, 1952, Legacy Tobacco Documents Online, University of California, San Francisco, Legacy.library.ucsf.edu, Bates number: 980300590/059 (accessed August 21, 2012).

33. D.C. Daniel, FTC, "United States of America Before Federal Trade Commission, Commissioners James M. Mead, Lowell B. Mason, John Carson, Stephen J. Spingarn, Albert A. Carretta, in the Matter Of Philip Morris & Company, Docket No. 4794, Decision of the Commission and Order to File Report of Compliance," December 29, 1952, Legacy Tobacco Documents Online, University of California, San Francisco, Legacy.library.ucsf.edu, Bates number: 980299310/9329 (retrieved August 30, 2006).

34. FTC "Hearing Examiner's Initial Decision," February 5, 1952, Legacy Tobacco Documents Online, University of California, San Francisco, Legacy.library.ucsf.edu, Bates number: 980299330/9331, (retrieved August 21, 2012).

35. FTC "Hearing Examiner's Initial Decision," February 5, 1952, Legacy Tobacco Documents Online, University of California, San Francisco, Legacy.library.ucsf.edu, Bates number: 980299330/9331 (retrieved August 21, 2012).

36. Commerce Clearing House, *Trade Regulation Reports* #67, 67,377 Cited 1952 Trade Cases, *FTC Vs. Liggett and Myers Tobacco Co.*, December 18, 1952, Legacy Tobacco Documents Online, University of California, San Francisco, Legacy.library.ucsf.edu, Bates number: 980295134/5159 (retrieved August 21, 2012).

37. FTC, "Chapter 2—Federal Trade Commission; Promotion of Export Trade and Prevention of Unfair Methods of Competition," *Federal Trade Commission Act Title 15—Commerce and Trade*, no date, FDA.gov (retrieved August 30, 2006).

38. Commerce Clearing House,

Trade Regulation Reports #67, 67,377 Cited 1952 Trade Cases, *FTC Vs. Liggett and Myers Tobacco Co.*, December 18, 1952, Legacy Tobacco Documents Online, University of California, San Francisco, Legacy.library.ucsf.edu, Bates number: 980295134/5159 (retrieved August 30, 2006).

39. Commerce Clearing House, *Trade Regulation Reports* #67, 67,377 Cited 1952 Trade Cases, *FTC Vs. Liggett and Myers Tobacco Co.*, December 18, 1952, Legacy Tobacco Documents Online, University of California, San Francisco, Legacy.library.ucsf.edu, Bates number: 980295134/5159 (retrieved August 30, 2006).

40. FTC Press Release, January 26, 1953, Legacy Tobacco Documents Online, University of California, San Francisco, Legacy.library.ucsf.edu, Bates number: 968091438/1439 (retrieved August 21, 2012).

41. FTC Press Release, January 26, 1953, Legacy Tobacco Documents Online, University of California, San Francisco, Legacy.library.ucsf.edu, Bates number: 968091438/1439 (retrieved August 21, 2012)

42. E.F. Howrey, L.B. Mason, J.M. Mead, R.T. Secrest, and J.W. Gwynne, "United States of America Before Federal Trade Commission; Commissioners: Edward F. Howrey, Chairman, Lowell B. Mason, James B. Mead, John W. Gwynne, Robert T. Secrest; in the Matter of Ligget & Myers Tobacco Company, a Corporation, on Appeal From Initial Decision," March 28, 1955, Legacy Tobacco Documents Online, University of California, San Francisco, Legacy.library.ucsf.edu, Bates number: 980295114/5123 (retrieved August 21, 2012).

43. Robert M. Parrish, "United States of America Before Federal Trade Commission, Commissioners: Edward F. Howrey, Lowell B. Mason, James M. Mead, John W. Gwynne, Robert T. Secrest, in the Matter of Philip Morris & Company, Ltd., Docket No. 4794, Decision Of The Commission," March 25, 1955, Legacy Tobacco Documents Online, University of California, San Francisco, Legacy.library.ucsf.edu, Bates number: 980299295/9296 (retrieved September 1, 2006).

44. Charles E. Grandey, FTC,

"Letter to Paul Hahn," September 14, 1954, Legacy Tobacco Documents Online, University of California, San Francisco, Legacy.library.ucsf.edu, Bates number: 968237949/7952 (retrieved August 21, 2012).

45. FTC, "The FTC Proposes Standards To Cigarette Companies," September 15, 1954, Legacy Tobacco Documents Online, University of California, San Francisco, Legacy.library.ucsf.edu, Bates number: 963016070/6071 (retrieved August 20, 2006).

46. FTC, "The FTC Proposes Standards To Cigarette Companies," September 15, 1954, Legacy Tobacco Documents Online, University of California, San Francisco, Legacy.library.ucsf.edu, Bates number: 963016070/6071 (retrieved August 30, 2006).

47. John E. Calfee, "The Ghost of Cigarette Advertising Regulation Past," *Regulation* 20, 1986, pp. 35–45.

48. John E. Calfee, "The Ghost of Cigarette Advertising Regulation Past," *Regulation* 20, 1986, pp. 35–45.

49. Paul M. Hahn, ATCO, "Letter to Charles M. Grandey Regarding the FTC's Proposed Advertising Standards," September 21, 1954, Legacy Tobacco Documents Online, University of California, San Francisco, Legacy.library.ucsf.edu, Bates number: 990774811/4812 (retrieved September 1, 2006).

50. Paul M. Hahn, ATCO, "Letter to Charles M. Grandley Regarding the FTC's Proposed Advertising Standards," September 21, 1954, Legacy Tobacco Documents Online, University of California, San Francisco, Legacy.library.ucsf.edu, Bates number: 990774811/4812 (retrieved September 1, 2006).

51. John E. Calfee, "The Ghost of Cigarette Advertising Regulation Past," *Regulation* 20, 1986, pp. 35–45.

52. Edward F. Howrey, Lowell B. Mason, James B. Mead, Robert T. Secrest, and John W. Gwynne, "United States of America Before Federal Trade Commission; Commissioners: Edward F. Howrey, Chairman, Lowell B. Mason, James B. Mead, John W. Gwynne, Robert T. Secrest; in the Matter of Ligget & Myers Tobacco Company, a Corporation, on Appeal From Initial Decision," March 28, 1955, Legacy

Tobacco Documents Online, University of California, San Francisco, Legacy.library.ucsf.edu, Bates number: 980295114/5123 (retrieved September 1, 2006).

53. Robert M. Parrish, "United States of America Before Federal Trade Commission, Commissioners: Edward F. Howrey, Lowell B. Mason, James M. Mead, John W. Gwynne, Robert T. Secrest, in the Matter of Philip Morris & Company, Ltd., Docket No. 4794, Decision Of The Commission," March 28, 1955, Legacy Tobacco Documents Online, University of California, San Francisco, Legacy.library.ucsf.edu, Bates number: 980299295/9296 (retrieved September 1, 2006).

54. Robert M. Parrish, "United States of America Before Federal Trade Commission, Commissioners: Edward F. Howrey, Lowell B. Mason, James M. Mead, John W. Gwynne, Robert T. Secrest, in the Matter of Philip Morris & Company, Ltd., Docket No. 4794, Decision Of The Commission," March 25, 1955, Legacy Tobacco Documents Online, University of California, San Francisco, Legacy.library.ucsf.edu, Bates number: 980299295/9296 (retrieved September 1, 2006).

55. Charles E. Grandey, "Letter to Horace Hitchcock," May 6, 1955, Legacy Tobacco Documents Online, University of California, San Francisco, Legacy.library.ucsf.edu, Bates number: 968237839/7840 (retrieved September 1, 2006).

56. John E. Calfee, "The Ghost of Cigarette Advertising Regulation Past," *Regulation* 20, 1986, 35–45.

57. T. Abrams, P. Crist, S. Kaczynski, and W. Marple, "Confidential Report Containing Legal Advice and Attorney Opinion Work Product Regarding Numerous Smoking and Health Issues Relevant to Litigation, Prepared by Outside Counsel for RJR, with Whom B&W Maintains A Common Legal Interest, and Forwarded to B&W in–House Counsel," no date, p. 286, TobaccoDocuments.org, Bates number: 681879254–681879715 (retrieved July 28, 2006).

58. T. Abrams, P. Crist, S. Kaczynski, and W. Marple, "Confidential Report Containing Legal Advice and Attorney Opinion Work Product Regarding Numer-

ous Smoking and Health Issues Relevant to Litigation, Prepared by Outside Counsel for RJR, with Whom B&W Maintains A Common Legal Interest, and Forwarded to B&W in–House Counsel" no date, p. 286, Tobacco Documents Online, TobaccoDocuments.org, Bates number: 681879254–68187 9715 (retrieved July 28, 2006).

59. Robert M. Parrish, "United States of America Before Federal Trade Commission, in the Matter of Philip Morris, a Corporation, Docket No. 6750," March 27, 1957, Legacy Tobacco Documents, Bates number: 963025756/5760 (retrieved September 1, 2006).

60. FTC, "Press Release, Publication," April 4, 1957, Legacy Tobacco Documents Online, University of California, San Francisco, Legacy.library.ucsf.edu, Bates number: 963025771/5772 (retrieved September 1, 2006).

61. Robert M. Parrish, "United States of America Before Federal Trade Commission, in the Matter of Philip Morris, a Corporation, Docket No. 6750," March 27, 1957, Legacy Tobacco Documents Online, University of California, San Francisco, Legacy.library.ucsf.edu, Bates number: 963025756/5760 (retrieved September 1, 2006).

62. FTC, "Press Release, Publication," April 4, 1957, Legacy Tobacco Documents Online, University of California, San Francisco, Legacy.library.ucsf.edu, Bates number: 963025767/5768 (retrieved September 1, 2006).

63. John E. Calfee, "The Ghost of Cigarette Advertising Regulation Past," *Regulation* 20, 1986, pp. 35–45.

64. John E. Calfee, "The Ghost of Cigarette Advertising Regulation Past," *Regulation* 20, 1986, pp. 35–45.

65. T. Abrams, P. Crist, S. Kaczynski, and W. Marple, "Confidential Report Containing Legal Advice and Attorney Opinion Work Product Regarding Numerous Smoking and Health Issues Relevant to Litigation, Prepared by Outside Counsel for RJR, with Whom B&W Maintains A Common Legal Interest, and Forwarded to B&W in–House Counsel," no date, p. 256, Tobacco Documents Online, TobaccoDocuments.org, Bates number: 681879254–6818 79715 (retrieved July 28, 2006).

66. John A. Blatnik, "The Medicine Man under the Eagle's Eye," *The Progressive*, November 1958, p. 6.

67. John A. Blatnik, "The Medicine Man under the Eagle's Eye," *The Progressive,* November 1958, p. 6.

68. John E. Calfee, "The Ghost of Cigarette Advertising Regulation Past," *Regulation* 20, 1986, pp. 35–45.

69. Thomas Whiteside, *Selling Death: Cigarette Advertising and Public Health* (New York: Liveright, 1971), p. 18.

70. John E. Calfee, "The Ghost of Cigarette Advertising Regulation Past," *Regulation* 20, 1986, pp. 35–45.

71. John E. Calfee, "The Ghost of Cigarette Advertising Regulation Past," *Regulation* 20, 1986, pp. 35–45.

72. Lee Loevinger, U.S. Dept. of Justice, "By Letter of May 20, 1963 (630520) You Have Submitted on Behalf of P. Lorillard Company a Proposed Series of Discussions Relating to Tobacco Advertising for Consideration in Relation to the Antitrust Laws," May 23, 1963, Tobacco Documents Online, TobaccoDocuments.org, Bates number: 502005761–502005762 (retrieved August 21, 2012).

73. Bruff Depo. Exh. 5; Harrington Depo. Exh. 9 (65009 0411), Tab 410, http://archive.tobacco.org/ Documents/jonesday2.html (retrieved August 21, 2012).

74. Lee Loevinger, U.S. Dept. of Justice, "By Letter of May 20, 1963 (630520) You Have Submitted on Behalf of P. Lorillard Company a Proposed Series of Discussions Relating to Tobacco Advertising for Consideration in Relation to the Antitrust Laws," May 23, 1963, Tobacco Documents Online, TobaccoDocuments.org, Bates number: 502005761–502005762 (retrieved August 21, 2012).

75. Atrr., "Restraints and Monopolies: Tobacco Code Gets Tentative Immunization from Criminal Antitrust Prosecution," no date, Tobacco Documents Online, TobaccoDocuments.org, Bates number: 2022975660–2022975661 (retrieved August 21, 2012).

76. Atrr., "Restraints and Monopolies: Tobacco Code Gets Tentative Immunization from Criminal Antitrust Prosecution," no date, Tobacco Documents Online, TobaccoDocuments.org, Bates number:

2022975660–2022975661 (accessed August 21, 2012).

77. John E. Calfee, "The Ghost of Cigarette Advertising Regulation Past," *Regulation* 20, 1986, 35–45.

78. T. Abrams, P. Crist, S. Kaczynski, and W. Marple, "Confidential Report Containing Legal Advice and Attorney Opinion Work Product Regarding Numerous Smoking and Health Issues Relevant to Litigation, Prepared by Outside Counsel for RJR, with Whom B&W Maintains A Common Legal Interest, and Forwarded to B&W in–House Counsel," no date, 294–295, Tobacco Documents Online, TobaccoDocuments. org, Bates number: 681879254–681879715 (retrieved July 28, 2006).

79. Stanley L. Temko, "The Tobacco Institute, Inc., Minutes of the Eighteenth Meeting of the Executive Committee," June 18, 1963 (est.), Tobacco Documents Online, TobaccoDocuments.org, Bates number: 2022975647–20229756 50 (retrieved August 21, 2012).

80. Stanley L. Temko, "The Tobacco Institute, Inc., Minutes of the Eighteenth Meeting of the Executive Committee," June 18, 1963 (est.), Tobacco Documents Online, TobaccoDocuments.org, Bates number: 2022975647–20229756 50 (retrieved August 21, 2012).

81. Hill & Knowlton, Public Relations Counsel, "Statement on College Advertising and Promotion," June 19, 1963, Tobacco Documents Online, TobaccoDocuments.org, Bates number: 202297 5651 (retrieved August 21, 2012).

82. Tobacco Institute and Stanley L. Temko, "The Tobacco Institute, Inc., Minutes of the Nineteenth Meeting of the Executive Committee," July 3, 1993 (est.), Tobacco Documents Online, TobaccoDocuments.org, Bates number: 2022975655–2022975656 (retrieved August 21, 2012).

83. Tobacco Institute and Stanley L. Temko, "The Tobacco Institute, Inc., Minutes of the Nineteenth Meeting of the Executive Committee," July 3, 1993 (est.), Tobacco Documents Online, TobaccoDocuments.org, Bates number: 2022975655–2022975656 (retrieved August 21, 2012).

84. Hill & Knowlton, "Former Governor Robert B. Meyner Selected as Administrator of Cigarette Advertising Code," June 8, 1964, Legacy Tobacco Documents Online, University of California, San Francisco, Legacy.library.ucsf.edu, Bates number: 500507202 (retrieved August 21, 2012).

85. T. Abrams, P. Crist, S. Kaczynski, and W. Marple, "Confidential Report Containing Legal Advice and Attorney Opinion Work Product Regarding Numerous Smoking and Health Issues Relevant to Litigation, Prepared by Outside Counsel for RJR, with Whom B&W Maintains A Common Legal Interest, and Forwarded to B&W in–House Counsel," no date, p. 295, Legacy Tobacco Documents Online, University of California, San Francisco, Legacy.library.ucsf.edu, Bates number: 681879254–681879715 (retrieved July 28, 2006).

86. T. Abrams, P. Crist, S. Kaczynski, and W. Marple, "Confidential Report Containing Legal Advice and Attorney Opinion Work Product Regarding Numerous Smoking and Health Issues Relevant to Litigation, Prepared by Outside Counsel for RJR, with Whom B&W Maintains A Common Legal Interest, and Forwarded to B&W in–House Counsel (Judge Depo. at 233)," no date, p. 295, Legacy Tobacco Documents Online, University of California, San Francisco, Legacy.library.ucsf.edu, Bates number: 681879254–68187 9715 (retrieved July 28, 2006).

87. T. Abrams, P. Crist, S. Kaczynski, and W. Marple, "Confidential Report Containing Legal Advice and Attorney Opinion Work Product Regarding Numerous Smoking and Health Issues Relevant to Litigation, Prepared by Outside Counsel for RJR, with Whom B&W Maintains A Common Legal Interest, and Forwarded to B&W in–House Counsel," no date, p. 295, Tobacco Documents Online, TobaccoDocuments.org, Bates number: 681879254–68187 9715 (retrieved July 28, 2006).

88. T. Abrams, P. Crist, S. Kaczynski, and W. Marple, "Confidential Report Containing Legal Advice and Attorney Opinion Work Product Regarding Numerous Smoking and Health Issues Relevant to Litigation, Prepared by Outside Counsel for RJR, with Whom B&W Maintains A Common Legal Interest, and Forwarded to B&W in–House Counsel," no date, p. 296, Tobacco Documents Online, TobaccoDocuments.org, Bates number: 681879254–68187 9715 (retrieved July 28, 2006).

89. Thomas Whiteside, *Selling Death: Cigarette Advertising and Public Health* (New York: Liveright, 1971), pp. 29–30.

90. Thomas Whiteside, *Selling Death: Cigarette Advertising and Public Health* (New York: Liveright, 1971), pp. 46–47.

91. "Cigarette Machine Vetoed," *The New York Times,* October, 26 1963, Legacy Tobacco Documents Online, University of California, San Francisco, Legacy.library.ucsf.edu, Bates number: 1003043510 (retrieved August 21, 2012).

92. "Smoking Ban Endorsed by Students," *Chronicle,* October 26, 1963, Legacy Tobacco Library, Bates number: 1003043510 (retrieved August 15, 2012).

93. "College Papers Doubt Tobacco Ad Cutoff Would Halt Teen Smoking," *World*, June 29, 1963.

94. "College Papers Doubt Tobacco Ad Cutoff Would Halt Teen Smoking," *World*, June 29, 1963.

95. "College Papers Doubt Tobacco Ad Cutoff Would Halt Teen Smoking," *World*, June 29, 1963.

96. Carol Almond, "Cigarette Firms to Withdraw Ads From College Publications," *Times*, July 4, 1963.

97. Carol Almond, "Cigarette Firms to Withdraw Ads From College Publications," *Times*, July 4, 1963.

98. "Second Week: U' Paper Surviving Ad Loss," *Star*, September 30, 1963.

99. Ann Shank-Volk, "College Newspaper Business & Advert.," October 20, 1981, Tobacco Documents Online, TobaccoDocuments. org, Bates number: 03019541–0301 9542 (retrieved August 12, 2012).

100. Tara Parker-Pope, *Cigarettes: Anatomy of an Industry from Seed to Smoke* (New York: The New Press, 2001), p. 99.

Chapter 4

1. The American Tobacco Company (ATC), "Agency Insertion Orders for Magazine and Cigarette Advertising," 1961, Legacy Tobacco Documents Online, Uni-

versity of California, San Francisco, Legacy.library.ucsf.edu, Bates number: 990876570/6575 (retrieved August 21, 2012); Batten, Barton, Durstine, & Osborn, Inc., for American Tobacco Co., "Lucky Strike College, 1954–1963," no date, Legacy Tobacco Documents Online, University of California, San Francisco, Legacy.library.ucsf.edu, Bates number: 990906328/6783, accessed August 21, 2012; William Etsy & Co., "College Newspapers, Your letter November 6th," November 15, 1933, Legacy Tobacco Documents Online, University of California, Legacy.library.ucsf.edu, Bates number: 50180 8112/8115 (retrieved August 21, 2012); Federal Trade Commission, "R.J. Reynolds Proceedings: Digest of Testimony," 1944, Legacy Tobacco Documents Online, University of California, San Francisco, Legacy.library.ucsf.edu, Bates number: MNATPRIV00040605-MNATPRIV00040926 (retrieved August 21, 2012); Lorillard Tobacco Co., LN, "Final Report on Old Gold College Test Campaign," June 1954, Legacy Tobacco Documents Online, University of California, San Francisco, Legacy.library.ucsf.edu, Bates number: 84439464/9491 (retrieved August 21, 2012); Elmo Roper and Associates for Phillip Morris, "A Study College Students' Cigarette Smoking Habits and Attitudes, Volume I," May 1956, Legacy Tobacco Documents Online, University of California, San Francisco, Legacy.library.ucsf.edu, Bates number: 990906328/6783 (retrieved August 21, 2012).

2. The American Tobacco Company (ATC), "Agency Insertion Orders for Magazine and Cigarette Advertising," 1961, Bates number: 990876570/6575 (retrieved August 21, 2012); Batten, Barton, Durstine, & Osborn, Inc., for American Tobacco Co., "Lucky Strike College, 1954–1963," no date, Legacy Tobacco Documents Online, University of California, San Francisco, Legacy.library.ucsf.edu, Bates number: 990906328/6783 (retrieved August 21, 2012).

3. Student Marketing Institute, "The American Tobacco Company Campus Campaign: Student Marketing Institute Recommendations for 1955–1956," 1955, Legacy Tobacco Documents Online, University of California, San Francisco,

Legacy.library.ucsf.edu, Bates number: 990992760/2775 (retrieved August 28, 2012); Student Marketing Institute, "Lucky Strike Campus Campaign–1953–1954 Analysis of: Survey Of Student Smoking, Cigarette Retail Sales Audit," 1953, Legacy Tobacco Documents Online, University of California, San Francisco, Legacy.library.ucsf.edu, Bates number: 990992810/2853 (retrieved August 28, 2012); Student Marketing Institute, "Student Marketing Institute Campus Campaign For The American Tobacco Company 1960–61, Faculty Supervisor Guide," 1961, Legacy Tobacco Documents Online, University of California, San Francisco, Legacy.library.ucsf.edu, Bates number: 990420449/0460 (retrieved August 28, 2012).

4. Student Marketing Institute, "Analysis of the Student Smoking Survey—73 non-campaign colleges," 1953, Legacy Tobacco Documents Online, University of California, San Francisco, Legacy.library.ucsf.edu, Bates number: 990992952/2970 (retrieved August 28, 2012); Student Marketing Institute, "American Tobacco Company, Campus Campaign Analysis Of The Student Smoking Survey, 147 Campaign Colleges" 1953, Legacy Tobacco Documents Online, University of California, San Francisco, Legacy.library.ucsf.edu, Bates number: 947220307/0366 (retrieved September 4, 2012).

5. Student Marketing Institute, "The American Tobacco Company Campus Campaign: Student Marketing Institute recommendations for 1955–1956," 1955, Legacy Tobacco Documents Online, University of California, San Francisco, Legacy.library.ucsf.edu, Bates number: 990992760/2775 (retrieved August 28, 2012).

6. Student Marketing Institute, Inc., "The American Tobacco Company Campus Campaign: Student Marketing Institute recommendations for 1955–1956," 1955, Legacy Tobacco Documents Online, University of California, San Francisco, Legacy.library.ucsf.edu, Bates number: 990992760/2775 (retrieved August 28, 2012).

7. Ronald E. Taylor, "A Six-Segment Message Strategy Wheel," *Journal of Advertising Research* 39(6), 1999, pp. 7–17.

8. Ronald E. Taylor, "A Six-

Segment Message Strategy Wheel," *Journal of Advertising Research* 39(6), 1999, pp. 7–17.

9. Image is not the original. Image recreated by the author.

10. Erwin P. Bettinghaus and M.J. Cody, *Persuasive Communication: Fifth Edition* (Fort Worth, TX: Harcourt Brace College, 1994), pp. 71–145.

11. H. Bruce Lammers, Laura Leibowitz, George Seymour, and Judith Hennessey, "Humor and Cognitive Response Stimuli," *Handbook of Humor Research*, P.E. McGhee and J.H. Goldstein, eds. (New York: Springer-Verlag, 1983).

12. G. Chronkhite and J. Liska, "The Judgment of Communicant Acceptability," in M. E. Roloff and G. R. Miller, eds. *Persuasion: New Directions in Theory and Research* (Beverly Hills: Sage, 1980), pp. 101–139.

13. Ellen Berscheid, "Opinion Change and Communicator-Comunicatee Similarity and Dissimilarity," *Journal of Personality and Social Psychology* 4, 1966, pp. 670–680.

14. Joanne R. Cantor, Herminia Alfonso, and Dolf Zillman, "The Persuasive Effectiveness of the Peer Appeal and a Communicator's First-Hand Experience," *Communication Research* 3, 1975, pp. 293–310.

15. Ellen Berscheid and Elaine Walster, "Physical Attractiveness," in L. Berkowitz, ed., *Advances in Experimental Social Psychology*, vol. 7 (New York: Academic Press, 1974), pp. 157–215.

16. Gary Chronkhite and Jo Ruth Liska, "The Judgment of Communicant Acceptability," in M.E. Roloff and G.R. Miller, eds., *Persuasion: New Directions in Theory and Research* (Beverly Hills: Sage, 1980), pp. 101–139.

17. Lynn R. Kahle and Pamela M. Homer, "Physical Attractiveness of the Celebrity Endorser: A Social Adaptation Perspective," *Journal of Consumer Research* 11, 1985, pp. 954–961.

18. Erwin P. Bettinghaus and Michael J. Cody, *Persuasive Communication*, 5th ed. (Fort Worth: Harcourt Brace College, 1994), pp. 71–145.

19. Erwin P. Bettinghaus and Michael J. Cody, *Persuasive Communication*, 5th ed. (Fort Worth: Harcourt Brace College, 1994), pp. 71–145.

20. Erwin P. Bettinghaus and Michael J. Cody, *Persuasive Communication*, 5th ed. (Fort Worth: Harcourt Brace College, 1994), pp. 71–145.

Chapter 5

1. Please note that the years listed on the graphs represent the first year of the academic year. For instance, the year 1920 represents the 1920–1921 academic year. The *Orange and White* is the student newspaper of the University of Tennessee. Although not a daily, its advertising frequency information is typical of most student newspapers.

2. "Briggs" Reedsburg, Wisconsin Website, 2000 (retrieved June 15, 2007).

3. *Orange and White*, April 26, 1928.

4. *Orange and White*, April 12, 1928.

5. *Orange and White*, April 5, 1928.

6. Jim Vadeboncoeur, Jr. "John Held Jr." *BPIB* (retrieved April 15, 2007).

Chapter 6

1. *The Daily Princetonian*, Princeton University, March 4, 1935.

2. *Orange and White*, April 13, 1933.

3. *Orange and White*, April 25, 1933.

4. *Orange and White*, May 9, 1933.

5. *Orange and White*, April 6, 1934.

6. *Orange and White*, March 9, 1934.

7. *Orange and White*, September 26, 1934.

8. *Orange and White*, February 9, 1934.

9. *Orange and White*, May 3, 1935.

10. *Orange and White*, September 26, 1934.

11. *Orange and White*, February 13, 1935.

12. *The Vassar Miscellany News*, January 23, 1935.

13. *Orange and White*, March 29, 1935.

14. *Orange and White*, April 16, 1935.

15. *Orange and White*, February 15, 1936.

16. *Orange and White*, November 6, 1931.

17. *Orange and White*, October 22, 1931.

18. *Orange and White*, February 4, 1937.

19. *Orange and White*, March 5, 1937.

20. *Orange and White*, February 26, 1937.

21. *Orange and White*, February 18, 1937.

22. *Orange and White*, March 26, 1937.

23. *Orange and White*, October 12, 1934.

24. *Orange and White*, October 19, 1934.

25. *Orange and White*, October 26, 1934.

26. *Orange and White*, November 23, 1934.

Chapter 7

1. The University of Tennessee paper changed its name from the *Orange and White* to *The Orange and White*.

2. *The Orange and White*, the campus paper of the University of Tennessee, is used as a case study for this book. The advertising appearing in this newspaper is representative of most student papers.

3. *The Orange and White,* October 3, 1947.

4. *The Orange and White*, October 8, 1947.

5. *The Orange and White*, October 15, 1947.

6. *The Orange and White*, October 22, 1947.

7. *The Orange and White*, October 29, 1947.

8. *The Orange and White*, October 3, 1947.

9. *The Orange and White*, December 10, 1947.

10. *The Orange and White*, January 14, 1948.

11. *The Orange and White*, February 20, 1948.

12. *The Orange and White*, January 16, 1948.

13. *The Orange and White*, December 1, 1948.

14. *The Orange and White*, November 19, 1948.

15. *The Orange and White*, October 22, 1948.

16. *The Orange and White*, October 27, 1948.

17. "Call for Phillip Morris!!!" Johnny's website—Bellhop.org (retrieved April 22, 2007).

18. *The Orange and White*, October 8, 1948

19. *The Orange and White*, February 12, 1947.

20. *The Orange and White*, January 24, 1947.

21. *The Orange and White*, February 26, 1947.

Chapter 8

1. M. Joycelyn Elders, *Preventing Tobacco Use Among Young People: A Report of the Surgeon General* (U.S. Department of Health and Human Services, 1997), p. 167.

2. M. Joycelyn Elders, *Preventing Tobacco Use Among Young People: A Report of the Surgeon General* (U.S. Department of Health and Human Services, 1997), p. 167.

3. Eugene Gilbert, *Advertising and Marketing to Young People* (Pleasantville, NY: Printer's Ink Books, 1957) p. 184.

4. Student Marketing Institute, Inc. "Lucky Strike Campus Campaign–1953–1954 Analysis of: Survey Of Student Smoking, Cigarette Retail Sales Audit," 1953, Legacy Tobacco Documents Online, University of California, San Francisco, Legacy.library.ucsf.edu, Bates number: 990992810/2853 (retrieved August 28, 2012).

5. *The Orange and White*, October 4, 1950.

6. *The Orange and White*, October 11, 1950.

7. *The Orange and White*, October 18, 1950.

8. *The Orange and White*, September 24, 1953.

9. *The Orange and White*, November 19, 1953.

10. *The Orange and White*, December 3, 1953.

11. *The Orange and White*, December 10, 1953.

12. *The Orange and White*, January 28, 1953.

13. *The Orange and White*, November 7, 1951.

14. *The Orange and White*, October 3, 1951.

15. *The Orange and White*, October 24, 1951.

16. *The Orange and White*, October 31, 1951.

17. *The Orange and White*, October 17, 1951.

18. *The Orange and White*, November 28, 1951.

19. *The Spectrum*, NDSU, April 7, 1950.

20. *The Spectrum,* NDSU, February 10, 1950.

21. *The Spectrum,* NDSU, January 20, 1950.

22. *The Orange and White*, November 7, 1958.

23. *The Orange and White*, October 24, 1958.

24. *The Orange and White*, October 17, 1958.

25. *The Orange and White*, October 10, 1958.

26. Max Shulman, "Adventures in Social Science: No. 1: Ad. No. 144—Req. No. 77198—2/3 page—45/8 x10 in.," December 15, 1958, Legacy Tobacco Documents Online, University of California, San Francisco, Legacy.library.ucsf.edu, Bates number: 1002760575 (retrieved July 28, 2006).

27.

28. *Vassar Miscellany News*, Wednesday, October 12, 1955.

29. *The Orange and White*, January 31, 1958.

30. *The Orange and White*, October 4, 1957.

31. *The Orange and White*, November 8, 1957.

32. *The Daily Iowan*, October 17, 1958.

Chapter 9

1. M. Joycelyn Elders, *Preventing Tobacco Use Among Young People: A Report of the Surgeon General* (Washington, D.C.: U.S. Department of Health and Human Services, 1997), p. 167; Ruth and Edward Brecher, Arthur Herzog, Walter Goodman, Gerald Walker, and The Editors of Consumer Reports, *The Consumers Union Report on Smoking and the Public Interest* (Mount Vernon, NY: Consumers Union, 1963).

2. *The Orange and White*, the campus paper of the University of Tennessee, is used as a case study for this book. The advertising appearing in this newspaper is representative of most student papers.

3. *The Daily Illini*, the University of Illinois, December 6, 1961.

4. *The Orange and White*, September 30, 1960.

5. *The Orange and White*, January 6, 1961.

6. *The Orange and White*, May 27, 1960.

7. *The Daily Illini*, The University of Illinois, December 8, 1961.

8. Roman lettering for dual.

9. *The Daily Illini*, The University of Illinois, December 8, 1961.

Chapter 10

1. Tina Eger, "Tobacco Card Series Included Carthage," *From the Vault,* no date, http://www.carthage.edu/news/carthage/2012/10/23/from-the-vault-an-unusual-artifact/ (retrieved July 22, 2013).

2. College Series, 51–75, Duke University Libraries, http://library.duke.edu/rubenstein/scriptorium/eaa/tobacco/D02/D0253/D0253-01–72dpi.html (Retrieved July 22, 2013).

3. Roy Nuhn, "Murad Cigarette Cards," *The Antique Shoppe Newspaper,* January 2010.

4. Michigan State University Archives Item #62 and Item #130.

5. CCNY, "CCNY in Souvenirs," Digital Archives, 2013.

6. "Luckies Runs College Drive," *Advertising Age* 24, no. 46 (1953), p. 99; M. Joycelyn Elders, *Preventing Tobacco Use Among Young People: A Report of the Surgeon General* (Washington, D.C.: U.S. Department of Health and Human Services, 1997), p.167.

7. Because advertisers ran one single advertisement for the entire season, ads are discussed thematically. No frequency information was collected because the numbers would be the same for most seasons because of the single insertion.

8. Lucky Strike College 1937–1953, Legacy Tobacco Documents Online, University of California, San Francisco, Legacy.library.ucsf.edu, Bates number: 990904548/5178. (retrieved June 5, 2013).

9. 1924 Football Program—UT vs. Carson-Newman, University of Tennessee Archives, October 18, 1924.

10. "Lucky Strike College 1937–1953," Legacy Tobacco Documents Online, University of California, San Francisco, Legacy.library.ucsf.edu, Bates number: 990904548/5178 (retrieved June 5, 2013).

11. 1935 Football Program—UT vs. Alabama, University of Tennessee Archives, October 19, 1935.

12. Lord & Thomas and American Tobacco Company, "All American Board of Football," March 24,

1936, Legacy Tobacco Documents Online, University of California, San Francisco, Legacy.library.ucsf.edu, Bates number: 634341771 (retrieved June 19, 2013).

13. Lord & Thomas and American Tobacco Company, "All American Board of Football," March 24, 1936, Legacy Tobacco Documents Online, University of California, San Francisco, Legacy.library.ucsf.edu, Bates number: 634341771 (retrieved June 19, 2013).

14. M. Joycelyn Elders, *Preventing Tobacco Use Among Young People: A Report of the Surgeon General* (Washington, D.C.: U.S. Department of Health and Human Services, 1997), p.167.

15. R.B. Walker, American Tobacco Company, "Letter dated September 19, 1955," Legacy Tobacco Documents Online, University of California, San Francisco, Legacy.library.ucsf.edu, Bates number: 990070239/0242 (retrieved June 5, 2013).

16. Don Spenser Company, Inc., "Letter to College Football Program Publishers," August 3, 1953, Legacy Tobacco Document Library, Bates number: 990078152 (retrieved June 19, 2013).

17. "Lucky Strike, Four Color, Two Color, Black & White, Sunday Comics, Sunday Supplements, 1956, 1944–1947," 1956, Legacy Tobacco Documents Online, University of California, San Francisco, Legacy.library.ucsf.edu, Bates number: 945141715/2002 (retrieved June 5, 2013).

18. Lucky Strike College, 1954–1963, Legacy Tobacco Documents Online, University of California, San Francisco, Legacy.library.ucsf.edu, Bates number: 798581/015 (retrieved June 5, 2013).

19. Circular Book, 1951, Legacy Tobacco Documents. Bates number: 947038669/8743 (retrieved June 5, 2013).

20. Lucky Strike College, 1954–1963, Legacy Tobacco Documents Online, University of California, San Francisco, Legacy.library.ucsf.edu, Bates number: 798581/015 (retrieved June 5, 2013).

21. R.B. Walker, American Tobacco Company, September 5, 1958, Legacy Tobacco Documents Online, University of California, San Francisco, Legacy.library.ucsf.edu, Bates number: 947039433/947039434 (retrieved June 5, 2013).

22. Lucky Strike College, 1954–1963, Legacy Tobacco Documents Online, University of California, San Francisco, Legacy.library.ucsf.edu, Bates number: 798581/015 (retrieved June 5, 2013).

23. F.X. Whelan, American Tobacco Company, "A Memorandum to Albert R. Stevens, Advertising Manager," February 18, 1958, Bates number: 968259369 (retrieved February 18, 1958).

24. Jesse Russell and Ronald Cohn, *The Tobacco Bowl* (Edinburgh, UK: Bookvika, 2012).

25. R. Gregg Cherry, game program for the *Piedmont—Tobacco Bowl Classic*, Durham, NC. VSU Library and Media Services (retrieved June 19, 2013) p. 1.

26. Game program for the *Piedmont—Tobacco Bowl Classic*, Durham, NC. Virginia State University Library and Media Services (retrieved June 19, 2013) p. 2.

27. R. Gregg Cherry, game program for the *Piedmont—Tobacco Bowl Classic*, Durham, NC, p.2, Virginia State University Library and Media Services (retrieved June 19, 2013).

28. James E. Shepard, game program for the *Piedmont—Tobacco Bowl Classic*, p. 3, Durham, NC. Virginia State University Library and Media Services (retrieved June 19, 2013) p. 3.

29. Robert C. Kennedy, "On this Day: July 27, 1897," *The New York Times*, July 27, 2001.

30. Ronald A. Smith, *Play-by-Play: Radio, Television, and Big-Time College Sport* (Baltimore: Johns Hopkins University Press, 2001), pp. 114–115.

31. Ronald A. Smith, *Play-by-Play: Radio, Television, and Big-Time College Sport* (Baltimore: Johns Hopkins University Press, 2001), pp: 114–115.

32. Ronald A. Smith, *Play-by-Play: Radio, Television, and Big-Time College Sport* (Baltimore: Johns Hopkins University Press, 2001), pp: 114–115.

33. "Television Continuity, Lucky Strike Football September—November 1947," November 1947, Legacy Tobacco Documents Online, University of California, San Francisco, Legacy.library.ucsf.edu, Bates number: 990005873/6454 (retrieved June 19, 2013).

34. "Television Continuity, Lucky Strike Football September—November 1947," November 1947, Legacy Tobacco Documents Online, University of California, San Francisco, Legacy.library.ucsf.edu, Bates number: 990005873/6454 (retrieved June 19, 2013).

35. "Television Continuity, Lucky Strike, Football, Sept.-Oct. 1949," 1949, Legacy Tobacco Documents Online, University of California, San Francisco, Legacy.library.ucsf.edu, Bates number: 945005079/5484 (retrieved June 19, 2013).

36. "Television Continuity, Lucky Strike, Football, Sept.-Oct. 1949," 1949, Legacy Tobacco Documents Online, University of California, San Francisco, Legacy.library.ucsf.edu, Bates number: 945005079/5484 (retrieved June 19, 2013).

37. "Lucky Strike Cigarettes BIG TEN Conference Basketball 1963 Season," January 8, 1963, Legacy Tobacco Documents (retrieved June 9, 2013).

38. "Memo to the Entire Sales Organization," November 7, 1958, Legacy Tobacco Documents Online, University of California, San Francisco, Legacy.library.ucsf.edu, Bates number: 968301571.

39. BBDO Television, "Television Closing Commercial—College #3" September 24, 1952, Legacy Tobacco Documents Online, University of California, San Francisco, Legacy.library.ucsf.edu, Bates number: 968301571/1575 (retrieved June 9, 2013).

40. E.A. Harvey, American Tobacco Company, "Dorothy Collins Point-of-Sale Material," January 12, 1951, Legacy Tobacco Documents Online, University of California, San Francisco, Legacy.library.ucsf.edu, Bates number: 990078422/8423 (retrieved June 19, 2013).

41. Dunning, E.R., American Tobacco Company, "Dorothy Collins Coffee Promotion," April 22, 1952, Legacy Tobacco Documents Online, University of California, San Francisco, Legacy.library.ucsf.edu, Bates number: 990078116/8117 (retrieved June 19, 2013).

42. American Tobacco Company, "No Title—Radio Commercials," 1931, Legacy Tobacco Documents Online, University of California, San Francisco, Legacy.library.ucsf.edu, Bates number: 990011932/2064 (retrieved June 19, 2013).

43. Liggett & Myers, "Chester-field," no date, Legacy Tobacco Documents Online, University of California, San Francisco, Legacy.library.ucsf.edu, Bates number: LG0502191 (retrieved June 19, 2013).

44. V.J. Boor, "Agreement between The American Tobacco Company and Ed Thorgersen," September 26, 1952, Legacy Tobacco Documents Online, University of California, San Francisco, Legacy.library.ucsf.edu, Bates number: 990567213/7217 (retrieved June 19, 2013).

45. "Television Continuity, Lucky Strike, This Is Show Business, Nov. 1952 Thru Jan. 1953" January 1953, Legacy Tobacco Documents Online, University of California, San Francisco, Legacy.library.ucsf.edu, Bates number, 945296739/7100 (retrieved June 19, 2013).

46. BBDO Television, "The American Tobacco Company Lucky Strike: Film Commercial College Survey, No. 57 (Time 1:30)," September 19, 1953, Legacy Tobacco Documents Online, University of California, San Francisco, Legacy.library.ucsf.edu, Bates number: 968301552/1554 (retrieved June 9, 2013).

47. BBDO Television, "The American Tobacco Company Lucky Strike: Film Commercial College Survey, No. 57 (Time 1:30)," November 19, 1953, Legacy Tobacco Documents Online, University of California, San Francisco, Legacy.library.ucsf.edu, Bates number: 945236636/7418 (retrieved June 9, 2013).

48. "The American Tobacco Company Lucky Strike College Radio One Minute Recorded Commercial," September 16, 1954, Legacy Tobacco Documents Online, University of California, San Francisco, Legacy.library.ucsf.edu, Bates number: 945085429/5950 (retrieved June 19, 2013).

49. Student Marketing Institute, "Campus Representative Activity Guide For The American Tobacco Company Campus Campaign, 1955–56," 1955, Bates number: 990992726/2759 (retrieved June 19, 2013).

50. Student Marketing Institute, "Campus Representative Activity Guide For The American Tobacco Company Campus Campaign, 1955–56," 1955, Bates number: 990992726/2759 (retrieved June 19, 2013).

51. E.F. Mooney, "To Selected Members of the Sales Organization," August 25, 1959, Legacy Tobacco Documents Online, University of California, San Francisco, Legacy.library.ucsf.edu, Bates number: 990091374/1408 (retrieved June 19, 2013).

52. F.X. Towers, "Dual Filter Tareyton Radio Sponsorship of Naval Academy Football Games," Legacy Tobacco Documents Online, University of California, San Francisco, Legacy.library.ucsf.edu, Bates Number 990091374/1408 (retrieved June 19, 2013).

53. R.B. Walker, "To Selected District Managers," October 11, 1960, Legacy Tobacco Documents Online, University of California, San Francisco, Legacy.library.ucsf.edu, Bates number: 947038544/8576 (retrieved June 19, 2013).

54. R.B. Walker, "To Selected District Managers," October 3, 1960, Legacy Tobacco Documents Online, University of California, San Francisco, Legacy.library.ucsf.edu, Bates number: 947038544/8576 (retrieved June 19, 2013).

55. BBDO Radio, "40-Second Transcribed Radio Commercial College Football, Frank Gifford #5—campus buildup," September 15, 1961, Legacy Tobacco Documents Online, University of California, San Francisco, Legacy.library.ucsf.edu, Bates number: 990627310/7323 (retrieved June 19, 2013).

56. R.B. Walker, "A Memorandum to Mr. Paul H. Hahn, President," July 29, 1960, Legacy Tobacco Documents Online, University of California, San Francisco, Legacy.library.ucsf.edu, Bates number: 990061998/2018 (retrieved June 19, 2013).

57. BBDO Television, "Men Who Make the Team—Tommy Trainer," December 22, 1960, Legacy Tobacco Documents Online, University of California, San Francisco, Legacy.library.ucsf.edu, Bates number: ATX01 0238825 (retrieved June 19, 2013).

58. BBDO Television, "Men Who Make the Team—Tommy Trainer," December 22, 1960, Legacy Tobacco Documents Online, University of California, San Francisco, Legacy.library.ucsf.edu, Bates number: ATX01 0238825 (retrieved June 19, 2013).

59. "Lucky Strike Cigarette BIG TEN Conference Basketball 1963 Season," January 8, 1963, Legacy Tobacco Documents Online, University of California, San Francisco, Legacy.library.ucsf.edu, Bates number: 990906328/6783 (retrieved June 19, 2013).

60. "The American Tobacco Company 1964 Lucky Strike Budget for Local TV and Radio," September 1, 1964, Legacy Tobacco Documents Online, University of California, San Francisco, Legacy.library.ucsf.edu, Bates number: 990697255/7261 (retrieved June 19, 2013).

61. BBDO, "The American Tobacco Company Radio—NCAA College Basketball," February 5, 1964, Legacy Tobacco Documents Online, University of California, San Francisco, Legacy.library.ucsf.edu, Bates number: 980293432/980293442 (retrieved June 19, 2013).

62. R.B. Meyner, "To All Members," September 15, 1965, Legacy Tobacco Documents Online, University of California, San Francisco, Legacy.library.ucsf.edu, Bates number: 980269086 (retrieved June 19, 2013).

63. Paul R. Dixon, "Report to Congress Pursuant to the Federal Cigarette Labeling and Advertising Act," June 30, 1968, Legacy Tobacco Documents Online, University of California, San Francisco, Legacy.library.ucsf.edu, Bates number: 3990360379/3990360461 (retrieved June 19, 2013).

64. Ronald A. Smith, *Play-by-Play: Radio, Television, and Big-Time College Sport* (Baltimore: Johns Hopkins University Press, 2001), pp. 114–115.

65. Robert B. Meyner, "Letter to Members Dated September 15, 1965," September 15, 1965, Bates number: USTC-00123116 (retrieved June 19, 2013).

66. Robert B. Meyner, "Letter to Members," December 2, 1965, Legacy Tobacco Documents Online, University of California, San Francisco, Legacy.library.ucsf.edu, Bates number: 3205134 (retrieved June 19, 2013).

67. Susan Wagner, *Cigarette Country: Tobacco in American History and Politics* (New York: Praeger, 1971), p. 168.

68. R.B. Meyner, "Letter to FCC Commissioner Paul Rand Dixon," April 11, 1967, Legacy Tobacco Document Library, Bates number: 50193–748 (retrieved June 19, 2013).

69. R.B. Meyner, "Letter to Code Members, May 9, 1967," May 9, 1967, Legacy Tobacco Documents Online, University of California, San Francisco, Legacy.library.ucsf.edu, Bates number: 6802742 48–680274248 (retrieved June 9, 2013).

70. Susan Wagner, *Cigarette Country: Tobacco in American History and Politics* (New York, NY: Praeger, 1971), p. 169.

71. Cornelia Pechmann, "Does Antismoking Advertising Combat Underage Smoking? A Review of Past Practices and Research," in *Social Marketing: Theoretical and Practical Perspectives*, M. E. Goldberg, M. Fishbein, and S. Middlestadt, eds. (Hillsdale, NJ: Lawrence Erlbaum Associates, 1997), pp. 189–216.

72. Susan Wagner, *Cigarette Country: Tobacco in American History and Politics* (New York: Praeger, 1971), p. 169.

73. Robert L. Rabin and Stephen D. Sugarman, *Regulating Tobacco* (New York: Oxford University Press) p. 85.

74. "Editorial Hits 'Conflicting Interests,'" *Broadcasting,* December 11, 1967, Legacy Tobacco Documents Online, University of California, San Francisco, Legacy.library.ucsf.edu, Bates number: TI25901769-TI25901770 (retrieved June 19, 2013).

75. "Editorial Hits 'Conflicting Interests,'" *Broadcasting,* December 11, 1967, Legacy Tobacco Documents Online, University of California, San Francisco, Legacy.library.ucsf.edu, Bates number: TI25901769-TI25901770 (retrieved June 19, 2013).

76. Susan Wagner, *Cigarette Country: Tobacco in American History and Politics.* (New York: Praeger, 1971). p. 169.

77. Robert L. Rabin and Stephen D. Sugarman, *Regulating Tobacco* (New York: Oxford University Press) p. 85.

78. R. B. Meyner, "Letter to Hon. Robert F. Kennedy," November 22, 1967, Tobacco Legacy Documents Library, Bates number: 68243286 (retrieved June 9, 2013).

79. "New Blast Hits Cigarette Ads: Kennedy Asks Industry, Football Leaders to Ban Cigarette Spots from Games," *Broadcasting,* Novem-

ber 22, 1967, Tobacco Legacy Documents Library, Bates number: T075457 (retrieved June 19, 2013).

80. Robert Kennedy, "Telegram Sent to Mr. Manuel Yellen of P. Lorillard Company," November 17, 1967, Legacy Tobacco Documents Online, University of California, San Francisco, Legacy.library.ucsf. edu, Bates number: 2075275383 (retrieved June 19, 2013).

81. R. B. Meyner, "Letter to Hon. Robert F. Kennedy," November 22, 1967, Tobacco Legacy Documents Library, Bates number: 68243286 (retrieved June 9, 2013).

82. "New Blast Hits Cigarette Ads: Kennedy Asks Industry, Football Leaders to Ban Cigarette Spots from Games," *Broadcasting,* November 22, 1967, Tobacco Legacy Documents Library, Bates number: T075457 (retrieved June 19, 2013).

83. "New Blast Hits Cigarette Ads: Kennedy Asks Industry, Football Leaders to Ban Cigarette Spots from Games," *Broadcasting,* November 22, 1967, Tobacco Legacy Documents Library, Bates number: T075457 (retrieved June 19, 2013).

84. *Times,* "RFK Challenges Tobacco Advertising," St. Petersburg, FL, December 9, 1967.

85. *Times,* "RFK Challenges Tobacco Advertising," St. Petersburg, FL, December 9, 1967.

86. *Times,* "RFK Challenges Tobacco Advertising," St. Petersburg, FL, December 9, 1967.

87. *Times,* "RFK Challenges Tobacco Advertising," St. Petersburg, FL, December 9, 1967.

88. Robert F. Kennedy, "Should Cigarette Advertising on Television Be Subjected to Stringent Regulations?" *Television Magazine,* December 8, 1967, p. 60

89. Earl C. Clements, "Should Cigarette Advertising on Television Be Subjected to Stringent Regulations?" *Television Magazine,* December 8, 1967, p. 61.

90. "NCAA's Plant Backs RFK's 'Anti' Moves," *Broadcasting,* December 11, 1967, p. 9

91. "Lorillard Surrendered Just after Thanksgiving," *Broadcasting,* February 12, 1968, p. 28.

92. *Broadcasting,* "Magnuson Sharpens Advertising Blade," February 5, 1968, p. 10.

93. *Advertising Age,* "Banzhaf Files Fraud Plaints on Cigaret Articles," March 25, 1968.

94. Robert B. Meyner, "Letter to FCC Chairman Dixon," May 15, 1968, p. 5, Legacy Tobacco Documents Online, University of California, San Francisco, Legacy.library. ucsf.edu, Bates number: 502429585 (retrieved June 9, 2013).

95. Robert B. Meyner, "Letter to FCC Chairman Dixon," May 15, 1968, Legacy Tobacco Documents Online, University of California, San Francisco, Legacy.library.ucsf. edu, Bates number: 50242 9585, pp. 5–6 (retrieved June 9, 2013).

96. Susan Wagner, *Cigarette Country: Tobacco in American History and Politics* (New York: Praeger, 1971), pp. 166–173.

97. Ronald A. Smith, *Play-by-Play: Radio, Television, and Big-Time College Sport* (Baltimore: Johns Hopkins University Press, 2001), pp. 114–115

98. Susan Wagner, *Cigarette Country: Tobacco in American History and Politics* (New York: Praeger, 1971), p. 209.

99. Susan Wagner, *Cigarette Country: Tobacco in American History and Politics* (New York: Praeger, 1971), pp. 209–210.

100. Susan Wagner, *Cigarette Country: Tobacco in American History and Politics* (New York: Praeger, 1971), p. 212.

101. Susan Wagner, *Cigarette Country: Tobacco in American History and Politics* (New York: Praeger, 1971), p. 212.

102. Ronald A. Smith, *Play-by-Play: Radio, Television, and Big-Time College Sport* (Baltimore: Johns Hopkins University Press, 2001), pp. 114–115

103. Mackay Yanagisawa, "Letter to the American Information Corporation," December 2, 1975, Legacy Tobacco Documents Online, University of California, San Francisco, Legacy.library.ucsf.edu, Bates number: 5017110 (retrieved June 19, 2013).

Chapter 11

1. Robert Sobel, *They Satisfy: The Cigarette and American Life* (Garden City, NJ: Anchor Press, 1978), pp. 35–45.

2. *Orange and White,* 1930–1931.

3. *The Orange and White,* March 10, 1943.

4. *The Miami Hurricane,* University of Miami, April 1, 1960.

5. *The Orange and White,* October 5, 1956.

6. *The Orange and White,* October 24, 1958.

7. *Orange and White,* November 15, 1932.

8. *Orange and White,* March 29, 1935.

9. *The Princetonian,* Princeton University, April 5, 1928.

10. *The Orange and White,* University of Tennessee, November 7, 1951.

11. *The Orange and White,* University of Tennessee, October 3, 1951.

12. *The Orange and White,* University of Tennessee, October 24, 1951.

13. *The Orange and White,* University of Tennessee, October 31, 1951.

14. *The Orange and White,* University of Tennessee, October 17, 1951.

15. *The Orange and White,* University of Tennessee, November 28, 1951.

16. *The Ram,* Fordham University, October 29, 1953.

17. *The Orange and White,* University of Tennessee, October 21, 1960.

18. *The Daily Iowan,* University of Iowa, October 4, 1960.

19. *The Daily Student,* University of Minnesota, October 7, 1960.

20. *Orange and White,* University of Tennessee, March 29, 1935.

21. *The Daily Illini,* University of Illinois, February 7, 1935.

22. *The Daily Iowan,* University of Iowa, March 3, 1935.

23. *The Tech,* M.I.T., October 26, 1934.

24. *The State College Aztec,* San Diego State University, May 6, 1936.

25. *Orange and White,* February 18, 1937.

26. *Orange and White,* February 26, 1937.

27. University of Tennessee.

28. University of Minnesota.

29. University of Iowa.

30. Fordham University.

31. SUNY-Buffalo.

32. M.I.T.

33. San Diego State University.

34. Princeton University.

35. *The Daily Princetonian,* Princeton University, February 12, 1935.

36. *Orange and White,* March 29, 1935.

37. *The Tech*, M.I.T. November 20, 1951.

38. *The Orange and White*, October 9, 1952.

39. *The Orange and White*, November 14, 1958.

40. *The Miami Hurricane*, University of Miami, April 1, 1960.

41. *The Miami Hurricane*, University of Miami, April 1, 1960.

42. "Biography for Jack Oakie," *IMDb* website, no date, http://www.imdb.com/name/nm0642988/ (retrieved June 15, 2007).

43. "Jack Oakie College," *Generic Radio Workshop Script Library*, May 11, 1937, http://www.genericradio.com/series.php?tag=jackoakie (retrieved June 15, 2007).

44. Stephen Fox, *The Mirror Makers: A History of American Advertising and Its Creators* (Chicago: University of Illinois Press, 1997), p. 116.

45. *The Minnesota Daily*, University of Minnesota, November 3, 1931.

46. *The Minnesota Daily*, University of Minnesota, November 10, 1931.

47. *Orange and White*, University of Tennessee, October 22, 1931, and February 5, 1932.

48. *The Daily Iowan*, University of Iowa, December 1, 1931.

49. *Orange and White*, University of Tennessee, February 12, 1932.

50. *Orange and White*, University of Tennessee, February 26, 1932.

51. *Orange and White*, University of Tennessee, March 4, 1932.

52. T. Abrams, P. Crist, S. Kaczynski, and W. Marple, "Confidential Report Containing Legal Advice and Attorney Opinion Work Product Regarding Numerous Smoking and Health Issues Relevant to Litigation, Prepared by Outside Counsel for RJR, with Whom B&W Maintains A Common Legal Interest, and Forwarded to B&W in–House Counsel," no date, 271, Legacy Tobacco Documents Online, University of California, San Francisco, Legacy.library.ucsf.edu, Bates number: 681879254–681879715 (retrieved July 28, 2006).

53. R.J. Reynolds Tobacco Co., "46 F.T.C. 706 (1950). modified, 192 F. 2d 535 (7th Cir. 1951) order modified 48 F.T.C. 682," 1955 (retrieved August 12, 2012).

54. 55 F.T.C. 354 (1958) (Bruff Depo. Exh. 7)

55. F.T.C., "Modified Order to Cease and Desist," January 17, 1952, Legacy Tobacco Documents Online, University of California, San Francisco, Legacy.library.ucsf.edu, Bates number: 980300590/059 (retrieved August 12, 2012).

56.

57. John E. Calfee, "The Ghost of Cigarette Advertising Regulation Past," *Regulation* 20, no. 3 (1997) (retrieved 28 July 2006).

58. John E. Calfee, "The Ghost of Cigarette Advertising Regulation Past," *Regulation* 20 no. 3 (1997) (retrieved July 28, 2006).

59. Stanley L. Temko, "The Tobacco Institute, Inc. Minutes of the Eighteenth Meeting of the Executive Committee," June 18, 1963 (est.), Tobacco Documents Online, TobaccoDocuments.org, Bates number: 2022975647–20229756 50 (retrieved July 20, 2006).

Chapter 12

1. Douglas S. Thompson, "Effective Approaches for Smoking Education Programs in Colleges," Presented at the National Interagency Conference on Smoking and Health, University of Maryland, College Park, Maryland, May 2, 1966, pp. 3–4, Legacy Tobacco Documents Online, University of California, San Francisco, Legacy.library.ucsf.edu, Bates number: 513337295 (retrieved July 22, 2013).

2. Douglas S. Thompson, "Effective Approaches for Smoking Education Programs in Colleges," Presented at the National Interagency Conference on Smoking and Health, University of Maryland, College Park, Maryland, May 2, 1966, pp. 3–4, Legacy Tobacco Documents Online, University of California, San Francisco, Legacy.library.ucsf.edu, Bates number: 513337295 (retrieved July 22, 2013).

3. Prepared for RJR by the Economic and Market Analysis Department, Eastman Chemical Products, "1969 Survey or Cigarette Smoking Behavior and Attitudes," 1969, Legacy Tobacco Documents Online, University of California, San Francisco, Legacy.library.ucsf.edu, Bates number: 508124318 (retrieved July 15, 2013).

4. Prepared for RJR by the Economic and Market Analysis Department, Eastman Chemical Prod-

ucts, "1969 Survey or Cigarette Smoking Behavior and Attitudes," 1969, p. 6, Legacy Tobacco Documents Online, University of California, San Francisco, Legacy.library.ucsf.edu, Bates number: 50812 4318 (retrieved July 15, 2013).

5. Prepared for RJR by the Economic and Market Analysis Department, Eastman Chemical Products, "1969 Survey or Cigarette Smoking Behavior and Attitudes," 1969, p. 18, Legacy Tobacco Documents Online, University of California, San Francisco, Legacy.library.ucsf.edu, Bates number: 50812 4318 (retrieved July 15, 2013).

6. Prepared for RJR by the Economic and Market Analysis Department, Eastman Chemical Products, "1969 Survey or Cigarette Smoking Behavior and Attitudes," 1969, p. 19 Legacy Tobacco Documents Online, University of California, San Francisco, Legacy.library.ucsf.edu, Bates number: 50812 4318 (retrieved July 15, 2013).

7. Prepared for RJR by the Economic and Market Analysis Department, Eastman Chemical Products, "1969 Survey or Cigarette Smoking Behavior and Attitudes," 1969, p. 26, Legacy Tobacco Documents Online, University of California, San Francisco, Legacy.library.ucsf.edu, Bates number: 50812 4318 (retrieved July 15, 2013).

8. "Smoking and Youth: College Poll Shows Students' Smoking Habits." *Tobacco Reporter*, 1971, pp. 72–74, Legacy Tobacco Documents Online, University of California, San Francisco, Legacy.library.ucsf.edu, Bates number: 2045207186 (retrieved July 10, 2013).

9. "Smoking and Youth: College Poll Shows Students' Smoking Habits." *Tobacco Reporter*, 1971, pp. 72–74, Legacy Tobacco Documents Online, University of California, San Francisco, Legacy.library.ucsf.edu, Bates number: 2045207186 (retrieved July 10, 2013).

10. Benjamin A. Toll and P.M. Ling, "The Virginia Slims Identity Crisis: An Inside Look at Tobacco Industry Marketing to Women," *Tobacco Control* 14, no. 3 (June 2005): 172.

11. The Roper Organization, "A Study of Smoking Habits Among Young Smokers, Prepared for Phillip Morris, Inc. 1975," 1975, p. 8.

12. Daniel H. Murphy, "Ethnic

Research—Black Smokers" June 25, 1979, Legacy Tobacco Documents Online, University of California, San Francisco, Legacy.library.ucsf.edu, Bates number: 501334546 (retrieved July 10, 2013).

13. Daniel H. Murphy, "Ethnic Research—Black Smokers" June 25, 1979, Legacy Tobacco Documents Online, University of California, San Francisco, Legacy.library.ucsf.edu, Bates number: 501334546 (retrieved July 10, 2013).

14. "Women's Cigarette Market," 1973, p. 6, Legacy Tobacco Documents Online, University of California, San Francisco, Legacy.library.ucsf.edu, Bates number: 502645875 (retrieved July 22, 2013).

15. "Women's Cigarette Market," 1973, p. 2, Legacy Tobacco Documents Online, University of California, San Francisco, Legacy.library.ucsf.edu, Bates number: 502645875 (retrieved July 22, 2013).

16. Hal Weinstein, "How an Agency Builds a Brand: The Virginia Slims Story," October 28, 1969, p. 31, Legacy Tobacco Documents Online, University of California, San Francisco, Legacy.library.ucsf.edu, Bates number: 0002430029 (retrieved July 22, 2013).

17. Hal Weinstein, "How an Agency Builds a Brand: The Virginia Slims Story," October 28, 1969, 20, Legacy Tobacco Documents Online, University of California, San Francisco, Legacy.library.ucsf.edu, Bates number: 0002430029, Retrieved: July 22, 2013.

18. Benjamin A. Toll and P.M. Ling, "The Virginia Slims Identity Crisis: An Inside Look at Tobacco Industry Marketing to Women," *Tobacco Control* 14, no. 3 (June 2005): 173.

19. Benjamin A. Toll and P.M. Ling, "The Virginia Slims Identity Crisis: An Inside Look at Tobacco Industry Marketing to Women," *Tobacco Control* 14, no. 3 (June 2005): 173.

20. Benjamin A. Toll and P.M. Ling, "The Virginia Slims Identity Crisis: An Inside Look at Tobacco Industry Marketing to Women," *Tobacco Control* 14, no. 3 (June 2005): 173.

21. Hal Weinstein, "How an Agency Builds a Brand: The Virginia Slims Story," October 28, 1969, p. 20, Legacy Tobacco Documents Online, University of California, San Francisco, Legacy.library.ucsf.edu, Bates number: 0002430029 (retrieved July 22, 2013).

22. Hal Weinstein, "How an Agency Builds a Brand: The Virginia Slims Story," October 28, 1969, p. 20, Legacy Tobacco Documents Online, University of California, San Francisco, Legacy.library.ucsf.edu, Bates number: 0002430029 (retrieved July 22, 2013).

23. Hal Weinstein, "How an Agency Builds a Brand: The Virginia Slims Story," October 28, 1969, p. 17, Legacy Tobacco Documents Online, University of California, San Francisco, Legacy.library.ucsf.edu, Bates number: 0002430029 (retrieved July 22, 2013).

24. Landor Associates, "Project Review and Cost Estimate Virginia Slims Ultra Lights Number 1630 100mm Flip Top Box Design," November 8, 1989, pp. 1–2, Legacy Tobacco Documents Online, University of California, San Francisco, Legacy.library.ucsf.edu, Bates number: 2044696148/6149 (retrieved July 22, 2013); Marketing Perceptions, "Virginia Slims Packaging," September 1998, Legacy Tobacco Documents Online, University of California, San Francisco, Legacy.library.ucsf.edu, Bates number: 2072242741 (retrieved July 22, 2013).

25. Benjamin A. Toll and P.M. Ling, "The Virginia Slims Identity Crisis: An Inside Look at Tobacco Industry Marketing to Women," *Tobacco Control* 14, no. 3 (June 2005): 173.

26. "Women's Cigarette Market," 1973, p. 10, Legacy Tobacco Documents Online, University of California, San Francisco, Legacy.library.ucsf.edu, Bates number: 502645875 (retrieved July 22, 2013).

27. "Women's Cigarette Market," 1973, p. 11, Legacy Tobacco Documents Online, University of California, San Francisco, Legacy.library.ucsf.edu, Bates number: 502645875 (retrieved July 22, 2013).

28. "Women's Cigarette Mar-

ket," 1973, p. 12, Legacy Tobacco Documents Online, University of California, San Francisco, Legacy.library.ucsf.edu, Bates number: 502645875 (retrieved July 22, 2013).

29. Young and Rubicam, "Eve Cigarettes," January 24, 1969, p. 1, Legacy Tobacco Documents Online, University of California, San Francisco, Legacy.library.ucsf.edu, Bates number: 0277865 (retrieved July 22, 2013).

30. Young and Rubicam, "Eve cigarettes," January 24, 1969, p. 1, Legacy Tobacco Documents Online, University of California, San Francisco, Legacy.library.ucsf.edu, Bates number: 0277865 (retrieved July 22, 2013).

31. "Women's Cigarette Market," (1973): p.12, Legacy Tobacco Documents Online, University of California, San Francisco, Legacy.library.ucsf.edu, Retrieved: July 22, 2013, Bates number: 502645875.

32. "Eve," Stanford School of Medicine Website (retrieved July 22, 2013).

33. "Women's Cigarette Market," 1973, p. 12, Legacy Tobacco Documents Online, University of California, San Francisco, Legacy.library.ucsf.edu, Bates number: 502645875 (retrieved July 22, 2013).

34. Young and Rubicam, "Promotional and Publicity Ideas: 'Eve' Cigarettes," January 21, 1969, pp. 1–9, Legacy Tobacco Documents Online, University of California, San Francisco, Legacy.library.ucsf.edu, Bates number: LG0277873-LG0277881 (retrieved July 22, 2013).

35. John Alcorn Studio website, "Cigarette Package Design Detail, 1970," (retrieved July 22, 2013).

36. Young & Rubicon, "Eve," October 24, 1968, p. 1, Legacy Tobacco Documents Online, University of California, San Francisco, Legacy.library.ucsf.edu, Bates number: 0277904 (retrieved July 22, 2013).

37. John G. Palmer, "Flair Cigarettes Sales Analysis," April 17, 1970, p. 2, Legacy Tobacco Documents Online, University of California, San Francisco, Legacy.library.ucsf.edu, Bates number: 501769506 (retrieved July 22, 2013).

38. L. W. Hall, Jr., "Embra v. Flair Package Show Test," February 19, 1970, p. 1, Legacy Tobacco Doc-

uments Online, University of California, San Francisco, Legacy.library.ucsf.edu, Bates number: 5010 77748 (retrieved July 22, 2013).

39. "A Historical Perspective on Female-Oriented Brands: Embra," November 25, 1980, p. 8, Legacy Tobacco Documents Online, University of California, San Francisco, Legacy.library.ucsf.edu, Bates number: 503550738–0738 (retrieved July 22, 2013).

40. R.J. Reynolds, "Embra. For My Woman," 1969, p. 1, Legacy Tobacco Documents Online, University of California, San Francisco, Legacy.library.ucsf.edu, Bates number: 501405342/5358 (retrieved July 22, 2013).

41. R.J. Reynolds, "More. Brand Positioning Statement," (January 1, 1975, or June 28, 1985—two different dates listed for the same document), pp. 1–9, Legacy Tobacco Documents Online, University of California, San Francisco, Legacy.library.ucsf.edu, Bates number: 50310 0077/0080 (retrieved July 22, 2013).

42. "More." Stanford School of Medicine website (retrieved July 22, 2013).

43. R.J. Reynolds, "Meet Winnie," October 31, 1974, p. 2, Legacy Tobacco Documents Online, University of California, San Francisco, Legacy.library.ucsf.edu, Bates number: 500734850/4868 (retrieved July 22, 2013).

44. R.J. Reynolds, "Meet Winnie," October 31, 1974, p. 2, Legacy Tobacco Documents Online, University of California, San Francisco, Legacy.library.ucsf.edu, Bates number: 500734850/4868 (retrieved July 22, 2013).

45. Dancer-Fitzgerald-Sample, "A qualitative assessment of women's reactions to Winnie campaign," December 19, 1974, p. 6, Legacy Tobacco Documents Online, University of California, San Francisco, Legacy.library.ucsf.edu, Bates number: 501167063/7095 (retrieved July 22, 2013).

46. Dancer, Fitzgerald, Sample, "A Qualitative Assessment of Women's Reactions to Winnie Campaign," December 19, 1974, p. 17, Legacy Tobacco Documents Online, University of California, San Francisco, Legacy.library.ucsf.edu, Bates number: 501167063/7095 (retrieved July 22, 2013).

47. Dancer-Fitzgerald-Sample,

"A Qualitative Assessment of Women's Reactions to Winnie Campaign," December 19, 1974, pp. 18–24, Legacy Tobacco Documents Online, University of California, San Francisco, Legacy.library.ucsf.edu, Bates number: 501167063/7095 (retrieved July 22, 2013).

48. R.J. Reynolds, "Announcing The First 120mm Cigarette for Women," (May 9, 1975): p. 1, Legacy Tobacco Documents Online, University of California, San Francisco, Legacy.library.ucsf.edu, Bates number: 01400877 (retrieved July 22, 2013).

49. "Introducing Dawn 120 Advertising," (1975), p. 1, Legacy Tobacco Documents Online, University of California, San Francisco, Legacy.library.ucsf.edu, Bates number: 502646547 (retrieved July 22, 2013).

50. Foote, Cone and Belding, "Introduction of Dawn 120mm Cigarettes to the San Francisco market," July 1975, p. 8, Legacy Tobacco Documents Online, University of California, San Francisco, Legacy.library.ucsf.edu, Bates number: 91547943 (retrieved July 22, 2013).

51. Foote, Cone and Belding, "Introduction of Dawn 120mm Cigarettes to the San Francisco market," July 1975, p. 8, Legacy Tobacco Documents Online, University of California, San Francisco, Legacy.library.ucsf.edu, Bates number: 91547943 (retrieved July 22, 2013).

52. Although some disciplines prefer the term African American, the term "Black" is used to be consistent with the terms used in the industry documents.

53. Kelvin Well and Caroline Jones, "Brand Mystique Among Blacks," *Madison Avenue Magazine*: 1975, p. 28. Legacy Tobacco Documents Online, University of California, San Francisco, Legacy.library.ucsf.edu, Bates number: 990678723/8724 (retrieved July 22, 2013).

54. Market Facts for Brown & Williamson, "1979 Black Smoker Study," December 1979, p. 4, Legacy Tobacco Documents Online, University of California, San Francisco, Legacy.library.ucsf.edu, Bates number: 468101991 (retrieved July 22, 2013).

55. Kelvin Well and Caroline Jones, "Brand Mystique Among Blacks," *Madison Avenue Magazine*, 1975, p. 28, Legacy Tobacco Docu-

ments Online, University of California, San Francisco, Legacy.library.ucsf.edu, Bates number: 99067 8723/8724 (retrieved July 22, 2013).

56. Richard L. Vandervoet, RJR, "Advertising to the Black Menthol Market," October 4, 1978, Legacy Tobacco Documents Online, University of California, San Francisco, Legacy.library.ucsf.edu, Bates number: 501381367/1372 (retrieved July 22, 2013).

57. Kelvin Well and Caroline Jones, "Brand Mystique Among Blacks," *Madison Avenue Magazine*, 1975, p. 28. Legacy Tobacco Documents Online, University of California, San Francisco, Legacy.library.ucsf.edu, Bates number: 990678723/8724 (retrieved July 22, 2013).

58. Kelvin Well and Caroline Jones, "Brand Mystique Among Blacks," *Madison Avenue Magazine*, 1975, p. 29, Legacy Tobacco Documents Online, University of California, San Francisco, Legacy.library.ucsf.edu, Bates number: 990678723/8724 (retrieved July 22, 2013).

59. William Esty for Lorillard, "Newport Cigarettes Business Analysis," October 19, 1976: 4, Legacy Tobacco Documents Online, University of California, San Francisco, Legacy.library.ucsf.edu, Bates number: 501199237/9311 (retrieved July 22, 2013).

60. William Esty for Lorillard, "Newport Cigarettes Business Analysis," October 19, 1976: 9, Legacy Tobacco Documents Online, University of California, San Francisco, Legacy.library.ucsf.edu, Bates number: 501199237/9311 (retrieved July 22, 2013).

61. William Esty for Lorillard, "Newport Cigarettes Business Analysis," October 19, 1976: 7, Legacy Tobacco Documents Online, University of California, San Francisco, Legacy.library.ucsf.edu, Bates number: 501199237/9311 (retrieved July 22, 2013).

62. "Cigarette Suit Says Maker Gave Samples to Children," *The New York Times,* June 27, 2004 (retrieved July 22, 2013).

63. Daniel H. Murphy, "Re: Ethnic Research—Black Smokers," June 25, 1979, Legacy Tobacco Documents Online, University of California, San Francisco, Legacy.library.ucsf.edu, Bates number:

501334546 (retrieved July 22, 2013).

64. R.J. Reynolds, "Menthol and the Black Smoker," 1974, Legacy Tobacco Documents Online, University of California, San Francisco, Legacy.library.ucsf.edu, Bates number: 500590125/0130 (retrieved July 22, 2013).

65. R.J. Reynolds, "Menthol and the Black Smoker," 1974, Legacy Tobacco Documents Online, University of California, San Francisco, Legacy.library.ucsf.edu, Bates number: 500590125/0130 (retrieved July 22, 2013).

66. "The Black Market," December 31, 1979, p. 1, Legacy Tobacco Documents Online, University of California, San Francisco, Legacy.library.ucsf.edu, Bates number: 501797442 (retrieved July 22, 2013).

67. R.J. Reynolds, "Menthol and the Black Smoker," 1974, Legacy Tobacco Documents Online, University of California, San Francisco, Legacy.library.ucsf.edu, Bates number: 500590125/0130 (retrieved July 22, 2013).

68. R.J. Reynolds, "Menthol and the Black Smoker," 1974, Legacy Tobacco Documents Online, University of California, San Francisco, Legacy.library.ucsf.edu, Bates number: 500590125/0130 (retrieved July 22, 2013).

69. Daniel H. Murphy, "Re: Ethnic Research—Black Smokers," June 25, 1979, Legacy Tobacco Documents Online, University of California, San Francisco, Legacy.library.ucsf.edu, Bates number: 501334546 (retrieved July 22, 2013).

70. "The Black Market," December 31, 1979, p. 5, Legacy Tobacco Documents Online, University of California, San Francisco, Legacy.library.ucsf.edu, Bates number: 50179 7442 (retrieved July 22, 2013).

71. "The Black Market," December 31, 1979, p. 1, Legacy Tobacco Documents Online, University of California, San Francisco, Legacy.library.ucsf.edu, Bates number: 501797442 (retrieved July 22, 2013).

72. "The Black Market," (December 31, 1979): p. 1, Legacy Tobacco Documents Online, University of California, San Francisco, Legacy.library.ucsf.edu, Bates number: 501797442 (retrieved July 22, 2013).

73. Daniel H. Murphy, "Re: Ethnic Research—Black Smokers," June 25, 1979, Legacy Tobacco Documents Online, University of California, San Francisco, Legacy.library.ucsf.edu, Bates number: 50133 4546 (retrieved July 22, 2013).

74. "The Black Market," December 31, 1979, Legacy Tobacco Documents Online, University of California, San Francisco, Legacy.library.ucsf.edu, Bates number: 50179 7442 (retrieved July 22, 2013).

75. R.J. Reynolds, "Menthol and the Black Smoker," 1974, Legacy Tobacco Documents Online, University of California, San Francisco, Legacy.library.ucsf.edu, Bates number: 500590125/0130 (retrieved July 22, 2013).

76. R.J. Reynolds, "Exploratory Research for Salem Cigarettes," 1974, p. 4, Legacy Tobacco Documents Online, University of California, San Francisco, Legacy.library.ucsf.edu, Bates number: 50072 7614 (retrieved July 22, 2013).

77. Neal L. Benowitz, Brenda Herrera, and Peyton Jacob III, "Mentholated Cigarette Smoking Inhibits Nicotine Metabolism," *Journal of Pharmacology and Experimental Therapeutics* 310, no. 3 (2004) p. 1208.

78. Ted Bates New York, "Report on Qualitative Study Among Black Smokers," July 1977, p. 11, Legacy Tobacco Documents Online, University of California, San Francisco, Legacy.library.ucsf.edu, Bates number: 670174482 (retrieved July 22, 2013).

79. Ted Bates New York, "Report on Qualitative Study Among Black Smokers," July 1977, p. 12 Legacy Tobacco Documents Online, University of California, San Francisco, Legacy.library.ucsf.edu, Bates number: 670174482 (retrieved July 22, 2013).

80. Ted Bates New York, "Report on Qualitative Study Among Black Smokers," July 1977, p. 12, Legacy Tobacco Documents Online, University of California, San Francisco, Legacy.library.ucsf.edu, Bates number: 670174482 (retrieved July 22, 2013).

81. Ted Bates New York, "Report on Qualitative Study Among Black Smokers," July 1977, pp. 8–9, Legacy Tobacco Documents Online, University of California, San Francisco, Legacy.library.ucsf.edu, Bates number: 670174482 (retrieved July 22, 2013).

82. Ted Bates New York, "Report on Qualitative Study Among Black Smokers," July 1977, Legacy Tobacco Documents Online, University of California, San Francisco, Legacy.library.ucsf.edu, Bates number: 670174482 (retrieved July 22, 2013).

83. Phillip Morris "Black Market Analysis," 1980, p. 2. Legacy Tobacco Documents Online, University of California, San Francisco, Legacy.library.ucsf.edu, Bates number: 1004891511 (retrieved July 22, 2013).

84. McCann-Erickson Research Department, "Opportunities Among Black Smokers," 1980, p. 9, Legacy Tobacco Documents Online, University of California, San Francisco, Legacy.library.ucsf.edu, Bates number: 660057871 (retrieved July 22, 2013).

85. David Harris, "Menthol Initiative Project—Brand Mystique," July 10, 1990, Legacy Tobacco Documents, Bates number: 507475461/5464 (retrieved July 22, 2013).

86. Richard W. Pollay and T. Dewhirst, "The Dark Side of Marketing Seemingly 'Light' Cigarettes: Successful Images and Failed Fact," *Tobacco Control* 11, sup. 1 (March 2002), pp. 18–31; A. Spears, "Re: Costs of Making Tobacco Products. Lorillard Document. Exhibit 14,009, *State of Minnesota and Blue Cross and Blue Shield of Minnesota v. Philip Morris, Inc., et al.*," November, 13, 1973, pp. 2–3, Legacy Tobacco Documents Library, Bates number: 80634636–80634637 (retrieved July 22, 2013).

87. Richard W. Pollay and T. Dewhirst, "The Dark Side of Marketing Seemingly 'Light' Cigarettes: Successful Images and Failed Fact," *Tobacco Control* 11, sup. 1 (March 2002), 18–31;

Oxtoby-Smith Inc., *A Psychological Map of the Cigarette World*. Prepared for Ted Bates and Brown & Williamson, August 1967, Legacy Tobacco Documents, Bates number: 777152126, 777152134, 777152 143 (retrieved July 22, 2013).

88. Merete Osler, Eva Prescott, Nina Godtfredsen, Hans Ole Hein, and Peter Schnohr, "Gender and Determinants of Smoking Cessation: A Longitudinal Study," *Preventive Medicine* 29, 1999, pp. 57–62.

89. Jacqueline M. Royce, Norman Hymowitz, Kitty Corbett,

Tyler D. Hartwel and Mario A. Orlandi, "Smoking Cessation Factors among African Americans and Whites," *American Journal of Public Health* 83, no. 2 (1993), pp. 220–226.

90. Jacqueline M. Royce, Norman Hymowitz, Kitty Corbett, Tyler D. Hartwel and Mario A. Orlandi, "Smoking Cessation Factors among African Americans and Whites," *American Journal of Public Health* 83, no. 2 (1993), pp. 220–226.

91. Arline T. Geronimus, Lisa J. Neidert, and John Bound, "Age Patterns of Smoking in U.S. Black and White Women of Childbearing Age," *American Journal of Public Health*, 83, no. 9 (1993), pp. 1258–1264.

92. "Women Show Little Desire to Give Up Smoking, Say Government Researchers," *U.S. Tobacco Journal*, February 18, 1971, p. 16.

93. "Smoking and Youth," *Tobacco Reporter,* March 1972, p. 54, Legacy Tobacco Documents Online, University of California, San Francisco, Legacy.library.ucsf.edu, Bates number: 500324147 (retrieved July 22, 2013).

94. Diane S. Burrows, "Re: Incidence of Smoking Among Young Adults and College Students," August 20, 1980, Legacy Tobacco Documents Online, University of California, San Francisco, Legacy.library.ucsf.edu, Bates number: 50123 3008 (retrieved July 22, 2013).

95. American Lung Association, "Trends in Tobacco Use," July 2011, p. 4.

96. H. Holbert for Phillip Morris USA, "Study of Cigarette Smoking among College Students," September 10, 1980, p. 1, Legacy

Tobacco Documents Online, University of California, San Francisco, Legacy.library.ucsf.edu, Bates number: 1002419176 (retrieved July 22, 2013).

97. Diane S. Burrows, "Re: Incidence of Smoking Among Young Adults and College Students," August 20, 1980, p. 1, Legacy Tobacco Documents Online, University of California, San Francisco, Legacy.library.ucsf.edu, Bates number: 50123 3008 (retrieved July 22, 2013).

98. "College Poll Shows Students' Smoking Habits," *Tobacco Reporter*, June 1971, Legacy Tobacco Documents Online, University of California, San Francisco, Legacy.library.ucsf.edu, Bates number: 2045207286 (retrieved July 22, 2013).

99. H. Holbert for Phillip Morris USA, "Study of Cigarette Smoking among College Students," September 10, 1980, pp.1–3, Legacy Tobacco Documents Online, University of California, San Francisco, Legacy.library.ucsf.edu, Bates number: 1002419176 (retrieved July 22, 2013).

100. "Smoking and Youth," *Tobacco Reporter*, March 1972, p. 54, Legacy Tobacco Documents, Bates number: 500324147 (retrieved July 22, 2013).

101. Cornelia Pechmann, "Does Antismoking Advertising Combat Underage Smoking? A Review of Past Practices and Research," in *Social Marketing: Theoretical and Practical Perspectives*, M. E. Goldberg, M. Fishbein, and S. Middlestadt, eds. (Hillsdale, NJ: Lawrence Erlbaum Associates, 1997), pp. 189–216.

102. "Smoking and Youth," *Tobacco Reporter*, March 1972, p. 54,

Legacy Tobacco Documents, Bates number: 500324147 (retrieved July 22, 2013).

103. Juliann Sivulka, *Soap, Sex, and Cigarettes: A Cultural History of American Advertising* (Belmont, CA: Wadsworth, 1998), p. 300.

104. Thomas H. Brandon, "Negative Affect as Motivation to Smoke," *Current Directions in Psychological Science* 3, no 2 (1994), pp. 33–37.

105. "Tobacco Industry: Market Research Reports, Statistics and Analysis," ReportLinker.com, 2010.

106. J. Brooks, "American Cigarettes Have Become a Status Symbol in Smoke-Saturated China," *Canadian Medical Association Journal* 152, 1995 pp. 512–13.

107. J. Brooks, "American Cigarettes Have Become a Status Symbol in Smoke-Saturated China." *Canadian Medical Association Journal* 152, 1995 pp. 512–13.

108. Shu-Hong Zhu, Dewei Li, Buoling Feng, Tong Zhu, and Christopher M. Anderson, "Perception of Foreign Cigarettes and Their Advertising in China: A Study of College Students from 12 Universities," *Tobacco Control* 7, 1998, pp. 134–140; Marvin E. Goldberg, "American Media and the Smoking-Related Behaviors of Asian Adolescents," *Journal of Advertising Research* 43, no. 1 (2003), pp. 2–11.

109. WHO, "World Health Organization Atlas," 2004 (retrieved August 1, 2013).

110. Georgia State University, "The 10 Countries Where People Smoke Most," 2013.

111. WHO, "WHO Report on the Global Tobacco Epidemic, 2013," 2013.

Bibliography

Altman, David G., et al. "How an Unhealthy Product Is Sold: Cigarette Advertising in Magazines, 1960–1985." *Journal of Communication* 37, (1987): 95–106.

Andreasen, Alan. "A Social Marketing Research Agenda for Consumer Behavior Researchers." In *Advances in Consumer Research*, vol. 20, Leigh McAlister and Michael Rothschild, eds. Provo, UT: Association for Consumer Research, 1993.

Avery, Donald R. "Advertising, 1900-Present: Capitalist Tool or Economic Necessity?" In *Perspectives on Mass Communication History*, Wm. David Sloan, ed. Hillsdale, NJ: Lawrence Erlbaum Associates, 1991, 243.

Bardin, Nelle. "History of The University of Tennessee Publications." *The University of Tennessee Magazine* (1920): 419–433.

Bernard, H. Russell, and Gery W. Ryan. "Text Analysis: Qualitative and Quantitative Methods." In *Handbook of Methods in Cultural Anthropology*, H. Russell Bernard, ed. Walnut Creek, CA: Alta Mira Press, 1998.

Bernays, Edward L. *Biography of an Idea: Memoirs of Public Relations Counsel Edward L. Bernays.* New York: Simon and Schuster, 1965.

Berscheid, E. "Opinion Change and Communicator-Communicatee Similarity and Dissimilarity." *Journal of Personality and Social Psychology* 4 (1966): 670–680.

Bettinghaus, Erwin P., and Micahel J. Cody. *Persuasive Communication*. 5th ed. Fort Worth, TX: Harcourt Brace College, 1994.

Blatnik, John A. "The Medicine Man under the Eagle's Eye." *The Progressive* 6 (November 1958), 6.

Botvin, Gilbert J., Catherine J. Goldbery, Elizabeth M. Botvin, and Linda Dusenbury. "Smoking Behavior of Adolescents Exposed to Cigarette Advertising." *Public Health Reports* 108, (1993): 217–224.

Brandon, Thomas H. "Negative Affect as Motivation to Smoke." *Current Directions in Psychological Science* 3 (2), (1994): 33–37.

Calfee, John E. and Debra J. Ringold. "What Can We Learn From the Informational Content of Cigarette Advertising? A Reply and Further Analysis." *Journal of Public Policy & Marketing* 9, (1990): 30–42.

Celebucki, Carolyn C., and K. Diskin. "A Longitudinal Study of Externally Visible Cigarette Advertising on Retail Storefronts in Massachusetts Before and After the Master Settlement Agreement." *Tobacco Control* 11, (2002): ii47–ii53.

Chronkhite, Gary, and Jo R. Liska. "The Judgment of Communicant Acceptability" in M. E. Roloff and G. R. Miller, eds., *Persuasion: New Directions in Theory and Research*. Beverly Hills, CA: Sage, 1980: 101–139.

Courtwright, David T. "'Carry on Smoking': Public Relations and Advertising Strategies of American and British Tobacco Companies Since 1950." *Business History* 47 (July 2005): 423.

Craig, Steve, and Terry Moellinger. "'So Rich, Mild, and Fresh': A Critical Look at TV Cigarette Commercials, 1948–1971." *Journal of Communication Inquiry* 25 (January 2001): 55–71.

Crimmins, James C. *Successful Publishing on the Campus.* New York: Newsweek, 1968.

Cummings, K. Michael, C. P. Morley, J. K. Horan, C. Steger and N-R Leavell. "Marketing to America's Youth: Evidence from Corporate Documents." *Tobacco Control* 11, (2002): 5–17.

Dalton, Madeline A., James D. Sargent, Michael L. Beach, Linda Titus-Ernstoff, Jennifer J. Gibson, M. Bridget Ahrens, Jennifer J. Tickle, and Todd F. Heatherton. "Effect of Viewing Smoking in Movies on Adolescent Smoking Initiation: A Cohort Study." *Lancet* (2003) 362: 281–85.

Devol, Kenneth Stowe. *Major Areas of Conflict in the Control of College and University Student Daily Newspapers in the United States.* Los Angeles: University of Southern California, 1965.

Duscha, Julius, and Thomas Fischer. *The Campus Press: Freedom and Responsibility.* Washington, DC: American Association of State Colleges and Universities, 1973.

Elders, M. Joycelyn. *Preventing Tobacco Use Among Young People: A Report of the Surgeon General.*

Washington, DC: U.S. Department of Health and Human Services, 1997.

Estrin, Herman A. "What is a College Newspaper?" In *Freedom and Censorship of the College Press*, Herman A. Estrin and Arthur M. Sanderson eds. Dubuque, IA: Brown, 1966.

Everett, Sherry A., Rae L. Schnuth, and JoAnne Tribble. "Tobacco and Alcohol Use in Top Grossing American Films." *Journal of Community Health* 23 (1998): 317–24.

Fairclough, Norman. *Analysing Discourse: Textual Analysis for Social Research*. New York: Routledge, 2003.

___, Bob Jessop, and Andew Sayer. "Critical Realism and Semiosis." *Journal of Critical Realism* 5 (2002): 2–10.

Feighery, Ellen C., Kurt M Ribisl, Nina Schleicher, Rebecca E. Lee and Sonia Halvorson."Cigarette Advertising and Promotional Strategies in Retail Outlets: Results of a Statewide Survey in California." *Tobacco Control* 10 (2001): 184–188.

Fox, Stephen. *The Mirror Makers: A History of American Advertisers & Its Creators*. Chicago: University of Illinois Press, 1997.

Geronimus, Arline T., Lisa J. Neidert, and John Bound. "Age Patterns of Smoking in U.S. Black and White Women of Childbearing Age." *American Journal of Public Health* 83 (9), (1993): 1258–1264.

Gilbert, Eugene. *Advertising and Marketing to Young People*. Pleasantville, NY: Printer's Ink Books, 1957.

Goldberg, Marvin E. "American Media and the Smoking-related Behaviors of Asian Adolescents." *Journal of Advertising Research* 43 (1), (2003): 2–11.

Hackbarth, Diana P., Barbara Silvestri, and William Cosper. "Tobacco and Alcohol Billboards in 50 Chicago Neighborhoods: Market Segmentation to Sell Dangerous Products to the Poor." *Journal of Public Health Policy* 16 (1995): 213–230.

Hawkins, Katherine and Audrey Curtis Hane. "Adolescents' Perceptions of Print Cigarette Advertising: A Case for Counteradvertising." *Journal of Health Communication* 5 (2000): 83–84.

Hazan, Anna R., Helene L. Lipton, and Stanton A. Glantz. "Popular Films Do Not Reflect Current Tobacco Use." *American Journal of Public Health* 84 (1994): 998–1000.

Ingelhart, Louis. *Freedom for the College Student Press: Court Cases and Related Decisions Defining the Campus Fourth Estate Boundaries*. Westport, CT: Greenwood Press, 1985.

Jacobson, Michael F., and Laurie A. Mazur. *Marketing Madness: A Survival Guide for a Consumer Society*. Boulder, CO: Westview Press, 1995.

Johnson, Burges. "Cigarette Advertising and Censorship." *School and Society* 32 (December 31, 1932): 856–856.

Jones, Ivan Livingston. *An Analysis of the Educational Problems Peculiar to School-Newspaper Advertising*. Seattle: University of Washington, 1961.

Kahle, Lynn R. and Pamela M. Homer. "Physical Attractiveness of the Celebrity Endorser: A Social Adaptation Perspective." *Journal of Consumer Research* 11 (1985): 954–961.

Kaplan, Howard B. *Patterns of Juvenile Delinquency: Social Origins, Continuities, and Consequences*. Newbury Park, CA: Sage, 1984.

King, Charles III, Michael Siegel, Carolyn Celebucki, and Gregory N. Connolly. "Adolescent Exposure to Cigarette Advertising in Magazines: An Evaluation of Brand-Specific Advertising in Relation to Youth Readership." *Journal of the American Medical Association* 279 (1998): 516–520.

Koop, C. Everett, David C. Kessler, and George D. Lundberg. "Reinventing American Tobacco Policy: Sounding the Medical Community's Voice." *Journal of the American Medical Association* 279 (1998): 550–552.

Krugman, Dean M., Margaret A. Morrison, and Yongjun Sung. "Cigarette Advertising in Popular Youth and Adult Magazines: A Ten-Year Perspective." *Journal of Public Policy & Marketing* 25 (2006): 197–211.

Laird, Pamela Walker. "Consuming Smoke: Cigarettes in American Culture." *Reviews in American History* 28 (2000): 96–104.

Lammers, H. Bruce, Laura Leibowitz, George Edward Seymour, and Judith Hennessey. "Humor and Cognitive Response Stimuli." In *Handbook of Humor Research*, P.E. McGhee and J.H. Goldstein, eds. New York: Springer-Verlag, 1983.

Lantz, Paula M., Peter D. Jacobson, Kenneth E. Warner, Jeffrey Wasserman, Harold A. Pollack, Julie Berson, Alexis Ahlstrom. "Investing in Youth Tobacco Control: A Review of Smoking Prevention and Control Strategies." *Tobacco Control* 9 (2000): 47–63.

Lincoln, Yvonna S., and Egon G. Guba. *Naturalistic Inquiry*. Beverly Hills, CA: Sage, 1985.

McGrew, Jane L. "History of Tobacco Regulation." Based on a paper prepared for the National Commission on Marihuana and Drug Abuse. Drug Library.org. http://www.druglibrary.org/schaffer/Library/studies/nc/nc2b.htm. Accessed July 19, 2005.

McNeil, Robert H. "Training on College Newspapers." *School and Society* 34 (March 30, 1929): 419–420.

Meyer, John A. "Cigarette Country." *American Heritage* 43, (1992): 72.

Miles, Robert H. *Coffin Nails and Corporate Strategies*. Englewood Cliffs, NJ: Prentice-Hall, 1982.

Miller, Karen S. "Smoking Up A Storm: Public Relations and Advertising in the Construction of the Cigarette Problem, 1953–1954." *Journalism Monographs* 36 (December 1992): 4.

___. *The Voice of Business: Hill & Knowlton and Postwar Public Relations*. Chapel Hill: University of North Carolina Press, 1999.

Neuberger, Maurine. *Smoke Screen: Tobacco and the Public Welfare*. Englewood Cliffs, NJ: Prentice Hall, 1963.

Nevins, Allan. *The Gateway to History*. New rev. ed. Garden City, NY: Doubleday, 1962.

Osler, Merete, Eva Prescott, Nina Godtfredsen, Hans Ole Hein, and Peter Schnohr. "Gender and Determinants of Smoking Cessation: A Longitudinal Study." *Preventive Medicine* 29 (1999), pp. 57–62.

Parascandola, Mark. "Public Health Then and Now: Cigarettes and the U.S. Public Health Service in the 1950s." *American Journal of Public Health* 91 (2), (2001): 196–205.

Park, Robert E. "The Natural History of the Newspaper." In *The City*, Robert E Park, Ernest W. Burgess, and Robert D. McKenzie, eds. Chicago: University of Chicago Press, 1925.

Parker-Pope, Tara. *Cigarettes: Anatomy of an Industry from Seed to Smoke*. New York: The New Press, 2001.

Pechmann, Cornelia, and S. Ratneshwar. "The Effects of Antismoking and Cigarette Advertising on Young Adolescents Perceptions of Peers Who Smoke," *Journal of Consumer Research* 21 (1994): 236–251.

Peracchio, Laura A., and David Luna. "The Development of an Advertising Campaign to Discourage Smoking Initiation among Children and Youth." *Journal of Advertising* 37 (1998), pp. 49–56.

Perry, Cheryl L. "The Tobacco Industry and Underage Youth Smoking: Tobacco Industry Documents From the Minnesota Litigation." *Archives of Pediatric and Adolescent Medicine* 153 (1999): 935–941.

Peterson, Bob. "Spartan Daily Debated at Friday Night Forum." *Spartan Daily* (San Jose State College, May 4, 1964).

Pierce, John P., Won S. Choi, Elizabeth A. Gilpin, Arthur J. Farkas, and Charles C. Berry. "Tobacco Industry Promotion of Cigarettes and Adolescent Smoking." *Journal of the American Medical Association* 279, (1998): 511–515.

Pollay, Richard W., and T. Dewhirst. "The Dark Side of Marketing Seemingly 'Light' Cigarettes: Successful Images and Failed Fact." *Tobacco Control* 11 (2002): 18–31.

Pollay, Richard W., S. Siddarth, Michael Siegel, Anne Haddix, Robert K. Merritt, Gary A. Giovino, and Michael P. Eriksen. "The Last Straw? Cigarette Advertising and Realized Market Shares Among Youths and Adults, 1979–1993." *Journal of Marketing* 60, no. 2. (1996): 1–16.

Potter, David M. *People of Plenty: Economic Abundance and the American Character*. Chicago: University of Chicago Press, 1954.

Pucci, Linda G. and Michael Siegel. "Exposure to Brand-Specific Cigarette Advertising in Magazines and Its Impact on Youth Smoking." *Preventive Medicine* 29 (1999): 313–320.

Ringold, Debra J., and J.E. Calfee. "The Informational Content of Cigarette Advertising 1926–1986." *Journal of Public Policy & Marketing* 8, (1989): 1–23.

Royce, Jacqueline M., Norman Hymowitz, Kitty Corbett, Tyler D. Hartwel, and Mario A. Orlandi. "Smoking Cessation Factors among African Americans and Whites." *American Journal of Public Health* 83 (2), (1993): 220–226.

Salmon, Lucy Maynard. *The Newspaper and the Historian*. New York: Oxford University Press, 1923.

Sargent, James D., Michael L. Beach, Anna M. Adachi-Mejia, Jennifer J. Gibson, Linda T. Titus-Ernstoff, Charles P. Carusi, Susan D. Swain, Todd F. Heatherton, and Madeline A. Dalton "Exposure to Movie Smoking: Its Relation to Smoking Initiation Among U.S. Adolescents." *Pediatrics* 116 (2005): 1183–1191.

Schooler, Caroline, Michael D. Basil, and David G. Altman. "Alcohol and Cigarette Advertising on Billboards: Targeting with Social Cues." *Health Communication* 8, (1996): 109–129.

Schoonover, Robert Andrew. *Working Relations of Faculty Advisers to Student Staffs on Collegiate Newspapers*. Washington, DC: American University, 1962.

Segrave, Kerry. *Women and Smoking in America, 1880–1950*. Jefferson, NC: McFarland, 2005.

Shudson, Michael. *Advertising, The Uneasy Persuasion*. New York: Basic Books, 1984.

Sivulka, Juliann. *Soap, Sex, and Cigarettes: A Cultural History of American Advertising*. Belmont, CA: Wadsworth, 1998.

Slosson, Edwin E. "The Possibility of a University Newspaper." *Independent* 72 (February 15, 1912).

Smith, Ronald A. *Play-by-Play: Radio, Television, and Big-Time College Sport*. Baltimore: Johns Hopkins University Press, 2001.

*Sobel, Robert. *They Satisfy: The Cigarette in American Life*. Garden City, NJ: Anchor Press, 1978.

Solow, John L. "Exorcising the Ghost of Cigarette Advertising Past: Collusion, Regulation, and Fear Advertising." *Journal of Macromarketing* 21, (2001): 135–145.

Startt, James D., and Wm. David Sloan. *Historical Methods in Mass Communication*. Hillsdale, NJ: Lawrence Erlbaum Associates, 1989.

Strang, Ruth. *Group Activities in College and Secondary School*. New York: Harper & Brothers, 1941.

Struder, Norman. "The New College Journalism." *Nation* 122 (May 26, 1926).

Taylor, Ronald E. "A Six-Segment Message Strategy Wheel." *Journal of Advertising Research* 39 (1999): 7–17.

Toll, Benjamin A., and P.M. Ling. "The Virginia Slims Identity Crisis: An Inside Look at the Tobacco Industry Marketing to Women." *Tobacco Control* 14 (2005): 173.

Tyas, Suzanne L., and Linda L. Pederson. "Psychosocial Factors Related to Adolescent Smoking: A Critical Review of the Literature." *Tobacco Control* 7, (1998): 409–420.

Wagner, Susan. *Cigarette Country: Tobacco in American History and Politics.* New York: Praeger, 1971.

Wakefield, Melanie A., Erin E. Ruel, Frank J. Chaloupka, Sandy J. Slater, and Nancy J. Kaufman. "Association of Point-of-Purchase Tobacco Advertising and Promotions with Choice of Usual Brand Among Teenage Smokers." *Journal of Health Communication* 7 (2002): 113–121.

Warren, Charles W., Leanne Riley, Samira Asma, Michael P. Eriksen, Lawrence Green, Curtis Blanton, Cliff Loo, Scott Batchelor, and Derek Yach. "Tobacco Use by Youth: A Surveillance Report from the Global Youth Tobacco Survey Project." *Bulletin of the World Health Organization* 78, no. 7 (2000).

Whitehead, Stanley G., and David A. Goodman. "A Saga of Cigarette Ads: Free Cigarettes and Tobacco Advertising are Fading From the College Scene." *America* (October 5, 1963): 387.

Whiteside, Thomas. *Selling Death: Cigarette Advertising and Public Health.* New York: NY, Liveright, 1970.

Zhu, Shu-Hong, Dewei Li, Buoling Feng, Tong Zhu, and Christopher M. Anderson. "Perception of Foreign Cigarettes and their Advertising in China: A Study of College Students from 12 Universities." *Tobacco Control* 7 (1998): 134–140.

Index